The Games

Britain's Olympic and Paralympic
Journey to London 2012

The Games

Britain's Olympic and Paralympic Journey to London 2012

Brendan Gallagher

WILEY

To Eileen Tully

A wonderful mum, sports enthusiast and armchair critic – RIP

Previous page

Sebastian Coe celebrates after winning a consecutive gold medal in the 1500m at the Los Angeles 1984 Games. he dominated the race and set a new Olympic record for the event.

Contents

Foreword

Tom Knight and Sybil Ruscoe
September 2011

A standard question for those athletes aiming to compete in the London 2012 Olympic and Paralympic Games requires them to come up with their earliest memory of the events. It never fails to amuse us when the answer features an event or person from recent times. Despite such reminders of the passing years, our early Olympic memories remain vivid.

Tom My earliest memory is not of an event or an athlete but a tune that I can still hum – even though it hails from the mid-Sixties.

Tokyo Melody, by the German composer Helmut Zacharias, was the theme music picked by the BBC for their daily coverage of the 1964 Olympic Games. Watching Cliff Michelmore introduce the grainy black and white pictures from Tokyo was something truly exotic and wonderful to a youngster in Hereford. It was clear, even then, that the Olympic Games were something extraordinary, and it is not surprising that the athletes I watched every teatime, all those years ago, remained special people.

Mary Rand became the first British woman to win an Athletics title when she triumphed in the Long Jump. Her teammate Ann Packer took the 800m gold with the sort of late run around the final bend that we would dearly love to see a Briton replicate at London 2012. I have interviewed them both but only by telephone, and I'm sure they would forgive me for saying that, even now, I see them as they were on the old television at home.

That cannot be the case with Lynn Davies, who danced out of the sandpit after winning the men's Long Jump in Tokyo with a British record of 8.07m. I still see Lynn these days, in his capacity as President of UK Athletics, and it doesn't take much for the ever-youthful and, dare I say, colourful Welshman to launch into a song. Together with the walker, Ken Matthews, they won Britain's only gold medals at the 1964 Games, and to have done that, against the best in the world, so far away from home, made them very special indeed.

Four years later and the same could be said of David Hemery, who won the 400m Hurdles with a world record. For Lord Coe, however, Chairman of the Organising Committee for London 2012, that race was more significant for the bronze medal awarded to another British athlete, John Sherwood. Like the young Coe, Sherwood was from Sheffield and chronicled within these pages is the memory of the moment that stayed with Coe until the time came to deliver his Games-winning speech to the International Olympic Committee in 2005.

Opposite

Mary Rand, gold medallist in the Long Jump at the Tokyo 1964 Olympic Games, competing in the Women's AAA Championship at the White City Stadium, July 1964. The Stadium itself was built to accommodate the first Olympic Games hosted by Great Britain in 1908, and was the focus of great national pride.

The names of the British champions from those Games of long ago have stayed with me. Almost like the music of the time, they encapsulate an era. As the screens of the televisions I watched became larger, so did the Olympic and Paralympic Games. I still remember the thrill of seeing the likes of the boxer, Chris Finnegan, the swimmer, David Wilkie, the three-day eventer, Richard Meade and the pentathlete, Mary Peters reach the pinnacle of their respective sports. In those days, of course, while we firmly believed that the England football team could win another World Cup, it was still rare to see a Briton on top of the Olympic podium.

I cannot claim to have been an aficionado of the Games in my student days, but I did take an interest in the young Steve Ovett because I was at Sussex University and he lived in Brighton. I often saw him in the town and tuned into the Montreal Olympic Games to witness the apparent coming of age of this brilliant talent. Yet, after his fifth place in the 800m – albeit behind the remarkable world record of Cuba's Alberto Juantorena – I also recall wondering what all the fuss had been about. But what did I know?

Nothing, it transpired. Ovett later wrote about how much he learned from that experience and we all saw the result of that, four years later at Moscow 1980. I have since also learned that winning Olympic gold medals has a lot to do with timing – the years of hard work and training can come to nothing if the moment is not right. There was no better illustration of this than Kelly Holmes' 800m/1500m double gold at Athens 2004. By then 34 and a mainstay of the British team for more than a decade, Holmes had seen her fair share of triumph and frustrations over the years and, if she knew her time had come, she kept it to herself. I shared a flight with Holmes from the team's holding camp in Cyprus to Athens, with the Games already in progress. The woman I remember striding from the airport and into the Greek sunshine for the short taxi ride to the Olympic Village certainly looked like an athlete on a mission. Most athletes

are lucky when everything falls into place for one Olympic Games, which makes the records of Steve Redgrave and Matthew Pinsent, Ben Ainslie and Chris Hoy all the more special.

Sybil I hope the London 2012 Olympic and Paralympic Games have the same effect on youngsters as watching the Olympic Games on television in 1972 had on me. Immediately after transmission, the small back garden of our house in Wem was transformed into our very own Olympic Stadium. There myself, my sister and friends would go through the trials and tribulations of competition, long-jumping over flower beds, hurdling an old desk and racing a circuit of our council estate. It was Belfast's smiling, gold medal-winning pentathlete, Mary Peters, who inspired us into athletic action. At Christmas, my pillow case was filled with a blue trendy Bukta tracksuit, a pair of white 'Geoff Hurst' training shoes and a black leotard.

It was the joy and precision of the tiny Russian gymnast Olga Korbut who made a leotard the 'must-have' Christmas present of 1972. Her energetic grin and cheeky flick of the foot at the end of her floor routine sent us leaping, tumbling and vaulting into the school hall for lunchtime and after school gym club. Athletics still appealed as well, and by the summer term of 1973, I was taking a discus home to practice with my Dad in a local field. I did in fact qualify for the Shropshire County Athletics finals, though sadly there's no record of the distance I threw. That Olympic Games in Munich 1972 certainly sealed my fate as a teenage sports-lover; in 1974, I even spent a week putting the high jump bar back up between the posts at the All England Schools Athletics Championships in Shrewsbury.

Fast-forward a couple of decades and I finally made it to the Olympic Games. In 1996 I covered the event in Atlanta for the BBC, and in 2000 I was lucky enough to be working for the *Daily Telegraph* at the Sydney Olympic Games. I'd come a long way from the grass track at Wem Secondary Modern School, growing into one of those sport-obsessed people who fail to make it as full-time athletes and go on to write and broadcast about sport instead.

While I never managed to emulate Mary or Olga's achievements, those athletes gave me a life-long love of Olympic and Paralympic sport and inspired me to have a go. As a Salopian, I am acutely aware of the Olympic legacy because the little playing field at Much Wenlock led to the resurgence of the modern Olympic Games. I am hoping that the Olympic and Paralympic Games of London 2012, and athletes such as Jessica Ennis, Nathan Stephens, Eleanor Simmonds, Kyron Duke, Tom Daley, Lee Pearson, Sarah Storey, Hannah England, Libby Clegg, Usain Bolt and Yohan Blake, to name just a few, will give the next generation the inspiration to love and take up sport.

Needless to say, there is no X Factor immediacy to becoming an Olympic or Paralympic champion. It is always the result of hard work and dedication, something that was as true for Wyndham Halswelle, the Scot and Boer War veteran who won his 400m gold medal with a 'walkover' in London's White City in 1908 as it was for Victoria Pendleton in taking the women's Sprint gold in the velodrome at Beijing 2008. That is often why the tears you see at the end of a gold medal-winning performance come as much from relief than anything else – a release of the enormous pressure that athletes put upon themselves, combined with the realisation that the years of work have finally paid off.

Britain's Olympic and Paralympic journey is now moving with real momentum towards London 2012. The hope in Britain, at least, is that more of its athletes than ever discover that, after all their hard work, the time is right for them to step up to the top of the medal podium. The celebrations will not just be about medal success, of course. The

Olympic and Paralympic Games may have travelled the world, but the first steps of Britain's journey were taken at home, with William Penny Brookes' Wenlock Games in 1850 and Dr Ludwig Guttmann's Stoke Mandeville Games for injured war veterans in 1948. The stories of both men – pioneers in their own right – are contained herein, and it is fitting that the story of Britain's participation will reach such a major staging post with the Olympic and Paralympic Games of London 2012. It is by no means the end of the movement's inspiring story, however. In 2016 the Games, with new competitors bringing their fresh hopes and dreams, will continue in Rio de Janeiro, and into the future.

Tom Knight is a sports journalist who has covered eight Olympic Games. Sybil Ruscoe is a journalist and broadcaster who has also covered past Olympic Games. They are the authors of *London 2012 Olympic and Paralympic Games – the Official Commemorative Book,* to be published by Wiley in October 2012.

Introduction

The most famous quotation about the Olympic Games is Baron Pierre de Coubertin's insistence that 'The most important thing in the Olympic Games is not winning but taking part; the essential thing in life is not conquering but fighting well.' The founding father of the modern Olympic Games first voiced this notion in 1908, a few days after hearing a visiting American bishop preach those same words at St Paul's Cathedral in London. The momentous Olympic Games that were taking place at the time gave his words particular resonance.

My own favourite, however, has always been Dawn Fraser's heartfelt explanation of exactly what the Games meant to her. 'The Olympic Games remain the most compelling search for excellence that exists in sport, and maybe in life itself,' mused the great Australian swimmer at the end of her very considerable Olympic career.

That nails it for me. Fraser's words also encapsulate the very essence of Britain's long and enduring relationship with the Olympic Movement – a remarkable journey that I attempt to chart in this book. In a pure sporting sense it is about performing as well as you can under the most testing circumstances against the best in the world – and pulling off that monumental task with a certain style and humility. Achieving the latter is often the biggest challenge of all, and the mark of a true Olympian or Paralympian. Britain's long association with the Games is full of such gold-encrusted stories, from those of humble origins and those born with every advantage in life – and indeed those who reached for the ultimate and fell just short.

But Britain's Olympic and Paralympic journey has stretched far beyond the sporting arena itself. When Dr William Penny Brookes organized his early 'Wenlock Olympian Games' at Much Wenlock, he was in effect conducting a great social experiment that has produced today's aspirational Games. Brookes sowed the seeds for a return of the Olympic Games as a means of bettering the physical, mental and possibly even spiritual well-being of his fellow men.

Such idealistic concepts are balanced by practicalities facing any nation hosting what has become the biggest show on earth. The approaches to staging past Games offer a fascinating snapshot of society in that country at that precise moment in time, never more so than in the case of Britain and London's Olympic past.

In late 1906 the Olympic Movement was facing the late withdrawal of Rome as hosts of the 1908 Olympic Games. With the luxury of hindsight you can argue that only Edwardian, imperial Britain had the financial muscle, confidence and organizing genius to stage the Olympic Games in the way they did at such short notice. They may have over-reached themselves slightly, but that is an Olympian trait in itself: striving way beyond what seems possible to discover what can actually be achieved.

In 1948, when no other nation in war-ravaged

Opposite

The Olympic Flame is passed between two Torchbearers on its journey to Wembley Stadium for the start of the London 1948 Olympic Games.

Europe could contemplate staging an Olympic Games, London stepped into the breach again. Battered by years of conflict, they still managed to deliver an understated, 'make and mend' Games – the perfect showcase for the country's great entrepeneurial spirit. The 1948 Games were a minor miracle, nothing less, and should be celebrated as such.

In 2012 London becomes the first city to host three Olympic Games, this time with plenty of notice but still in challenging circumstances. Designers, architects, engineers, constructors and event organizers have been challenged in 'the most compelling search for excellence' they will ever experience in their professional careers. Everybody concerned has been stretched at every level.

With the world economic downturn budgets have had to be closely watched, and the need for legacy is a political fact of life, vital to the London 2012 vision. As well as a sporting festival the likes of which we have never seen before in Britain, there has to be a tangible return for the wider community. This may be in enhanced facilities or a general raising of the bar for the next sporting generation, at both competitive and recreational levels. An even wider recognition and appreciation of Paralympic sport will also be key to London 2012's success.

The Paralympic Games now share central stage and are an integral part of the event – very different from London's previous Olympic Games. Britain's role in the promoting of Paralympic sport and the Paralympic Games themselves is second to none. The inspired work of Dr Ludwig Guttmann and colleagues at Stoke Mandeville in establishing the value of Paralympic sport is one of this nation's finest achievements, sporting or otherwise. There will be a real sense of 'coming home' in 2012 when the finest Paralympic athletes in the world gather in London.

Britain is the only nation to have been represented at all the Olympic Games since 1896 – and indeed to have won a gold medal at every one, although there were a couple of close calls: in both 1952 and 1996 Great Britain took only a solitary gold medal. Great Britain didn't officially send a team to the St Louis 1904 Games on financial grounds, but their record was preserved in a roundabout fashion. The world's greatest all-round athlete, Thomas Kiely from Ballyneal, travelled to the United States hoping to compete for Ireland. Despite his Irish roots he was only allowed to participate if he competed in British colours – so he swallowed his pride and stormed his way to the gold medal in the Athletics all-round competition (the forerunner to the Decathalon).

Kiely was legally a British citizen and the IOC's decision was undoubtedly correct, given the politics of the time. Many of the early 'great' athletes from the USA and Canada were in fact Irish athletes, and the whole Irish situation, now largely forgotten, formed a major issue during the first two decades of the modern Olympic Games. It is certainly an important aspect of Britain's Olympic journey.

As a core member of the modern Olympic Movement Britain has faced all of the concerns that have confronted the Games from the start. Nationality has been a huge issue, as the case of Kiely demonstrates; it was 1924 before Great Britain and Ireland became separate entities at the Games to reflect the new political realities. Britain has never been alone in grappling with such matters, however – there have been wars and dramatic political changes in Europe and the Eastern bloc. Competing nations, including Britain, have had to face calls to boycott the Olympic and Paralympic Games at periods of international tension. Whatever your politics, Britain's view – that Olympic and Paralympic sport should always transcend politics – has been consistently upheld. The British Olympic Association (BOA) and the athletes they represent refused to support a possible boycott of the Berlin 1936 Games. In 1980, under much stronger pressure, the majority of Great Britain's teams declined to join an

American-led boycott of the Moscow Olympic Games after the Soviet Union's invasion of Afghanistan in 1979.

Britain, like every other competing nation, has had to grapple with the Olympian ideal of amateurism, a principle to which it adhered longer than almost any other country. After the Second World War the massive state funds diverted to sport by the Soviet Union and the Eastern bloc changed the face of Olympic competition for ever. Britain had to decide how to respond. The decline of amateurism was a patchy process. Some sports, such as athletics, went 'open' worldwide in a de facto fashion long before the Olympic Games was officially declared 'open' to professionals in 1992. Top British athletes were earning a living out of their sport – although precious little more – before 1992.

The majority of British Olympic sports clung to 'amateurism' right up to the Atlanta 1996 Games. Britain returned home from the Olympic Games with just one gold medal, a perceived 'failure' that prompted a massive rethink. If the country was to remain competitive, Olympic and Paralympic athletes (the latter having been significantly more successful at the 1996 Games), had to be allowed to compete on an equal footing. The nettle had to be grasped. Two years later Lottery funding started began to come online, with immediate and startling effect.

The wining of gold medals has necessarily, to a certain extent, taken a more businesslike and scientific approach. Yet the Olympic and Paralympic sprit burns on. Sir Chris Hoy was an aspiring Olympian long before Lottery funding was available; he has changed not a jot since his three gold medals in Beijing opened up a number of hard-earned commercial opportunities. Hoy remains a true Olympian who gives everything in the pursuit of excellence, but is the first to congratulate the other bloke on the rare occasions that he loses.

Another great Olympian is Nicole Cooke. Her brilliant Cycling gold medal in the women's Road Race in Bejing started the British gold rush in the 2008 Games.

Nobody trains harder and more scientifically than Cooke, nobody prepares more assiduously, and there are few more determined and focussed competitors. A few weeks after the Olympic gold I remember interviewing her as this thoroughly modern Olympian waded through the thousands of congratulatory letters and emails sent in by the British public.

'It really touched a nerve as I read them all,' recalled a humbled Cooke. 'There are hundreds and thousands of people out there in Britain who achieve something fantastic every day and win their 'Olympic Games'. Doctors and nurses who get the treatments of their patients absolutely right, rescue services, people making a breakthrough in business or science, journalists trying to write the best article they can. The list is endless.'

'Their achievements can go completely unrecognized and uncelebrated, with often only the individual concerned knowing they did something very special in their field. Sometimes in the past, as women's cycling struggled to make an impact, I've ridden in races that only I and those very close to me will have known were as perfect as I could manage that day. When that moment, in whatever field you operate in, is suddenly recognised, it's an extraordinary feeling.'

The compelling search for excellence in sport and life. It defines the Olympic and Paralympic Games, the occasional wart and all, and inspires all those who look to these great Movements. Britain can be proud of the role it has played in its long Olympic and Paralympic journey. It is one that the nation will continue to play, through the excitement and anticipation of London 2012 to the colour and drama of Rio de Janeiro 2016, far long beyond.

Brendan Gallagher September 2011

Overleaf

Delighted crowds in Trafalgar Square celebrate the success of Britain's Olympic and Paralympic athletes at Beijing 2008.

Photo Credits

Chapter 1
Early Days

Early Days

AS BEFITS A NATION THAT CLAIMS, WITH SOME JUSTIFICATION, TO HAVE INVENTED AND DEVELOPED MANY OF THE WORLD'S MOST POPULAR SPORTS AND TEAM GAMES, BRITAIN'S CONTRIBUTION TO THE MODERN OLYMPIC MOVEMENT HAS PROVED DEEP-ROOTED AND CONSTANT. IT HAS ALSO BEEN INSPIRATIONAL, WITH A SELF-EFFACING ENGLISHMAN – DR WILLIAM PENNY BROOKES – HAVING SIGNIFICANT INFLUENCE ON FRANCE'S BARON PIERRE DE COUBERTIN, THE ACKNOWLEDGED FOUNDER OF THE MODERN OLYMPIC GAMES.

De Coubertin, a man of great vision and energy, admired the strong emphasis placed on physical education by British public schools. He considered that robust and sometimes harsh system to be the basis of Britain's military superiority throughout the nineteenth century – as did many Britons. De Coubertin desired the same for France, who had come off a poor second best against the stronger and well-drilled Prussian troops in the Franco-Prussian War of 1870–71. Initially De Coubertin saw sport in the pragmatic terms of physical fitness, rather than the ancient Greek approach that believed sporting prowess played a part in spiritual as well as physical development.

De Coubertin was not alone, however. A dynamic, well-connected entrepreneur and showman, he drew on the pioneering work of Dr Brookes, founder of the curiously named Wenlock Agricultural Reading Society in Shropshire. Brookes was both a far-seeing visionary and a busy GP, possessed of an invaluable practical ability simply to get things done. An erudite and talented medical man, he trained at Guys and St Thomas's Hospitals before continuing his studies in Padua, where there was a noted School of Medicine at the University, and Paris. He was, however, a countryman at heart and when his father, Dr Brookes senior, died in 1830 it needed little persuasion for him to return home from Paris a year later and assume his father's former role of GP for Much Wenlock. He also quickly became a JP.

An enthusiastic Philhellene, a lover of all things ancient Greek, Brookes was firmly convinced of the democratic ideals of ancient Greek society. His support for the working classes started at the intellectual and educational level. In 1841 he formed the Wenlock Agricultural Reading Society (WARS) and wrote successfully to high profile individuals such as the Duke of Wellington and Benjamin Disraeli, requesting books and other donations to his cause. Then, on 25 February 1850, the Society resolved to establish an Olympian Class 'for the moral, physical and intellectual improvement of

> **'Sport is part of every man and woman's heritage, and its absence can never be compensated for'**
>
> Baron Pierre de Coubertin

Charles Ainsworth is crowned with olive leaves at the 37th Wenlock Olympian Games, held in 1887, by the Queen of Beauty, Miss Serjeantson. Ainsworth won tilting-at-the-ring – an equestrian event similar to jousting where the rider, at full gallop, has to unhook a small iron ring with his lance.

Wenlock and Severn Junction Railway Company

A man of extraordinary energy and innovation, Brookes and his brother Andrew were also closely involved with the Wenlock and Severn Junction Railway and its associated company. The line formed part of the Wellington to Craven Arms Railway, and was operated for much of its working life by the Great Western Railway. Although it had not been officially opened, the first train on the railway was used to transport fans and competitors to the 1861 Wenlock Olympian Games. A modern day Olympic Movement of sorts was up and running, even before De Coubertin was born.

the inhabitants of the town and neighbourhood of Wenlock and especially of the working classes by the encouragement of outdoor recreation and by the award of prizes annually at public meetings for skill in athletics exercises and proficiency in intellectual and industrial attainments.' Brookes strongly felt that some sort of physical education should be compulsory at all schools, not just England's sports-orientated public schools, and sought to make participation in the Games open to men and boys from all walks of life. His Class was an early prototype of a modern Olympic Games, designed for the moral and physical benefit of 'every grade of man'.

The Wenlock Games

The Wenlock Olympian Class (WOC) was born and their first sporting gathering was held at Wenlock Racecourse on October 1850. It proved a notable success, developing into a thriving annual sports and cultural gathering preceded by a spectacular opening ceremony and parade through the town. Brookes insisted from the outset that his Games be open to all-comers – working men and artisans –as well as the leisured amateurs and gentlemen who had considered the sporting fields their own.

The core activities of the Wenlock Olympian Games were initially traditional English sports such as football, cricket and quoits. By 1852 a big

English surgeon Dr William Penny Brookes is often seen as one of the key men in the resurgence of the Olympic Games. A doctor from the English town of Much Wenlock, Shropshire, he founded the Wenlock Olympian Society in 1860 which held annual Games that became an inspiration for Baron Pierre de Coubertin to launch the modern Olympic Games.

'These Olympic Games bring together different classes and make them sociable and neighbourly'

Dr William Penny Brookes describes the benefits of the 1852 Much Wenlock Olympian Games

athletics element had been introduced, however, including races over 220 yards and the half mile and a number of throwing and jumping events. The very new sport of cycling also appeared early on at the Wenlock Olympian Games. At this stage prize money was also on offer, ranging from 2 shillings to 22. Although looking to promote athletic excellence the canny Brookes also wanted to remain inclusive, to ensure that none of those living locally felt barred from competition. Less serious competitions were thus established to keep the crowds entertained, such as a wheelbarrow race, pig chases and – the only female event – an old ladies' race for a pound of tea.

At the 1852 Games Brookes addressed the gathering. He explained that 'these Olympic Games bring together different classes and make them sociable and neighbourly' and that they maintained

'good feeling between high and low, rich and poor'. Within a decade of their inception the Games were attracting crowds of between four and five thousand, with competitors coming from Birmingham, Shrewsbury and Wolverhampton.

Meanwhile in Athens Evangelis Zappas, a wealthy Greek-Albanian-Romanian benefactor, seemed to be thinking along much the same lines. His response was to organise another 'Olympian Games' in an Athens city square in 1859. Brookes acted as an advisor to those Greek Games via Sir Thomas Wyse at the British Embassy, sending a copy of the 1858 Wenlock Olympian Games schedule and timetable to help the Athens project get off the ground. The Greek Olympian Games were not hugely successful, but Zappas was undeterred, funding the restoration of the Panathinaiko Stadium with a view to staging bigger and better versions of his Games in years to come. Brookes was always receptive to new ideas and the unlikely cross-fertilisation between Much Wenlock and Athens continued apace. On reading reports of the 1859 Games in Athens, Brookes introduced a number of events into the existing format of the Wenlock Olympian Games. The Wenlock Olympian Society (WOS) was formally founded on 15 November 1860.

Although best known as a cricketer, W.G. Grace was an outstanding athlete as a young man. In August 1866 he won the 440 yards hurdles at the National Olympian Games at Crystal Palace. Grace was also known to play football for the Wanderers, an amateur club in Surrey, on occasion.

Forging the Olympic Ideal

The concept of moving the 'Olympic Games' from city to city was also based on another of Brookes' ideas. As well as his town contest, the doctor had helped establish the National Olympian Association (NOA) in 1865, which featured yearly sporting festivals held across England. Each year the NOA Games were held in a different town or city, and the place that hosted them financed the meeting, as is the case with the Olympic Games today. Between 1862 and 1867 Liverpool – a real hotbed of the early Olympic Movement – held a grand annual 'Olympic Festival', organised by John Hulley and Charles Melly in conjunction with Brookes. Another three-day Olympic festival took place at London's Crystal Palace in 1866, with a young W.G. Grace winning the 440 yards hurdles in front of an estimated crowd of 10,000. Grace had been playing for an England XI against Surrey at the Oval, but was excused fielding duties on race day to make the short journey to Crystal Palace and compete. There is no record as to what contingency plans were in place had England and Grace been batting – he was not a man who lightly gave up his place at the crease.

Back at Wenlock in Shropshire, Brookes was fine-tuning his Olympian Games. He took the key decision that they must become amateur, with prize money and prizes being abolished. From now on it was medals, with an inscription from Pindar ('There are rewards for the glorious deeds'), and cups only. Competitors also had to swear an oath renouncing commercial reward: 'I will never compete for money, nor with professionals, nor ever make athletic exercise or contests as a means of livelihood.'

From 1859 the Wenlock Games, drawing inspiration from the Athens event of the same year, included a much-coveted all-round Pentathlon event. This consisted of the high jump, long jump, hurdles, a 55-foot rope climb and putting a stone of 35lb weight – the basis of a truly Olympian event that was soon to develop into the Decathlon. The silver medal that was struck in the early Games for the winner still exists, combining what appears to be a Maltese Cross with a winged figure of Nike, the Greek goddess of victory, holding a crown of olive leaves. Pindar's words were used for the inscription and the cross is suspended on an emblematic bar with the motto *Arte et Veribus* – skill and strength. The connection with the ancient world, especially Greece, was manifest, reflecting a sentimental attachment markedly different from the young De Coubertin's plans towards the end of the century.

Brookes was on a mission as his event gathered momentum and recognition. At the 1866 Wenlock Games he made a notable speech roundly criticising Parliament for its 'great and culpable neglect of physical education in England'. With a GP's insight, he argued that the simple 'drill' sessions in the playground of ordinary schools – in effect, marching in formation – should be replaced by competitive sport. Brookes sent a petition to Parliament to this effect in 1868, but it was rejected. He tried again in 1890, but again met with no success.

Running parallel to these 'Olympian' meetings in Britain, the Panathinaiko Stadium hosted two domestic Greek Games in 1870 and 1875. Brookes, perceiving there could be an international element to such an event, began a correspondence with John Gennadius, the Greek chargé d'affaires in London, to that effect. It caught Gennadius's imagination and in 1883 he wrote to Brookes, 'As a Greek I cannot but feel indebted to you that you continue with this idea, the project of a revival of the Olympic Games … I feel you will find a very sympathetic response in Greece.'

Enter the young De Coubertin, aged just 27 in 1890 but already formulating his own ambitious ideas on an international gathering of sportsmen. He visited a number of British public schools on a fact-finding mission and paid handsome tribute to the work of Brookes at a conference on the subject of physical education. In particular he praised Brookes'

speech of 1866 highlighting the need for compulsory sport in state schools. On hearing this Brookes immediately invited the Frenchman to the 40th Wenlock Games that summer, but he was unable to attend. However, De Coubertin agreed to attend an autumn version of the Games, specially arranged in his honour, so that he could witness exactly how such a gathering and sports festival worked.

The following 12 sports appeared in some of the first modern Olympic Games, but have now vanished from the event programme:

Basque pelota 1900 Games; demonstration sport in 1924, 1968 and 1992

Cricket 1900 Games. Team from England beat team from France – mostly English British Embassy employees

Croquet 1900 Games. Featured first women to take part in the Olympic Games

Jeu de paume (Real tennis) 1908 Games; demonstration sport in 1900

Lacrosse two Olympic Games in 1904 and 1908; demonstration sport in 1928, 1932, 1948

Polo five Olympic Games in 1900, 1908, 1920, 1924, 1936

Water Motorsports 1908 Games. Held off Southampton, speeds of 19mph achieved; six out of nine events cancelled owing to bad weather

Roque (hard surface form of croquet) 1904 Games

Rackets 1908 Games. Great Britain won all three medals in both the Singles and Doubles

Tug of war five Olympic Games in 1900, 1904, 1908, 1912, 1920

Golf, played in two Olympic Games (in 1900 and 1904) and

Rugby Union, played in four Olympic Games (in 1900, 1908, 1920 and 1924) are both due to return to the Olympic programme at Rio 2016.

De Coubertin stayed with Brookes and his wife for four days and, despite almost continuous rain during the two days of competition, the visit was judged a great success. He certainly received the red carpet treatment throughout as the ageing Brookes sensed a final opportunity to promote his bigger concept of an Olympian Games to a like-minded and influential member of the French aristocracy. A huge arch of flowers was constructed proclaiming, 'Welcome Baron Pierre de Coubertin and Prosperity to France', which De Coubertin asked if he could take back to France with him. At the end of the visit he dined with Brookes and about 60 other members of the Wenlock Olympian Society at the Raven Inn, planting a tree to commemorate the occasion on the Linden Fields, which flourishes to this day. Soon after his return to Paris, De Coubertin formed the International Olympic Committee. The venerable Brooks was duly invited to attend the inaugural meeting of the IOC, held at the Sorbonne in June 1894, where it was decided to press on with plans to hold a modern day Olympic Games in 1896. Brookes, however, was by now in poor health and he was unable to attend.

He died in 1895, aged 86, just five months before the 1896 Games in Athens.

Minutes from that original IOC meeting of 1894 suggest that the 79 delegates from 12 countries initially voted for London as the site of the inaugural 1896 Games. De Coubertin opposed this and, not sensing any support for his native Paris which was his first choice as a venue, instead suggested Athens. Delegates are minuted as objecting to this as well. However the British delegate, a Mr Herbert, was not present at the meeting, for reasons unknown, so could not instantly confirm whether London could accept the honour of hosting the Games. Eventually Athens emerged as the compromise venue. Despite the confusion of ad hoc committee room politics, a start had been made. The modern Olympic Movement was in its infancy and feeling its way.

De Coubertin was a free-thinking and highly intelligent individual with his own ideas for an Olympic Movement to suit the modern age. He borrowed heavily from the work of both Brookes and Zappas to shape that Movement and to address the practicalities of staging such a large and diverse sports gathering. In an obituary written immediately

The two mascots of London 2012, Wenlock (left) and Mandeville (right), during the opening of the London 2012 shop in Paddington Station on 1 November 2010. Wenlock is named after the Shropshire town, Much Wenlock, that played such a big part in the creation of the modern Olympic Movement and Mandeville is named after Buckinghamshire's Stoke Mandeville Hospital that led to the formation of the first Stoke Mandeville Games in 1948.

after Brookes' death, De Coubertin acknowledged his debt, 'If the Olympic Games that modern Greece has not yet been able to revive still survives today, it is due not to a Greek but to Dr William Penny Brookes'. Nearly a century later Juan Antonio Samaranch, then the long-serving President of the IOC, visited Much Wenlock in 1994. He laid a wreath at Brookes' grave and paid handsome tribute to the humble GP's contribution. 'I came to pay homage and tribute to Dr Brookes, who really was the founder of the modern Olympic Games.' Such an endorsement would have delighted the dedicated GP whose pioneering work will also be recognised at the London 2012 Games. One of the two official Mascots has been named 'Wenlock' to honour the role that small town has played in Britain's Olympic heritage. The other, Mandeville, honours the fundamental founding role that Britain, and especially Stoke Mandeville, has played in the development of the Paralympic Games.

The Athens Olympic Games, 1896

And so to 1896 and Athens, where Zappas and his cousin Konstantos had left the Greek government a trust fund to help finance any future Olympic Games that might occur. The Greek government contributed nothing itself, but another wealthy individual – businessman Georgios Averoff – also donated one million drachma towards a further upgrade for the beautiful Pananthinaiko Stadium. The Greek Organising Committee, led by Crown Prince Constantine, raised money by selling souvenir stamps and medals. From the very outset finance and commercial considerations loomed large for any nation wishing to host the Games.

There were concerns in many quarters that such demands would compromise the ideals of the original Olympic Games, an offering of physical prowess to the gods. An American professor of Greek and Latin, Basil L. Gildersleeve, described his initial scepticism at such a resurrection, 'We must not forget the great altar that dominates Olympia … The year was a sacred year; the poems that celebrated the victories were sacred poems … is there anything left of the old spirit, or can anything of the old spirit be evoked? Will the new Olympic Games be anything more than athletic sports?' He arrived in Athens only towards the end of the Games where his initial reservations were confounded by the carnival atmosphere he encountered. Although no longer charged with religious sentiment, a passionate patriotism set these Games apart from any ordinary competition.

The success of Great Britain and Ireland, as it remained until 1922, at these first Games was modest. A small team of 10 competitors attended, most of whom arrived on the SS *Congo* from Marseilles, having travelled by train to the south of France. They returned with seven medals in total – two gold, three silver and two bronze – a decent enough tally, although nothing to set the world alight. The USA set the pace with a total of 20 medals, including 11 gold.

'I declare the opening of the first international Olympic Games in Athens. Long live the Nation. Long live the Greek people'
King George I of Greece opens the first modern Olympic Games in 1896

Previous page A gathering of members of the International Olympic Committee, 10 April 1896 (four days into the first modern Olympic Games in Athens). They are (standing left to right) Willibald Gebhardt, IOC member for Germany, Jiri Guth-Jarkovsky, IOC member for Bohemia, Ferenc Kemény, IOC member for Hungary, Viktor Balck, IOC member for Sweden; (sitting left to right) Baron Pierre de Coubertin of France, Secretary General of the IOC, Demetrius Vikelas of Greece, President of the IOC, and General Alexey Dmitriyevich Butovsky, IOC member for Russia.

Launceston Elliot

Described in many journals as one of the handsomest men of his generation, Launceston Elliot caused a minor sensation in Athens. The official report into the 1896 Olympic Games noted, 'this young man attracted universal admiration by his uncommon beauty. He was of impressive stature, tall, well proportioned, his hair and complexion of surprising fairness. His handsome figure procured for him an offer of marriage from a highly placed lady.' Trained by the founder of body building Eugen Sandow, Elliot went on to win the one hand lift and came a debatable second in the two hand event. An all-round sportsman, he finished third in his 100m heat and lost in the first round of the Wrestling to Germany's Carl Schuhmann, winner of three Gymnastic events including the Wrestling. Elliot did not take that defeat well, having to be escorted out of the building as he protested long and hard. His final event was rope climbing, in which he finished fifth of five competitors. After the Athens 1896 Olympic Games Elliot won four British titles before becoming a professional 'strongman' in 1905. He emigrated to Australia in 1923.

An artist's impression of the start of the first 100m final at the Athens 1896 Olympic Games. The race was won in 12.0 seconds by American Thomas Burke, depicted here crouched down in the red shorts. Second was Fritz Hofmann, of Germany, in 12.2 with Francis Lane, also of America, and Alajos Szokolyi of Hungary sharing third in 12.6.

The first Briton ever to compete in an Olympic event was Charles Gmelin, a teacher from Oxford later to take Holy Orders. Gmelin finished third in the first heat of the 100m, won by Francis Lane of the USA who amazed the Greek crowd with his 'crouch' start, a position not seen in Europe before. The final was won by another American, Thomas Burke from Boston, using a similar starting technique. Gmelin fared much better in his specialist event, the 400m, where he finished third in the final behind Burke and another American, Herbert Jamison. At these inaugural modern day Olympic Games no medals were presented to athletes who finished in third position, although they have retrospectively been included in medal tables. In Athens the winners received a silver medal, a crown of olive branches and a diploma, while the runners-up received a bronze medal, an olive wreath crown and a diploma.

Britain's two champions were an interesting

duo – indeed many of these early winners seem to be exotic, larger than life characters. Weightlifter Launceston Elliot was the first. The son of a colonial Scottish family, his great-grandfather was a former Governor of Madras on the east coast of India and his grandfather, Sir Charles Elliot, was once the Governor General of remote St Helena in the South Atlantic – the prison of Napoleon for a number of years. Conceived in Launceston, Tasmania, Elliot himself was initially brought up in India where his father was a civil servant before the family returned to settle in Essex. Trained by the renowned Edwardian strongman and showman Eugen Sandow, he developed very quickly as a lifter. Aged just 21, Elliot won the one hand lift and came second in the two hand lift at the Games. Elliot was a little unlucky in the latter as he lifted the same weight (111.5kg) as Denmark's Viggo Jensen, only for Greece's Prince George, acting as a judge, to award the Dane first place because he had completed the lift more 'stylishly'. In the one-handed competition that followed straight afterwards, Elliot, most probably annoyed by the earlier decision, easily defeated the Dane, hoisting 71kg to Jensen's 57.

The other champion, John Mary Pius Boland, won the men's Singles at the Tennis tournament. He was a dapper Dublin lawyer who sat at Westminster as MP for South Kerry between 1900 and 1918 in which role he was a strong supporter of Irish nationalism. A graduate of Christ Church, Oxford, Boland was a talented games player who was simply visiting his friend Thrasyvoulos Manaos in Athens at the time of the Olympic Games. He had no intention of participating but Manaos, a member of the Greek Organising Committee, had other ideas. Soon Boland found himself competing in the men's Singles, where he defeated Friedrich Traun of Germany in the first round, Evangelos Rallis of Greece in the second and Konstantinos Paspatis of Greece in the semi-finals before accounting for Dionysios Kasdaglis of Egypt in the final 6-2,

6-2. Much encouraged, he then joined forces with Germany's Friedrich Traun, who had travelled to Athens mainly to run in the 800m. Together they went on to win the unofficial Doubles tournament, defeating Kasdaglis and Petrokokkinos 5-7, 6-3, 6-3 in a highly entertaining match.

The great set-piece event of the 1896 Athens Games – and an event that has maintained its status throughout the history of the modern Olympic Games – was the Marathon. Contrary to popular belief, such a long-distance endurance race had never been part of the ancient Greek games, although a legend of that time provided its inspiration. The messenger Pheidippides is said to have run from the town of Marathon to Athens to announce to the Athenians that their army had won the battle of Marathon. Allegedly his last word, before collapsing and passing away was 'Nenikiamen' – Greek for 'we have conquered'. French philologist Michel Bréal, credited as the founder of modern semantics, was much taken by the story and its resonance with the

The marble Olympic Stadium, depicted during competition in 1896, has remained in magnificent condition and was used at Athens 2004 for the Archery competition 108 years after the first modern Olympic Games in the same stadium.

Greek people. When the 1896 revival Games were confirmed Bréal suggested to his friend De Coubertin that a long-distance event to celebrate the epic run should be held in Athens. No sooner said than done: the idea struck an immediate chord with De Coubertin and plans were put in place.

To trial the new event the Greeks ran two marathons in March 1896 with the eventual victor at the Olympic Games, Spyridon Louis, finishing fifth in the second race – a promising if not startling debut. Less than three weeks later he was competing in the first Olympic Marathon, with Greece still clamouring for its first Athletics winner. This time the Greek water carrier was a man inspired. Fuelled along the way, as he recalled, by spectators offering milk, beer, and Easter eggs, and wine from his father-in-law, he beat off the French favourite Albin Lermusiaux and Australia's Edwin Flack – neither of whom finished – to win the 40km race (as it then was) in 2:58:50.

The official Olympic report reflected his reception as he received his medal: 'Here the Olympic victor was received with full honour; the King rose from his seat and congratulated him most warmly on his success. Some of the King's aides de camp and several members of the committee went as far as to kiss and embrace the victor, who finally was carried in triumph to the retiring room under the vaulted entrance. The scene witnessed inside the Stadium cannot be easily described and even foreigners were carried away by the general enthusiasm.'

One foreigner who relished the experience was the American hurdler Thomas P. Curtis. Almost 40 years later he vividly recalled watching thousands of white pigeons released into the sky as Spyridon Louis approached the finishing line. Another visitor overwhelmed by the

spectacle was the classics professor Basil Lanneau Gildersleeve, who reached Athens to witness the great celebrations that were greeting the news of Louis's victory. They made a powerful impression: 'the coast-line of Greece did not speak to the soul as did the simultaneous joy of a hundred thousand men and women with blood in their veins and the light of gladness on their faces. I have seen the light of battle on the soldier's face, but I have never seen faces more brilliantly illuminated than the countenances of the throngs that pervaded the streets of Athens.'

The King offered Louis any gift he would care to ask for, but all he could think of was a humble donkey-drawn carriage for his water-carrying business. He never ran another marathon, but returned instead to his hometown of Marousi, later in life becoming the local police officer. Louis was the guest of honour at the Berlin 1936 Olympic Games where he carried the standard of the Greek team at the Opening Ceremony and, ironically, received an olive branch from Adolf Hitler.

The Marathon event and its Greek victor caught the imagination of many, not least the British. They had no runner at the Athens 1896 Marathon, but still believed themselves to be the best long-distance runners in the world – due in part to well-established cross-country running at public schools and fell running in mountainous parts of the country. Well over a century later, however, despite a continuing addiction to the race, we are still waiting for the first British winner.

Another physical 'marathon' took place on the Cycling track, where Britain's Frederick Keeping came second in the 12-hour race. The event was immediately discontinued, however – the main objection apparently that it was simply too boring for

'Catch him, Louis. You've got to beat him. Hellas! Hellas!'

The Greek crowd's enthusiastic support for Spyridon Louis in the Marathon of 1896

'I slurped down the wine and felt much stronger'

Spyridon Louis acknowledges his future father-in-law's contribution to his Marathon victory

the spectators as competitors endlessly lapped the 333m Velodrome. It was clearly an event for tough endurance athletes; competitors drove themselves to the limit, with only two out of the seven competitors completing the race. After a cold wet day's racing that started at 5am the winner, Adolf Schmal from Austria, finished with Keeping just one lap behind after 314.66km of racing. In his book *The First Modern Olympics* Richard D. Mandell wrote, 'Neither had eaten and had only sipped liquid. They were squalid from excreta and delirious from fatigue … their legs swollen gruesomely … both could be heard weeping.' Both Keeping and Edward Bartell, Britain's other competitor, were listed as working as servants at the British Embassy, and as such there were objections to their participation as they could not be considered amateurs and gentlemen. The objection was overruled.

The only other British athlete to claim second place at the Athens 1896 Games was Grantley Goulding in the 110m Hurdles. Born into a wealthy Gloucestershire farming family, Grantley created something of a stir and accusations of arrogance by pinning medals from previous races to his waistcoat as he paraded around Athens. In the event Goulding was pipped at the post by Thomas Curtis from the USA. Two of the four finalists withdrew on the morning, and to this day Goulding remains the only Olympic athlete to both come second and finish last in the race.

A Greek water carrier by trade, a sporting legend by ability, Spyridon Louis made history when he became the winner of the first Olympic Marathon in Athens in 1896. He victory over the 40km distance was in a time of 2:58.50 in a race of 17 runners. Some 40 years later, in one of his last public appearances, Louis was a guest of honour at the Berlin 1936 Games.

Medal table from the 1896 Olympic Games

Country	Gold	Silver	Bronze	Total
USA	11	6	2	19
Greece	10	17	18	45
Germany	6	5	2	13
France	5	4	2	11
Great Britain	2	3	3	8
Hungary	2	1	3	6
Austria	2	1	2	5

The First Olympic Medals

There were no gold medals in the 1896 Games. Winners were awarded a silver medal engraved with the face of the ancient Greek god Zeus, holding a globe surmounted by the winged goddess Victory. They also received an olive wreath and a diploma. Those in second place were given a copper medal, a laurel wreath and a diploma, and every competing athlete received a commemorative medal. The first gold medals were awarded at the St Louis 1904 Games and they remained solid gold until Stockholm 1912, when they became guilded silver instead. Today's winners receive medals made from gold-plated silver, although each medal must contain at least six grams of pure gold.

Curtis himself, the winner of the 110m Hurdles, thoroughly enjoyed his time in Athens. He and his teammates were applauded by locals in the streets and partook enthusiastically of local hospitality, on occasion competing while nursing hangovers. For them the Games were a time of adventure and conviviality rather than intensely focused competition, as well as a chance to exchange ideas. Among Curtis's fondest memories was a recollection of teaching the Crown Prince of Greece the rudiments of baseball, aided by a walking stick and an orange.

Despite their impressive medal tally, the ad hoc arrangements in Athens were sometimes too much for the Americans. One of Curtis's teammates, diving fearlessly into the sea in a Swimming event, encountered a startling chill. He emerged with a horrified cry of 'Jesu Christo! I'm freezing' before beating a hasty retreat to the float. 'Wild swimming' continued in several of the early Olympic Games, only ending with the 'cutting edge' facilities of London's White City Stadium in 1908.

The Paris 1900 Olympic Games

Although it had its problems, the Athens 1896 Olympic Games, by most criteria, has to be considered a significant success as a start-up event. Certainly the crowds in Athens flocked to watch the main events in the Panathinaiko Stadium, even if one or two other competitions, notably the Tennis, attracted little attention. Afterwards there were many who felt perhaps Athens now ought to be established as a permanent home, but De Coubertin, who had always longed to bring the Olympic Games to his home city of Paris, resisted this idea. Such was his influence in committee at the IOC in those early days that his wishes carried the day, a decision that in retrospect set back the Olympic Movement by a decade or more. The 1900 Games became

'Jesu Christo! I'm freezing!'

An American swimmer takes the plunge in the 1896 Olympic Games

incorporated into the 1900 World's Fair, set to be staged in Paris at the same time. De Coubertin and the IOC effectively lost control of the Games, with the World's Fair organisers almost reluctantly working the sporting events into their schedule to suit themselves.

The Olympic Games became a very distant second. There was no sense of occasion and virtually no effort was made by the World's Fair organisers to invest in sporting facilities. The Athletics 'arena'

At Paris 1900, Britain's Charlotte Cooper became the first woman champion of the Olympic Games when she won the Tennis Singles. She had already won three of her five Wimbledon championships at the time and went on to win the Mixed Doubles at these Games with Reginald Doherty.

The Paris 1900 Games were quite a time for the Doherty brothers. Lawrence (right) won gold in the men's Singles with Reginald (left) taking bronze and the pair then combined to win the Doubles. Reginald also won the Mixed Doubles gold with Charlotte Cooper.

Best of British

Charlotte Cooper

The formidable Charlotte Cooper became Britain's first female Olympic gold medallist, and the world's first women's Olympic champion in any sport, when she won the women's Singles in the 1900 Games. She defeated Hélène Prévost of France in straight sets in the final before taking a second title in the Mixed Doubles with Reginald Doherty. She had already won the Wimbeldon Singles title in 1895, 1896 and 1898 (the first won after cycling to Wimbledon from her home in Ealing with her racket attached to the front bracket). Cooper took two more titles after the 1900 Games, in 1901 and 1908 when, aged 37 years and 282 days, she became the oldest woman to win the Single's title, a record that still stands. Cooper became one of four mothers to win the women's Singles title and was runner-up in six Wimbledon finals, the last in 1912.

was a simple grass track at the Bois de Boulogne, as the Parisian authorities were unwilling to lay down a cinder track on such hallowed turf. The events took place over an interminable five-month period with very little press coverage, leaving the citizens of Paris virtually unaware that anything out of the ordinary was being staged. Strangely no medals, laurel crowns or diplomas were awarded, although the winners of most competitions did receive a trophy.

As ever, the competitors themselves – including for the first time 22 women – rose to the occasion, managing in part to rescue the Olympic Games with the quality of their performances. Britain was well to the forefront with a total of 30 'medals', including 15 gold. This placed them third in the unofficial medal table that had begun to be compiled, a task always diligently undertaken by officials from the teams enjoying a successful games.

Britain dominated the Tennis tournament. Charlotte Cooper became the nation's first female gold medallist when she won the women's Singles and Lawrence Doherty won first the men's Singles and then, in tandem with brother Reginald, the men's Doubles. Meanwhile Reginald, having withdrawn from the men's Singles rather than compete against his brother, partnered Cooper in the Mixed Doubles and won that as well. A splendid week's work which all of them regarded as a pleasant diversion from the more serious business of acquiring Wimbledon titles.

Elsewhere Britain won three of the yachting titles, immediately establishing a strong tradition in that sport that continues today. A deal of controversy surrounds the entire Paris regatta, held largely on the River Seine at Meulan, with the two biggest classes contested at Le Havre. Some Olympic historians argue that they cannot be considered authentic Olympic events as prize money was offered in all seven classes and races were operated under a handicap system. Such conditions of competition were the norm in yacht racing at the time, however,

Best of British

John Jarvis

John Jarvis, born in 1872, was the first in a line of great British swimmers at the forefront of the sport during the early Olympic Games. He won his first Olympic title at the Paris 1900 Games, beating Austrian Otto Wahle by over a minute in the 1000m Freestyle. He took a second win in the 4000m Freestyle with an even more emphatic victory, finishing about 11 minutes ahead of Zoltán Halmay from Hungary. Often dubbed the 'world's greatest swimmer', Jarvis was also a keen water polo player; he represented Britain internationally for 11 seasons and won a third medal as a member of the winning Great Britain team at the 1900 Games. Britain's refusal to travel to St Louis for the 1904 Games prevented Jarvis from taking a similar haul there, but he was still competitive in the Intercalated Games in Athens two years later, although these medals are not recognised by the International Olympic Committee. Jarvis enjoyed a long and varied career, but his glory days had gone by the Olympic Games of 1908, when he failed to finish in his 1500m semi-final.

Right Britain's John Jarvis was one of the stars of the Paris 1900 Games. The Swimming events took place in the River Seine and Jarvis won gold medals in two of the long distance events: the 1000m Freestyle and the 4000m Freestyle.

although it is less easy to explain why more than one 'final' was held in a number of the classes, with winners and a gold medallist being declared after each race. For the record, Britain's three gold medals came in the ½–1 ton class, the 3–10 ton class and the Open class. Crewing on two of those gold medal-winning teams was John Gretton, later to become 1st Baron Gretton CBE. He still holds the unique distinction of being the only athlete to also be a serving MP to win an Olympic title for Great Britain, having been elected as the Conservative member for Derbyshire South in 1895. Gretton later served as the MP for Rutland and completed a marathon 48 years in the House by serving for 25 years as the MP for Burton.

National teams, although commonplace, were not compulsory at this stage. As a result another British yachtsman, Edward William Exshaw, won both finals and gold medals in the 2–3 ton class, competing in a mixed Anglo/French team alongside Frédéric Blanchy and Jacques le Lavasseur. Despite such confusion it is clear that Britain, an island nation with a proud naval tradition, was generally going to be one of the teams to beat at Olympic regattas. And so it has proved. According to the IOC's own medal tables – which do recognise those three gold medals from 1900 – Britain is historically ranked as the number one sailing nation in the world, with 24 gold medals at all Olympic Games and 49 medals in total.

If there was drama on the River Seine during the yachting, perhaps we should spare a thought for the swimmers who used the same waters in their bids for glory. Strong currents helped the swimmers to unusually quick times, with the Leicester-born John Jarvis taking the men's 1000m freestyle and the 4000m freestyle. Hailed as the 'Amateur Swimming Champion of the World', Jarvis claimed 108 major championships throughout a long career. Along with Joey Nutall, the English professional swimming champion, he developed an idiosyncratic

overarm sidestroke – a one-armed freestyle –that was complemented by a strong side-kick. Known throughout the sport as the Jarvis-Nutall kick, this became a very useful style for lifesavers and beachguards. Later a swimming instructor and life-saver, Jarvis once famously rescued a pair of twin sisters from drowning. He was posthumously inducted into swimming's international Hall of Fame in Fort Lauderdale in 1968, an event attended by his three daughters, all themselves swimming instructors.

Although generally outclassed by the powerful Americans in track and field, Great Britain did produce a notable 1500m champion in Charles Bennett – a native of Shapwich in Dorset who worked as a train driver in Bournemouth. Bennett was aided by the absence of American John Cregan, the pre-race favourite, who refused to compete on Sunday, but he also reduced his personal best by 18 seconds in the final en route to victory over local favourite Henri Deloge. Bennett came second in the 4000m steeplechase, behind fellow team member John Rimmer, and also won a gold in the 5000m team race. The latter does not count in the official medal table, however, as the British quartet had to recruit an Australian sprinter, Stanley Rowley, to run as their fifth man against the French. In the event Rowley dropped out after a couple of leisurely laps, leaving Bennett to win the race from Alfred Tysoe.

Stan Rowley

Born in 1876, Stanley Rupert Rowley was an Australian sprinter who won both 100 yards races at the bi-annual Australian championships in 1897 and 1899. He raised funds by private subscription to travel to Paris for the Olympic Games, where he took bronze medals in the 60m, 100m and 200m. Rowley then joined a British 'mixed' team to compete against the French in the now-defunct 5000m team race. The four existing runners needed a fifth man to enter the event, and were so confident of success that they were not concerned about taking on a sprinter for a distance race. Rowley joined the team and they did indeed win the race, aided by 1500m champion Charles Bennett.

British train driver and Olympic athlete Charles Bennett wins the 1500m event at the Paris 1900 Olympic Games in Bois de Boulogne on 15 July. Bennett's winning time of 4:06.2 set a new world and Olympic record.

Medal table from the 1900 Olympic Games

Country	Gold	Silver	Bronze	Total
France	26	39	30	95
USA	18	14	14	36
Great Britain	15	6	8	29
Belgium	5	5	5	15
Germany	4	2	1	7
Italy	2	2	0	4
Australia	2	0	3	5

Tysoe had completed a middle distance double for Britain in the 800m, at which he was already the world record holder, by defeating Cregan. He and Bennett were feted on their return to Britain and a compromise race of 1,320 yards was organised, which Tysoe won. Sadly Tysoe, who had also been part of the 5000m team race with Bennett, died the following year of pleurisy, aged only 27 – a hugely talented athlete still some way short of his peak. Joining that much vaunted duo was the less heralded John Rimmer, who won the 4000m steeplechase. He, Bennett and Sidney Robinson ran together and tried to cross the line together, but Rimmer was awarded the race – while the trio also ran together in the 5000m team race with Tysoe.

Although Britain's middle-distance runners reigned supreme, the outstanding figure of the Paris 1900 Games was undoubtedly the American Alvin Kraenzlein. He set a record that still stands, being the only Olympian ever to win four individual Athletics events at a single Games. The flamboyant Kraenzlein, a dental student from the University of Pennsylvania, was of German extraction, and his enduring fame lies in the fact that he invented and perfected the technique of hurdling using a leading leg rather than a two-legged jump. That technical mastery saw him win both Hurdles events – the 110m Hurdles and the 200m Hurdles – and he also pipped his fellow dental student and Penn colleague Walter Tewksbury in the 60m. The fourth event, the Long Jump, brought together both Kraenzlein, a former world record holder, and his American colleague Meyer Prinstein, a Polish-born jumper and the existing world record holder. As captain of the devout Syracuse University track

'In loving memory of Alfred Ernest Tysoe, champion amateur half mile runner of the world. Brief life is here our portion, brief sorrow, short-lived care. The life that knows no ending, the tearless life is there'

Inscription on the gravestone of Paris 1900 800m champion and world record holder Alfred Tysoe, who died aged 27.

team Prinstein had been warned by his Dean not to compete in the final round of the Long Jump, scheduled to be held on a Sunday. Prinstein believed he had an informal agreement with Kraenzlein that he too would not jump on a Sunday and that the results of the qualifying round, which in those days could be carried forward to the finals, would be used to separate them. On the Saturday afternoon in qualifying Prinstein lead with a jump of 7.17m, but to the surprise of many Kraenzlein appeared the next day and duly bettered the jump by 1cm to win the event. Legend has it that Prinstein, on hand to watch the event, reined a volley of punches on Kraenzlein, although some observers insist he was restrained by colleagues and no punches actually landed! Kraenzlein then refused Prinstein's challenge of a jump-off the following day and became a controversial victor.

The Marathon provided a huge focus of interest as ever. In 1900 it was a fairly chaotic affair, with numerous runners getting lost on a poorly marked course through winding Parisian streets. American Richard Grant claimed afterwards he was run down by a cyclist and his compatriot, a bemused Arthur Newton, was credited with fifth place despite his insistence that he had not been passed by a single runner en route. Michel Théato was finally declared the winner and the French immediately claimed him as one of their own, running up the Tricoleur at the Victory Ceremony and playing the 'Marseillaise'. Afterwards Théato, a cabinet-maker who ran for the St-Mandé athletics club in Paris, admitted that he was from Luxembourg. He remained a Belgian citizen for the rest of his life.

Left Alvin Kraenzlein, of the USA, on his way to winning the 110m Hurdles in 15.4, an Olympic record, at the Paris 1900 Games. Kraenzlein went on to win three more events at the Games: the 60m, 200m Hurdles and Long Jump.

Cricket Gold

Victory in the cricket competition of the 1900 Games was awarded to Great Britain, one of only two teams in the tournament. The Devon and Somerset Wanderers, largely composed of Blundell School old boys and members of the Castle Cary Cricket Club, took on the 'French Athletic Club Union', which consisted of two Paris clubs largely made up of British ex-pats. Montagu Toller was one of the two Wanderers cricketers who played for Somerset at county level, Alfred Bowerman being the second, and it was Toller's vigorous bowling attack which sealed the win for his team, wresting it from the jaws of a draw with only five minutes to spare.

'I do not know why my leg gave way. I then seemed to lose control of it, and suddenly it gave out, throwing me on my face. But that is one of the fortunes of sport and I cannot complain'

Arthur Duffey, favourite for the 100m, who collapsed after 50m in the 1900 Games

Previous page
The Marathon at the Paris 1900 Games was incredibly confusing, with cyclists and runners 'mingling' in the backstreets of Paris. The American Arthur Newton thought he had won, but Michel Théato, a Belgian living in France, had finished an hour earlier.

The 1904 Olympic Games took place in St Louis, USA, to coincide with the World Fair. Here pictured is Miss Alice Roosevelt, daughter of the President, who is watching the events taking place at the Fair.

Wild Swimming

Swimming events at the early Olympic Games had no sophisticated Aquatics stadia. Instead they took place in open water, leaving competitors to battle with cold, mud and swirling currents. At the 1896 Games Swimming events were held in the Mediterranean, in the chilly waters of the Bay of Zea off the Piraeus coast. In Paris they took place in the River Seine, where fast currents impacted on the competitors' times, and in 1904 in an artificial lake in Forest Park, in the western area of St Louis. Only in the 1908 Games did the Swimming competition first enjoy a purpose-built pool, within the track of the main White City Stadium.

The St Louis 1904 Olympic Games

With 30 gold medals in the first two Olympic Games, the USA was already established as the most powerful Olympic nation. De Coubertin wanted to reward their support and excellence by allowing them to stage the 1904 Games, a decision resulting in a disappointing Games that nearly brought the emerging modern day Olympic Movement to a grinding halt. Originally the IOC awarded the Games to Chicago, but a domestic row immediately erupted within the USA. St Louis, the scheduled venue for the World's Fair in 1904, felt that it should stage the Olympic Games in conjunction with the Fair, following the example of Paris four years previously – although the experience there should perhaps have

set the alarm bells ringing. The Fair was planned to be an impressive spectacle, with over 1,500 buildings connected by over 120km of roads and walkways spread over a 485-hectare site. More than 60 foreign nations mounted exhibits, and it was later said that a visitor would need more than a week to give even a cursory glance at all that was on display.

The St Louis Fair organisers, to press their point, aggressively threatened to stage a competing international sports competition to rival a Chicago Olympic Games. A stand-off developed and President Theodore Roosevelt eventually intervened. Seeking to secure the obvious economic benefits of the World's Fair, he unsurprisingly came down on the side of St Louis. The organisers duly proceeded to repeat most of the mistakes of the Paris 1900 Olympic Games, not least spreading the Games over four months. Significantly, David Francis, President of the Louisiana Purchase Exposition, declined to invite any IOC dignitaries to participate in the functional Opening Ceremony of the Olympic Games; he preferred to do it himself.

The 1904 Games attracted negligible press or spectator interest, not least because of the Fair's direct competition. De Coubertin, sniffing the wind well in advance, didn't even bother to attend himself, nor did many of the European nations who had begun to show an interest in the concept of Oympic sport. Some 24 nations had sent competitors to Paris, but only 12 nationalities were represented in St Louis, and some of those only nominally. Of the 651 athletes participating, 523 were known to have come from the USA. Unsurprisingly many of the events amounted to little more than a domestic USA championships. Of the 84 gold medal events, 42 did not include competitors from outside of the USA. The USA won 23 of the 25 track and field titles contested.

Officially Britain did not send a team to the USA. The cost of travelling and accommodation was considered prohibitive, the fear of organisational chaos was another big deterrent, and there were also some doubts expressed about the amateur status of some of the American athletes. In the end, however, the record books credit Great Britain and Ireland with a single gold medal, earned by one Tom Kiely – a remarkable all-rounder and one of Ireland's most famous sons, even if his crowning achievement brought glory to Britain.

And thereby hangs a tale and a source of some controversy and a storyline that was to be a major part of Great Britain's participation at the early Games. Kiely was Irish through and through, a proud son of Ballyneal just outside Carrick-on-Suir, County Tipperary. A quite exceptional athlete, pictures of Kiely in his pomp show a physique that could have been honed in a twenty-first-century gym. There was a great local tradition in Tipperary of weight and stone throwing and the young Kiely developed initially as a thrower. He was fleet-footed as well, though, and gradually turned to what was then termed the 'all-rounder' event, which we would recognise as the modern day Decathlon. At the turn of the century the 10 events contested were the 100 yards, shot put, high jump, 880 yard walk, hammer throw, pole vault, 120 yards hurdles, 56lb weight throw, long jump and 1 mile.

Contemporaries agreed that Kiely was no rampant 'Irish nationalist', but he was an active playing member of the highly politicised GAA and definitely considered himself Irish, not British. Politically of course the two countries were as one during his career, considered legally indivisible until 1922. For various reasons Kiely chose not to attend the 1896 and 1900 Games when he was at his peak. At neither of those Games was there an 'all-rounder' event, but he was perfectly capable of entering a number of throwing events had he wished. He decided to stay away. By 1904 however, opportunity came to the 34-year-old Kiely with the appearance of the all-rounder event on the programme in St Louis. He impulsively decided that he would finally like to compete in the Olympic Games before his powers deserted him entirely.

> ## 'Most of the athletes had never been near a World's Fair and naturally wanted to see the sights'
>
> Emil Breitkreutz on the mix of business and pleasure at the St Louis 1904 Olympic Games

Medal table from the 1904 Olympic Games

Country	Gold	Silver	Bronze	Total
USA	72	79	75	216
Germany	4	6	5	15
Cuba	4	2	3	9
Canada	4	1	1	6
Hungary	2	1	1	4
Great Britain	1	1	0	2
Switzerland	1	0	1	2

Tom Kiely's Decathlon Gold Medal Winning Performance	
100 yards	11.2
shot put	10.82m
high jump	1.52m
800 yard walk	3:59
hammer	36.76m
pole vault	2.74m
120 yard hurdles	17.8
56lb throw	8.91m
long jump	5.94m
1 mile	551.0
Points total	**6036**

Kiely made it quite clear, however, that he would not accept offers of financial assistance from Great Britain or indeed the USA, both of whom in the preceding years had badly wanted the Tipperary man to declare for them and officially compete under their flag.

A true son of the soil, Kiely's all-round strength and athleticism were developed during long days as a teenager helping his father William on their small farm at Curraghdobbin near Ballyneal in County Tipperary. It was his good fortune to live near the Davin brothers – Pat, Tom and Maurice, who were notable early all-round athletes and throwers and took him under their wing. For the Paris 1900 Olympic Games he did briefly have a notion to reluctantly compete for Great Britain in the Hammer – he had won a succession of hammer titles and had set a world record of 49.38m the previous year – but at the AAA Championships in 1900 he endured the one really bad day of his long career and finished a distant second to fellow Irishman John Flannagan, competing for the USA. Much discouraged he determined then to stick to his original conviction and not participate at the Olympic Games for Great Britain. Yet as 1904 approached and a career that had included 36 Irish and GAA titles (not to mention 28 world record marks) drew to its conclusion, he decided the time had come.

Kiely had decided to finance the trip himself and reportedly sold some of the 3,000 trophies he had won during his career to pay for the May sea voyage. On arrival in St Louis the USA redoubled their efforts to recruit him – many talented Irish American athletes were already covering themselves in glory for their adopted country – but again Kiely resisted. Whenever the press came calling his message was clear, namely that he was in St Louis to represent Tipperary and Ireland. Come the competition day, however, and it was again made quite clear to Kiely by IOC officials that he would only be able to compete if he registered as a British

Tom Kiely (left), of Ireland, was the first hero of the multi-events after winning the All-Round – the forerunner of the Decathlon – at the St Louis 1904 Games. Pictured with teammate J.J. Holloway, Kiely triumphed in a discipline whose all 10 events were held on the same day.

competitor. Like it or not in 1904, in the eyes of the world and not just the IOC, he was a citizen of Great Britain. Ireland at the time was not an independent country and Dublin was often labelled as the second city of the Empire.

Keily was between a rock and a hard place. He wrestled with his conscience, but having made such an effort to travel to St Louis it would have been perverse to do anything other than compete. In those days the USA was not just an eight-hour flight away, it was a journey you made just occasionally in your career. It was a huge undertaking and to have returned home to Ireland without contesting the issue was ultimately unthinkable. Everybody knew his affiliations in any case, and perhaps winning the gold medal would highlight his pride in Ireland and Tipperary to the world at large. That's how he rationalised his decision anyway.

The competition was held on a horribly wet July day in St Louis, when a rainstorm battered the competitors from dawn to dusk and the unforgiving muddy cinder track tested everybody to the full. Times and distances were way down, survival and getting through the day was the priority. A shamrock on his vest demonstrated where Kiely's true loyalties lay, but for a day – all 10 events were completed in one day – he put nationality issues to one side and concentrated on proving himself to be the world's greatest all-round athlete. Kiely made the worst possible start in the 100 yards, slipping badly and finishing last. He recovered his poise to win four of the 10 events in the Decathlon – the 880 yard walk, 120 yard hurdles, hammer throw and 56lb weight throw – to comfortably take the gold medal with a total of 6,036 points from America's Adam Gunn, a four-time All-American guard with the Penn State Football team. Another Tipperary man, John Holloway from Bansha, finished fourth that day.

The St Louis 1904 Olympic Games were not quite Kiely's swansong – two years later he crossed the Atlantic one last time and once more defeated all of the top American athletes to claim the 'World title'. Later that year he decided to get married and gave his wife a girdle stitched with a double row of his various medals as a wedding present – as you do when you are the world's greatest all-round athlete.

Just to emphasise a confusing situation, middle-distance runner John Daly from Galway won a second medal for Great Britain at the St Louis Games, a silver in the steeplechase, over the curious distance of 2590m. Daly had recently emigrated to the USA and, like Kiely, wanted to be recognised as an Irish competitor. The Olympic officials would not be swayed in his case either and again he was

formally listed as a Great Britain competitor.

Kiely apart, the story that interested the British readership – when the story was eventually relayed – was again the Marathon, which developed into an extraordinary saga with the added interest that it was eventually won by a British-born runner, although Thomas Hicks was unambiguously a US citizen by the time he competed. The Marathon was run on a sweltering August afternoon, with temperatures hitting the mid-90°F. The situation was exacerbated by the posse of automobiles and horses that rode ahead to clear the dry roads, who kicked up a dust storm for the runners to negotiate along the 24.85-mile course, which included seven steep inclines – anathema to marathon runners.

There were immediately some big name casualties including Frederick Lorz, a tough American who was to win the Boston marathon

Left Tom Kiely competing in the high jump, where he jumped 1.52m. He was only joint fifth in the high jump, but went on to win four of the 10 events to take the overall title.

later in his career. Lorz was forced to quit after nine miles, when his manager stopped to give him a lift to the finish in his car. Unfortunately the car then broke down close to the running track at Francis Field, so he was forced to jog the final five miles back to reclaim his clothes and valuables. High farce then took over with Lorz, arriving alone in the stadium three hours and 13 minutes after he started, being acclaimed as the winner when he walked into the 'arena'. Highly amused by the entire scenario, Lorz played along with the joke and was about to receive the laurel wreath from Alice Roosevelt, daughter of the President, when he admitted the deception. He was disqualified and subsequently banned for life by the AAU although this was later to be reduced to 12 months.

Meanwhile, in the race proper, the British born

'I would rather have won this race than be President of the United States'

Thomas Hicks after his controversial Marathon victory in the 1904 Olympic Games

Hicks who had settled in Cambridge, Massachusetts, duly arrived at the finishing line after 3:28:35 to win the gold medal, but only after dramatic interventions from his trainers. He seemed to be on the point of collapse seven miles from the stadium, and then again four miles back, when they twice fed him a cocktail of strychnine and brandy to revive him. The 'remedy' worked in the short term, but Hicks collapsed again shortly after reaching the finish line and had to be carried away. There was no such thing as 'doping' at the time and although strychnine would now be considered an illegal drug its use was commonplace in those days, certainly among long-distance runners and cyclists. Like Spyridon Louis before him, Hicks was never to run another marathon again.

Below The start of the Marathon at the St Louis 1904 Games. The eventual winner, Hicks, is on the left wearing number 20. Next to him, wearing number 31, is Lorz. Wearing number 3, Carvajal, who ran wearing his ordinary clothes, is towards the centre of the line up.

For much of the race, the Marathon had been led by an impoverished Cuban postman Andarín Carvajal. He had begged in the streets of Havana to raise the ferry fare to the USA and then arrived in St Louis on the day of the race. Carvajal was tired, hadn't eaten for over a day and had no specialist running clothes with him although he had his running shoes. Martin Sheridan, the giant Irish American athlete, took pity on the diminutive Cuban in the athletes' changing room and sat down with a pair of scissors patiently to fashion a pair of running shorts out Carvajal's trousers. The Cuban was a talented performer and immediate crowd favourite with his habit of briefly running backwards as he turned to acknowledge cheers of encouragement. He featured prominently for much of the race, but – famished – unwisely stopped at an orchard to eat an apple, which immediately gave him severe stomach cramps. He eventually overcame that handicap to finish a battling fourth.

Just to complete a notable afternoon in so many ways, the St Louis 1904 Marathon featured the first appearance of a black African athlete at an Olympic Games, in fact two. Is it any wonder that the Marathon has always captured the public's imagination? Len Taunyane and Jan Mashiani, both students from the Orange Free State, had travelled to the USA to attend the trade exposition as part of a Boer War exhibit, and both decided on spec to enter the Marathon. Both completed the torturous course, Taunyane in ninth and Mashiani in 12th, and the long tradition of brilliant African distance runners had made a modest start.

The Intercalated Games of 1906

After the 1900 Games in Paris a strong lobby favoured returning the Olympic Games to Athens on a permanent basis. De Coubertin headed off such

OFFICIAL SOUVENIR
WORLD'S FAIR - ST. LOUIS 1904

Government Building.

A souvenir postcard for for St Louis 1904 Olympic Games, the third of the modern era, depicts. the government building in city.

a move, but to preserve the link with Athens, and to tap into the enthusiasm they displayed for the 1896 Games, it was decided to stage an interim Intercalated Games there, midway through every four-year Olympic cycle. The 1906 Intercalated Games, the only one that ever happened, duly took place in Athens. It was a well contested event, featuring over 903 competitors from 20 nations – a welcome opportunity for international competition for those unable to travel to St Louis two years earlier. However, the Intercalated Games is not regarded as an official Games by the IOC. None of the results or medal winners count as official Olympic records or statistics. The Intercalated Games is remembered now only as a sporting curiosity from a time of experiment in which the Olympic Movement was still finding its feet.

The Games saw an encouraging scattering of gold medals for Britain. At the Velodrome, John Matthews and Arthur Rushen won the tandem event and William Pett took the 20km. Henry Taylor, whose finest moments were to come two years later at the 1908 Games in London, made light of choppy waters to win the 1 mile freestyle in the swimming, while Greek-born brothers Gerald and Sidney Merlin both won gold medals at the trap shooting, with Gerald winning the single shot competition and Sidney the double shot. John Jarvis proved he was still competitive, taking a silver medal in the one mile freestyle and two bronze medals, one in the 400m freestyle and another in the 4 x 250m freestyle relay. As mentioned, however, none of these medals now appear in official Olympic records.

The main dramas, however, were reserved for the Athletics arena, held at the beautiful Panathanaiko Stadium, where the horseshoe track was a strange 192m in length. In the absence of Britain's best middle-distance runner Alf Shrubb, who had been ruled professional and therefore ineligible, Lieutenant Henry Hawtrey was a convincing winner of the 5 miles race, although third-placed John Daly, the

At the 1906 Intercalated Games in Athens, the British cycling team of William Pett, Arthur Rushen, John Matthews, Herbert Bouffler and Herbert Crowther, won two gold medals between them.

Irishman who won a silver medal in St Louis, was disqualified for blocking a Swedish runner. Long jumper Peter O'Connor, the world record holder from Wicklow, caused further controversy by fixing an Irish national flag to the top of a 20ft flagpole during the Victory Ceremony, at which he was awarded a silver medal. The concept of political protest at a sporting event had been established, even at this early stage, and it was to take firm root in the years that followed.

Chapter 2
The 1908 Olympic Games

The 1908 Olympic Games

OVER A CENTURY LATER WE CAN LOOK BACK ON LONDON 1908 AS THE OCCASION WHEN THE MODERN OLYMPIC GAMES, IN A FORMAT THAT WE WOULD RECOGNISE, STARTED TO TAKE DEFINITIVE SHAPE. IT WAS IN MANY WAYS AN OUTRAGEOUS SUCCESS, A SPECTACULAR GAMES STAGED AT SHORT NOTICE AGAINST OVERWHELMING ODDS AND HIGHLIGHTING THAT VERY BRITISH GENIUS FOR COMBINING METICULOUS DETAIL WITH SPUR OF THE MOMENT IMPROVISATION. IF BRITAIN AND LONDON HAD NOT ANSWERED AN EMERGENCY CALL FROM THE INTERNATIONAL OLYMPIC COMMITTEE (IOC) IN 1906, THE MODERN GAMES MIGHT HAVE FIZZLED OUT ALTOGETHER, BEING NOW ONLY A SPORTING CURIOSITY THAT BRIEFLY STRADDLED THE NINETEENTH AND TWENTIETH CENTURIES.

> 'The curtain descended on the Tiber's stage and rose soon after on that of the Thames'
>
> Lord Desborough

As it was a total of 2,008 competitors, including 37 women, from 22 nations gathered to contest 24 sports over six months. Time was not rationed in those days, and for those who had made the effort to travel from afar, possibly making a six week sea voyage from Australasia, there was generally no rush to get home. For the first time the volume of entries required heats and semi-finals, while the appearance of Ice Dancing as a sport presaged the eventual creation of a Winter Olympic Games.

The 1908 Games was a groundbreaking sporting pageant on a previously unimagined scale – effectively becoming the template for the event in the century that followed. The Games spawned a high profile 'celebrity' in Italian Marathon runner Dorando Pietri – the man who became a 'victor' in defeat, infinitely more celebrated for losing than he would ever have been for winning. The London Games also saw the first African American gold medallist, with 400m runner John Taylor being a member of the successful USA Medley Relay team. There were iconic sporting moments aplenty, although the Games was also a somewhat argumentative affair.

Nationalistic overtones were unsurprising at a time when Edwardian Britain, at the very height of Empire, dominated much of the globe. London was the greatest city in the world, the world's financial and commercial powerhouse. The Royal Navy ruled the seas; the Merchant Navy serviced the Empire with enviable efficiency; and British explorers had that very year discovered oil in what is now Iran. The 1908 Games established one or two themes that were to play out through most of the twentieth century, not only in the Olympic and Paralympic Games but in international sport generally. It raised the bar massively, increasing people's hopes and expectations and inflaming the passions of competitors and spectators alike.

Crucially all this was played out during a lively circulation war between American newspapers that saw the level of sports coverage radically increase. Several national British newspapers – notably the *Mirror*, *Daily Mail*, *The Times* and *The Daily Telegraph*, plus many other popular periodicals of the day – also gave extensive coverage to the Games. The *Daily Telegraph* didn't print by-lines in those days, but their Olympic correspondent was in fact none other than Theodore Andrea Cook, a former captain of the English Fencing Team and a key man on the British Olympic Association (BOA) organising committee in London. Predictably some of his reports attempted to gloss over the controversies, or at least reduce their impact.

Pathé News was also present throughout, filming much of the action and distributing it through their pay-to-watch booths. Unfortunately only a small

Lord Desborough

The 1908 Games proved a remarkable personal triumph for Lord Desborough, the pinnacle of an extraordinary career of achievement and service. Desborough's sporting credentials were impeccable: a member of the Harrow XI, he held the school mile record for over 60 years and rowed for Oxford against Cambridge in the famous Dead Heat of 1877. A former President of the MCC, Desborough was a big game sportsman in the Rockies and in India. He had swum at the foot of the Niagara Falls and had cheated death when working as a war correspondent in Egypt.

Desborough served as a British representative of the IOC until 1913, when he unexpectedly resigned. Two of his sons were killed within a month of each other in the First World War, serving on the Western Front, and in 1926 his surviving son died in a car crash. He turned away from public life to garden on his Taplow Court estate and oversee the construction of the Desborough Cut, a channel in the Thames that opened in 1935. When he died in January 1945, aged 80, the family name and title went with him, but the 1908 Olympic Games remained as a lasting legacy.

percentage of the footage survives, although we can trace almost the entire Dorando Pietri story through moving images – one reason why he became an early global sporting star. From those small beginnings we now have a situation, over a century later, whereby the Olympic and Paralympic Games have become the ultimate television event, packaged and distributed live to over 200 nations.

Edwardian Britain was a nation that made things happen – and the Olympic Games proved no exception to this rule. There was a great urgency about life then that we sometimes underestimate. Britain was a land of constant achievers, talented individuals impatiently pushing back the boundaries in commerce and industry, exploring all four corners of the earth geographically and creating sporting norms and institutions that survive to this day. London 1908 was their interpretation of the Olympic Games concept that was still far from being fully formed.

Events had begun to unfold at Athens in 1906 as the first, and last, Intercalated Games drew to a close. It was becoming clear that spring that the recent eruption of Mount Vesuvius, on 7 April, and the consequent loss of life would seriously hinder Italy's ability to stage the 1908 Games: any available philanthropic funds had to be channelled towards survivors. Baron Pierre de Coubertin, President of the IOC, sensing a crisis brewing, cleverly put out feelers in the direction of Lord Desborough, a member of the British Fencing team and a charismatic high achiever with an impeccable sporting record. He was on to a winner almost instantly as Desborough – wealthy, influential and possessed of boundless energy – found the career-defining challenge of staging the Olympic Games irresistible.

Desborough was soon animatedly discussing De Coubertin's proposal with fellow members of the Fencing team, all staying aboard Lord Howard de Walden's private yacht, the SS *Branwen*, anchored in the Bay of Athens. Those on board included Charles

Baron Pierre de Coubertin, the Frenchman who revived the Olympic Games, was a man of outstanding perception. At Athens 1896, the first modern Games, there were 241 competitors from 14 nations; at London 2012, there will be over 11,000 from up to 204, proving that De Coubertin's vision has created the greatest sports show in the world.

Newton-Robinson and Theodore Cook (the same Cook who was to report on the games anonymously for the *Daily Telegraph*), both members of the Council of the BOA. De Walden himself also contributed to the discussion, together with Edgar Seligman and Sir Cosmo Duff-Gordon, who in 1912 survived the sinking of the *Titanic* despite the Captain's orders that women and children should be saved first. To a man they offered their support to the idea of Britain staging the 1908 Games. Fortunately Edward VII – a personal friend and, as Prince of Wales, a witness at Desborough's wedding – was also attending the

Captain MacDonnell, W. Bean and Sir Cosmo Duff-Gordon, non-competing members of the British Fencing Team at the London 1908 Games. Interestingly, all three hold dueling pistols.

Games, and the two old friends spoke at length on the subject. The monarch was happy to give his seal of approval to the project, but only if Desborough could assure him that it would not cost the British government a penny.

That wish was eventually fulfilled, although not without considerable difficulty. Desborough's first task was to get all the British governing bodies and federations of the various sports on board, which he achieved with the very considerable administrative help of Rev. Robert Stuart de Courcy Laffan, BOA Honorary Secretary. Desborough was,

of course, Chairman, and both served as Britain's representatives on the IOC. Then came a huge stroke of luck, or happy coincidence as Desborough preferred to call it. After the briefest of negotiations an agreement was reached with the entrepreneur and ringmaster of the Franco-British Exhibition, Imre Kiralfy. He was to receive a percentage of the gate takings in return for building a Stadium to host most of the major sports at the London 1908 Games. Desborough was delighted, and on 19 November 1906 he formally accepted the invitation of the IOC to host the Games of the IV Olympiad.

Gastronomic Delights

The Amateur Athletic Association really went to town in entertaining IOC members and friends at the Empire Rooms at London's Trocadero in 1908. Their eight-course meal included:
Suprême de sole palace
Filet de boeuf piqué Richelieu
Ris de veau florentine
canteon d'Aylesbury
Pêche Melba dessert

So far so good, but it became evident very quickly in the spring of 1908 that more funds were needed for the day-to-day running of such a huge event – not least for a series of seven lavish banquets to be laid on for the visitors. Desborough launched a public appeal in June 1908, which raised £2,840 from 200 subscribers who were mainly his personal friends, but greater funds were urgently needed. He then approached Lord Northcliffe, owner of the *Daily Mail*, who immediately re-launched the appeal, which this time reached almost £16,000.

The biggest single donation came from the Prussian strongman and founder bodybuilder Eugene Sandow, who had become a star turn on Britain's lucrative music hall circuit. The Prince of Wales and the Maharajah of Cooch Behar offered substantial amounts, the Football Association coughed up £250 and a group of 30 MPs had a whip round, contributing the somewhat underwhelming sum of £30. Of the grand total of monies raised, well in excess of £18,000 if you include Desborough's initial call to arms, a staggering £5,300 was subsequently spent on entertainment and hospitality. In stark contrast to the 'ration book' austerity Games hosted only 40 years later, such post-competition dining contributed to London's success as a Host City. Edwardian London had earned a reputation as a gastronomic capital second only to Paris. Such 'rest and relaxation' was undeniably hard earned, with an enormous amount of work going into making the 1908 Games a reality and a commercial success. Which in the end it was, with the BOA reporting an operational profit of £6,000.

The White City

Starting from scratch in 1906, when Britain's involvement with the 1908 Games began, this state-of-the-art sports complex with a capacity of 93,000 was erected in 10 months flat in West London. Brainchild of the extraordinary Hungarian-born

The newly created White City Stadium in West London, a focus of national pride, in 1908, proved popular with crowds at the London 1908 Games.

The White City Stadium saw the historic finish of the 1908 Marathon when Dorando Pietri collapsed. The venue was built especially for the Games and for the next 60 years it remained one of the most famous athletics stadia in the world.

Kiralfy, who had forged a reputation in America with showman P.T. Barnum, White City was regarded for a while as the eighth wonder of the world. The 57-hectare site – eight times larger than the Great Exhibition of 1851 site in Hyde Park – had been obtained for the Franco-British Exhibition, which for a while seemed likely to be staged in 1907. Then the well connected Desborough convinced those involved that the exhibition should effectively merge with the 1908 Olympic Games, with the world's greatest new Stadium staging the main event. Thus at a stroke the 1908 Games became a probability rather than a possibility – a good day's work from the splendid Desborough, and the single most important factor in the 1908 Games happening at all. Crucially, Desborough also ensured that the Games, despite owing their existence to the Franco-British Exhibition, did not get taken over by them; his own strong personality, interwoven with diplomacy and charm, ensured equal partner status. The lessons of the Paris 1900 Games, and those of St Louis 1904, had been learned.

The exhibition site consisted of a collection of elegant domes, spires and pavilions celebrating every aspect of life in the British and French empires. Complete with Irish and Sengalese 'villages', it

Right The cover of the programme for the London 1908 Olympic Games, illustrated by Arthur Stockdale Cope.

became a source of great national pride, glistening like a massive tented town when the sun shone – admittedly a rare occurrence in 1908, one of the wettest summers on record. White City, in short, spoke of wealth, permanence, imagination, power, mission and a resolutely can-do attitude. It was constructed in a frenzy throughout 1907 with the first stone being laid on 2 August by Lady Desborough, and early 1908, with up to 12,000 labourers on site at the busiest times and work going on throughout the night under floodlights. They made their deadline just in time for the official

> **'Lord Desborough is in every respect an ideal representative of English sport in its best sense – tall, well set up, a commanding presence, yet utterly devoid of arrogance'**
>
> *Empire*, 2 June 1908, commending Lord Desborough, chairman of the British Olympic Association

opening by the Prince and Princess of Wales on 14 May, although the *Westminster Gazette* rather pointedly suggested that some work was still to do: 'The weather was as bad as it could well be; the crowd was a dense one … roads and pathway were ankle deep in mud … and yet one heard very little grumbling.' Like everything else around it, the White City Stadium was constructed at an extraordinary pace and seemingly went up overnight. Its actual construction broke all records, on a schedule that would be impressive even with today's technology and resources.

'I do not approve of the participation of women in public competitions. In the Olympic Games their primary role should be to crown the victor'

Baron Pierrre de Coubertin

In fact 37 women competed in the 1908 Games, 25 of them in the Archery competition. Two British women, archer 'Queenie' Newall and Lottie Dod, won gold and silver medals while figure skater Madge Syers also won a gold medal and a bronze.

The feat certainly helped forge a reputation for excellence by the builder George Wimpey, a name that lives on.

The construction of the main sporting arena for the Olympic Games, which became known as the White City Stadium, was just a part of the much bigger overall project. Kiralfy delivered a cutting edge Stadium for the BOA, with space for 17,000 spectators under cover. It included a 100m swimming pool and movable diving tower within the infield of the 536m running track, 24 feet wide and three laps to the mile. The track itself was laid down by Charles Perry, groundsman at Stamford Bridge and previously responsible for the track at the Athens 1896 Games.

Perry went on to supervise the tracks and field for the Stockholm Games in 1912 and Antwerp in 1920. Around the outside of the athletics track was a 600m cycling piste, on which the organisers confidently expected new world record times to be set in every race. The reported cost of this phenomenon was £80,000, although some historians feel the real cost was almost double that.

Within the confines of the White City Stadium was staged the Rugby Union final between Australia and Britain (represented with disastrous results by county champions Cornwall). Other events and finals took place within the vast infield of the athletics track – not least the Gymnastics, Archery, Hockey, lacrosse and Wrestling. As well as a Royal Box in the main stand there were four other boxes, sited in prime viewing positions. The IOC, the Franco-British Exhibition and the BOA all had their own boxes. So did the Comité d'Honneur, composed of three representatives of each competing nation. There were cordoned-off areas for the judges and press although these were not under cover, much to the latter's chagrin when the Athletics programme was marred by bad weather during the early stages of the Games. The better-heeled members of London society were made temporary members of the Imperial Sports Club, connected to the Stadium and boasting a fine clubhouse and two sumptuous dining areas within the White City grounds, as well as the reading rooms and other facilities associated with a gentleman's club. Fourteen massive dressing rooms for competitors were set up under the main stand, while five cafes served the spectators. For the duration of the Athletics competition a sportsman parade was created around the Stadium, featuring vendors selling every known form of

1908 Rugby Fnal: Australia v ... Cornwall

Following disagreement among the Home Unions and a last minute withdrawal from France, the RFU approached county champions Cornwall to compete at the 1908 Olympic Games. The Cornish, who had just lost to the tourists 18–5 at Camborne, had no realistic prospect of victory and understandably decided to enjoy the event. On match day they undetook a coach tour of London, followed by a long lunch at the Garden Club, hosted by the president of the Cornish Union. They then dragged themselves off to a dank White City Stadium to encounter a pumped-up Australian side who defeated them 32–3. The bedraggled team headed for a consolation dinner at the House of Commons, leaving the press to complain. As *The Times* lamented, 'Cornwall completely failed to find their game, their forwards executed a few good rushes but their backs, without exception, were not only too slow but continually failing in their fielding. One expected better football from the champion county side.'

Opposite page and left

Danish gymnasts produce a routine at White City during the London 1908 Games, but their performance was only an exhibition. Women's gymnastics did not become an Olympic medal event until 20 years later in Amsterdam.

Bottom right Britain's Richard Gunn achieved a landmark moment in London in 1908 when he beat Boxing teammate Charles Morris to lift Feather Weight gold. His victory at the age of 37 years and 254 days has made him into the oldest fighter to win an Olympic title.

Far Right Tug of war might no longer be an Olympic sport, but in 1908 it sparked controversy. The USA team, pictured in action during the Games, faced the Liverpool Police in the first round and were beaten within a few seconds. The Americans protested that the police used illegal footwear and, after their protest had failed, they withdrew from the competition.

sporting equipment and associated literature. Ahead of the Olympic Games national British championships were held for Athletics, Cycling and Swimming by way of test events.

Legacy was not a big issue back in 1908 and nobody had really considered what might happen to the Stadium afterwards. The Exhibition site itself kept busy enough for a while – it staged a Japan-British Exhibition in 1910, a Latin-British Exhibition in 1912 and an Anglo-American Exhibition in

1914, the last featuring a mini New York, the Grand Canyon and a Wild West show. With the onset of the First World War, however, it began to struggle, and when hostilities ceased there seemed no more appetite for such frivolity. Eventually, in 1936, most of the exhibition showgrounds were sold to Hammersmith Borough Council. The White City Stadium enjoyed a more varied post-Games career before demolition in 1985 to make way for the BBC's new Broadcasting Centre.

The Last Years of White City

The White City Stadium became a greyhound racing track and a speedway circuit, and an annual 'Dorando marathon' was staged every year. It was the main venue of the 1934 Empire Games and hosted the annual AAA championships between 1932 and 1970, as well as becoming a major boxing venue. Chris Chataway set a world record in the 5000m there in 1954, in a novelty athletics match between London and Moscow, and a World Cup pool football match between Uruguay and France was attended by a crowd of 40,000 in 1966. The Stadium was a clearing station in the Second World War after the evacuation of Dunkirk, and it later staged rodeos and even cheetah racing. The final event was the last race at a greyhound meeting on 22 September 1984, won by Hastings Girl.

Anglo-American Rivalry

The 1908 Olympic Games, although attended by 22 nations, was dominated by the clash between Great Britain and the USA, who between them accounted for 79 of the 110 gold medals on offer. The British had, rather provocatively, suggested a national league table based on points accrued across the board by all competitors in all events – a none too subtle demonstration of the effortless supremacy of Empire. The Americans, and others with much smaller teams and with their resources very much concentrated on certain sports, resisted this, but the idea took root. In subsequent Olympic Games the official Medal Table, taking in silver and bronze medals as well, has become an important indicator as to how respective countries have performed.

The American team won no less than 16 of the 27 Athletics gold medals on offer, taking a total of 34 track and field medals, while Britain won seven golds and 17 total medals. With a team of nearly

700 competitors the hosts did predictably dominate the Games elsewhere, taking every gold medal on offer at the Boxing, Rowing, Sailing and Tennis in a final haul of 56 golds which was more than double the Americans' tally. Numbers were not the full story, however. At the White City Stadium, in the sport that really mattered above all others to the watching world, the Americans cleaned-up in impressive fashion and took most of the plaudits.

They also received a good deal of criticism for contesting just about every official decision they could and complaining endlessly about the facilities. The USA team and its outspoken management seemed to go out of their way to agitate their hosts, in part a response to a backdrop of simmering nationalism. The stakes had been raised at London 1908, where for the first time competitors were entered as representatives of their nation, inevitably involving a selection process. Previously any talented individual could enter, and although medals were listed by country, that was almost an afterthought. Now this had all changed.

James E. Sullivan, son of an Irish construction worker and for many years the all-powerful Secretary of the Amateur Athletic Union (AAU) in the US, proved a fierce and authoritarian team manager. A former journalist and publisher, he was a hard-nosed operator who saw athletics as a part of a bigger sports business and demanded a much more 'professional' approach from his athletes. His battle

The final of the 110m Hurdles at the 1908 Olympic Games, on 25 July 1908. Forrest Smithson (second right) is on his way to victory with a time of 15.0 The USA delivered a clean sweep in the event, with teammate John Garrels coming second in 15.7 and Arthur Shaw third in 15.8.

with the British at the 1908 Games took the form of official complaints, lodged at the rate of one a day. Pole vaulters were unable to dig small holes in which to plant their poles; certain competitions were scheduled for Sunday, which was problematic for some of the American athletes; the American team had allegedly been offered 'inferior' accommodation, and so on. Their dispute over Sunday competition spawned the legend that the devout theology student Forrest Smithson – who won the 110m Hurdles in a world record of 15.0 seconds – ran the race with a small Bible in his left hand. Unfortunately the official records show that the race was contested on the final Saturday of the Athletics competition, although Smithson was certainly photographed in training holding the good book in his left hand.

Sullivan also accused the top Canadian Marathon runner Tom Longboat of being a professional – rather below the belt as competing for a living was virtually a way of life for many American College students. Some also perceived his comments as racist, Longboat being a member of the Onondaga tribe from the Six Nations reserve near Brantford, Ontario. Needless to say all of these complaints – many of which had more than a germ of truth in them – tended to appear in the American press before the British officials were aware of them. 'I just could not understand Sullivan's attitudes,' noted De Coubertin in his *Mémoires Olympiques*. 'He shared his team's frenzy and did nothing to try and calm them down.'

In defence of the Americans it should be noted that the home nation was providing all the judges and officials, as had been the custom in the three

'Remember you are heroes for just ten days. When that time is up, drop the hero business and go to work'

President Theodore Roosevelt addressing the returning American team on his Oyster Bay estate

previous modern Olympic Games. That hadn't remotely been a factor in St Louis 1904, as very few international athletes travelled to America and the Olympic Games became virtually a domestic affair, but it did escalate in the much bigger and more cosmopolitan London 1908 Games. Initially it was a practical issue – nearly 800 judges were needed for the Games and it was simply easier for the organisers to use home-based judges who all spoke the same language. However, the weakness of this system was twofold: Britain clearly opened itself up to accusations of bias and the rules of any sport were those then pertaining in the host nation. Sport was becoming truly international, and this needed to be reflected at the Olympic Games. As a direct result of these and other incidents, in which British objectivity was called into doubt, the International Association of Athletics Federations (IAAF) was formed immediately after London 1908. Its role was to govern the sport of athletics and to provide neutral officials for major athletics competitions.

The returning American team received an unashamedly nationalistic ticker-tape reception in New York, with American and Irish patriotism being celebrated simultaneously and in equal measure. The flags of both were in evidence, and the Irish contingent's victories at the Olympic Games undoubtedly caused the ethnic stock of the Irish in America to rise considerably. The *New York Times* quoted Sullivan as saying the attitude of certain English officials towards American competitors was 'outrageous', leaving the host nation in danger of becoming 'athletically degenerate'. Bearing this in

---

A Critical Time

Oh! British Empire great and free
Attend! The moment's psychic;
Rome fell, and so it seems shall we
Unless we win the high kick

Our fame, one great, will wholly go
To pot – a thought that curdles –
If in the sprints we make no show
And fall across the hurdles

Men will forget out Art, our Laws
Our trade (secured by jumping)
If for some maybe trivial cause
An alien wins the jumping

'Tis said 'tis pity to achieve
What many would find baffling
And fail because we can not heve –
Free style – the blooming javelin.

A popular ditty published in *Bystander* magazine, July 1908

American Martin Sheridan was one of the early stars of Olympic track and field events. Shown here throwing the discus, at the London 1908 Games he won with 40.89m, having also taken the title at St Louis 1904 with 39.28m.

mind, he thought the American team's victory was 'undoubtedly the greatest in the history of Amateur sport in the world'. A note of realism was introduced by President Teddy Roosevelt, however, who received the entire squad at his summer estate at Oyster Bay. 'Remember you are heroes for just ten days,' advised the wily politician. 'When that time is up, drop the hero business and go to work.'

'This Flag Dips To No Earthly King'

American anger had been evident right from the opening ceremony before the Athletics events. It was sparked by a hapless minor British official who forgot to raise the Stars and Stripes on the main stand of the White City arena as the crowd and teams gathered. The same official also forgot to raise the Swedish flag to join those of the other competing nations. The Swedes were sufficiently irritated not to attend the royal march past later that day, after which they considered the matter closed and competed fully in the Games without further rancour.

Not so Sullivan and the Americans, however. They raged behind the scenes and a couple of hours later, during the teams' march past, made a point of not dipping their flag when they passed King Edward VII and Queen Alexandra in the Royal Box. Nor had the Americans dipped the flag when the teams gathered in the centre of the White City and the British National Anthem was played. King Edward was so outraged that he refused to attend another event during the Olympic Games, leaving official duties to the more diplomatic Queen Alexandra. The American moment of non-compliance in flag-dipping spawned a tradition that exists to this day. In 1942, this refusal to lower the Stars and Stripes to any head of state was enshrined in law by Congress (Public Law 829). In 1908, of course, it was perceived by the British public and indeed one or two American commentators themselves as arrogant and insulting to the hosts.

The flag dipping controversy becomes even more complicated the deeper you dig. The American team contained a large Irish American contingent of quite exceptional athletes and significant influence. The most outstanding was Martin Sheridan from Bohola in County Mayo, a discus specialist who introduced a novel wind-up, completing two turns before releasing the discus. He was also a phenomenal all-round athlete with the versatility to finish third in the standing long jump in the 1908 Games as well as winning the discus throw proper and the classical discus.

At 1.9m and 88kg, Sheridan would have been a star athlete in any era. He won three Olympic gold medals and one bronze, and was a huge focus within the American team. He spent his first 18 years living at home in Mayo, when Ireland was part of the United Kingdom, before emigrating to the USA to join his brother Richard, also a very useful Discus thrower. Like many Irish immigrants to New York, Martin Sheridan became a New York City policeman – and a very good one at that, as he has a bravery award named in his honour – who was personally assigned to security details whenever the Governor of New York was in town. Yet whether the famous quote

Members of the American track and field team, including the enormous Ralph Rose (far left), who took gold in the Shot Put at the London 1908 Games. Rose caused some controversy at the Opening Ceremony by refusing to dip the American flag when he passed the Royal Box.

of 'This flag dips to no earthly king' can accurately be attributed to him is a moot point. Sullivan seems to have been an understated, humorous individual, a model policeman not given to throwing his weight around away from the sporting arena. At the St Louis Games, it was he who had put a kindly arm around the Cuban Marathon runner Félix Carvajal and took the trouble to hurriedly transform his trousers into shorts so that he would not overheat. A suspicious mind might think that the wording of Public Law 829 'That no disrespect should be given to the flag of the United States, the flag should not be dipped to any person or thing' is uncannily close to what Sheridan was supposed to have said.

Some early reports claimed it was actually Sheridan who carried the flag, but this can be dismissed. Photographic evidence shows that it was his friend and fellow strong man, the massive Ralph Rose – who at 2m tall and weighing 125kg went on to win the gold medal in the Shot Put – who pointedly refused to lower the flag as he carried it past the Royal Box. Rose was a controversial choice for the job within the USA team. He was far from being the most popular member of the team and had been thrown out of the University of Michigan in 1904 for persistent rowdy behaviour. He had also achieved notoriety soon after the 1904 Games when he challenged World Heavy Weight Boxing champion James J. Jeffries to a bout, causing much embarrassment in both Athletics and Boxing circles.

Rose was an unpredictable maverick, the loosest of cannons and the refusal to dip the US flag may have simply been his angry, tit-for-tat protest at the earlier oversight. Whatever the motivation, the immediate effect was to enrage the home crowd, who interpreted the action as a deliberate insult to their monarch and by extension to Britain. Although the British press tried initially to turn a blind eye, American athletes from that moment onwards were frequently jeered and booed whenever they competed, and their many protests given short shrift from those in the Stadium.

It all became fractious as the 'Irish' contrived to be everywhere and to make their presence known at London. The talented Tim Ahearne, from Athea, County Limerick, won the Triple Jump for Britain; Con Leahy from Cregane, County Limerick took silver in the High Jump. A Cork man, the absolutely massive George 'Con' O'Kelly (who dwarfed even Ralph Rose), took the Heavy Weight Freestyle Wrestling title, again for Britain. His son, Con O'Kelly, Jr, subsequently represented Britain in the Heavy Weight Boxing competition at the Paris 1924 Games before retiring to become a priest. And yet another athlete with Irish connections was Canada's 200m gold medallist Bobby Kerr. He originally hailed from Enniskillen, but had tired of the complex politics and emigrated to Canada. Meanwhile Rose's firm friends and drinking partners also included two gregarious Irishmen who won medals in the Hammer Throw for the USA at London – John Flanagan from Kilbreedy in County Limerick, who won his third consecutive Olympic

'The most important thing in the Olympic Games is not to win but to take part'

Ethlebert Talbot, visiting bishop of Bethlehem, Pennsylvania, preaching at St Paul's Cathedral, 1908

title in London, and silver medallist Matt McGrath from Nenagh, County Tipperary. McGrath went on to win the title at the Stockholm Games in 1912 . Just for good measure, Canada's bronze medallist in the Hammer Throw at London was Con Walsh from County Cork.

The complicated Irish situation was mirrored in part by the humiliating sight of Finnish athletes – whose nation was occupied by Russia at the time – having to march behind the Russian flag, although they took care to walk a few paces back from their conquerors. Austria-Hungary also competed as one nation, much to the chagrin of the Hungarians. Bohemia, which approximates to the modern day Czech Republic, did daringly send its own team, although it too was officially part of the Austria-Hungarian Empire. De Coubertin, a firm ally of Bohemia's IOC representative Dr Jirí Stanislav Guth-Jarkovský, had assured his friend that he would raise no objections if Bohemia was represented. An astute observer, testing the political temperature at the 1908 Olympic Games, might well have predicted that serious political trouble lay just around the corner.

Boots and All

Quite how the two most powerful nations on earth could fall-out over a tug of war contest remains something of a mystery, even a century later. But in 1908 tensions were running high and every minor disagreement or spat was magnified out of all proportion, not least by an American press seeking to score points against rival publications. One of the best ways to achieve this was to take offence on American's behalf, and so the tug of war incident came to belligerent life.

In 1908 the tug of war was an Olympic discipline. Its origins lay in the Tang dynasty in China, but it had been perfected as a competitive sport by the British, to be used as a form of team training and bonding and physical exercise in the

The American team preparing to compete in the tug of war at the White City Stadium, London 1908, when they pulled against the Liverpool Police in the first round and were beaten in a few seconds. The Americans, unpractised in the event, protested that the police used illegal footwear. They refused the Liverpool Police's offer of a re-run in stockinged feet.

army, navy and most of the county police forces. In 1908 it was considered a curious adjunct to the Olympic Athletics programme, attracting just seven entries, of whom five actually participated. Three of those were British police teams, the others being national teams from the USA and Sweden. Surprisingly, to the non-expert eye, the sport owed little to brute strength and almost everything to technique and getting the full weight of eight sturdy men pulling at exactly the same instant. The tug of war was a specialised event and leading contenders such as the London City Police, for example, had been training intensively for the five months leading into the Games.

The Americans, deciding to enter a team at short notice, included some of their huge 'Irish whales', such as Hammer Throwers John Flanagan and Matt McGrath and the 20-stone shot-putter Ralph Rose, he of the flag-dipping controversy. Discus champion Martin Sheridan was also on hand for their opening best-of-three contest against Liverpool Police, although Olympic historians are agreed that his was a non-playing captaincy role. Certainly the few pictures that exist of the one American pull do not show him in their line-up. Curiously Sheridan discovered shortly before the contest that Jim Clarke, his first cousin, was pulling for the Liverpool Police team – a quirk typical of the 1908 Games with their curious blend of gentle village fete and elite international sport.

It had been raining heavily on the morning of the competition, but the Americans wore just their lightweight athletics shoes, as if preparing to run or jump. Much consternation arose in their ranks when the Liverpool Police eight appeared in their normal police boots, which had small steel rims on their heels. An official complaint was immediately made as the rules, especially drawn up and formalised in the weeks preceding the 1908 Games, stated that, 'No competitor shall wear prepared boots or shoes or boots or shoes with any projecting nails, tips, sprigs, points, hollows, or projections of any kind.' This was rejected, however, on the grounds that the boots has not been especially prepared in any way and were entirely 'normal' footwear – they were actually discarded police boots, retired from regular foot patrols but perfectly adequate for tug of war contests. A century on one could concede, objectively, that the Liverpool Police team may have been 'trying it on' a little, although they may not have been aware of the new rules.

'The English team wore shoes as big as North River ferryboats'

American Martin Sheridan on the controversy of the tug of war

The USA reluctantly agreed to compete, but were easily pulled across the line in the first heat, which cruelly exposed their lack of collective technique and training. The biggest and strongest men in the world were no match for the Liverpool Police, anchor man Ralph Rose even failing to wrap the rope around himself in the traditional fashion. There was a suggestion that the Americans 'gifted' the contest to their opponents and didn't pull properly to underline their complaint, but photographic evidence seems to suggest that the USA were pulling for all their worth, albeit inexpertly.

It wasn't all a matter of shoes. As Theodore Cook wrote in his official report on the Games, 'The Americans were magnificent athletes, but were not aware of how to tie an anchor or how to place their men. They were, in fact, not used to the game at all and were very naturally surprised to find how little their strength availed against skilful combination.'

A second American protest was lodged and disallowed. The Liverpool Police offered to conduct a second pull in their stockinged feet to ensure absolute fair play, but by now the disgruntled Americans were no longer interested. They had stormed off in high dudgeon, to jeers from the crowd, as a Stadium announcer rather insensitively informed the spectators that 'the Americans have had enough' via his massive megaphone. The Liverpool Police team later defeated the Swedish national team, but then lost in the final against the London City Police. Still, Jim Clarke won a silver medal to add to little Bohoa's growing roll of honour over in County Mayo.

Meanwhile the anger and dismay of the USA team was taken up by the American press and rumbled on for months. On their return to the USA Sheridan – probably in jest although the joke may have got lost along the way – told American reporters that 'the English team wore shoes as big as North River ferryboats' and that they 'had to waddle out on the field like of a lot of County Mayo ganders going down to the public pond for a swim.' The *New York Sun* appeared to be the sole American paper that, like Sheridan, saw the funny, or at least the ironic, side of the debate, commenting that, 'the American protest must have been due to ignorance of this form of sport in which it is a great speciality of the British Police to wear heavy boots. To wear athletics shoes in a tug of war would be regarded as the same error as to wear heavy boots for a sport.'

'The Americans have had enough'

Stadium announcer, via megaphone, after the American team's defeat in the tug of war by the Liverpool Police

At any other time the incident might have been treated as amusing knock-about stuff between old friends and rivals trying to score a few points off each other in the name of sport. In the heated atmosphere of the 1908 Games the boots incident quickly became a cause célèbre, taking far longer than it should have done to die down. Yet this was nothing compared with the sporting controversy of the 400m final, which produced a furore on a scale unmatched until England's 1932 'Bodyline' Ashes tour of Australia.

American athlete John Carpenter after his controversial performance in the 400m final, when he was judged to have forced Britain's Wyndham Halswelle to go wide.

Tempers Flare in the 400m

The 400m had been one of the most widely anticipated events of the entire Athletics programme. There had been a huge entry for the event, requiring 16 heats, which together with the semi-finals were conducted in an orderly enough fashion. The ever vigilant USA manager Sullivan was, of course, in a state of high alert. He had complained long and hard throughout the Games about American runners 'always' being drawn against each other in heats and semi-finals and therefore knocking each other out. Yet he was strangely mute as the Briton Wyndham Halswelle prepared to contest a semi-final including two other top British runners and medal hopes, Edwin Montague and George Nicol. No favouritism in evidence there.

As was widely expected the qualifiers for the final were Halswelle, who set an Olympic record of 48.4 seconds in his heat after a sparkling run, and three crack Americans – namely John Carpenter from Cornell University, William Robbins, a recent graduate of Trinity College, Oxford, and John Taylor, a graduate of the Pennsylvania School of Veterinary Medicine. Taylor was attempting to become the first black athlete from any nation to win an Olympic gold medal, a feat he later achieved in the medley relay. He tragically died of typhoid only a few months later.

The scene was set for one of the 1908 Games' last and most obvious showdowns between the USA and Britain. With a numerical advantage of three athletes to one and no marked out lanes in those days, British pressmen and officials immediately sensed the opportunity for the Americans to employ 'team tactics' and gang up on Halswelle. In America it was perfectly normal for the 400m to develop into something of a rough house. A fair degree of barging and leaning on an opponent was tolerated as part of the appeal of the race – rather as modern 800m races can sometimes be highly tactical and physical as runners fight for position and try to cover moves from opponents. In Europe, however, the

Wyndham Halswelle

Wyndham Halswelle, born in London and educated at Charterhouse and Royal Sandhurst, is still the only competitor to have won a gold medal by virtue of a walkover in an Olympic final. Of Scottish stock, he won the 100 yards, 220 yards, 440 yards and 880 yards in one afternoon in 1906 at the Scottish Championships, and in 1907 he set a world record of 31.2 seconds for the 300 yards. At the 1908 Games he qualified for the 400m final in a very brisk 48.4 seconds, becoming the pre-race favourite and raising conjecture that his three American opponents would work as a team to 'baulk' him. After Carpenter was disqualified and his American teammates withdrew from the rerun in protest, Halswelle competed alone to take the gold medal. He left the sport soon after.

400m race was much more gentlemanly in style; it was considered a pure test of running, almost a time-trial, with little tactical acumen required.

Pre-race rumours quickly circulated the Stadium that the 'Yankee gang' would be trying to baulk Halswelle, considered the pre-race favourite. Before the race the starter, Mr Harry Goble, spoke firmly to the runners and warned them that any wilful stalling or baulking would see the race abandoned and the miscreant instantly disqualified. Officials, all of them British, were posted at 20-yard intervals around the track to police the situation – a most unusual event that raised the tension further. The simmering Anglo-American rivalry, not exclusively connected with sport, seemed focused on just one race and four individuals.

What happened next is still debated. We know that Carpenter took the lead, followed by Robbins, with Halswelle tracking the race in third place. Taylor took his habitual position at the rear where he liked to run untroubled in the early part of any race before unleashing his much feared late finish. The 'incident' occurred coming off the final bend when it appeared that Robbins, and in particular Carpenter, cut across the Briton's line and forced Halswelle to run wide. Some observers claimed that Halswelle was forced across two-thirds of the width of the track as he attempted to overtake the two Americans with a final sprint down the home straight. Briefly Halswelle, also known for his later spurts, appeared to be on the point of passing Carpenter when the latter again

The start of the first 400m final at the 1908 Olympic Games. It featured three Americans, William Robbins, John Taylor and John Carpenter, and Wyndham Halswelle of Great Britain (second from left), the pre-race favourite.

apparently forced the British runner to go wide. British judges on the spot claimed that the American shouldered Halswelle and also made contact with him, elbowing him in the torso.

Uproar broke out. The race umpire Roscoe Badger immediately shouted 'foul' and an unidentified official at the finish broke the woollen tape to signify that the race had been abandoned. Robbins and Halswelle slowed down, but Carpenter kept running at full speed and passed to finish in 48.4 seconds – a time equalling Halswelle's Olympic record.

Clerk to the course Jack Andrew, using a megaphone nearly as large as he was, immediately informed the spectators that Carpenter had been disqualified and the race declared null and void. At no time were the three American runners or officials invited to give their version of events or appeal the decision, and fierce arguments broke out in the crowd. Other British officials studied the footprints on the cinder track, which allegedly showed that Halswelle had almost been forced onto the cycle track. Photographs of this were faithfully printed in the *Daily Mirror* the following day, as if amassing evidence for a criminal investigation as chaos and controversy took hold.

The *New York Evening Post* quoted the USA's Irish trainer, Mike Murphy, 'It shows what the boasted fairest sportsmen in the world will do to win', and other American newspapers weighed in along similar lines. The *New York Times* bucked the trend, however, with a much more sanguine view: 'The only thing that can be said is that interfering with another runner is considered fair in America and that Carpenter saw nothing wrong in acting on that principle. However, as the race was run in England, where tactics of this kind are contrary alike to the rules that govern sport and to our notions of what is fair play, the committee has no choice but to punish the offender and order the race to be run over again.'

Britain's Wyndham Halswelle, sole participant in and winner of the re-run 400m final.

The British press had previously taken a much more relaxed attitude to other American complaints, but on this occasion they stood foursquare behind Halswelle, taking the complaints about biased British judges as a national insult. *The Sportsman*, a popular London journal, went into bat for the British, describing the 400m as 'one of the most disgraceful exhibitions of foul play ever witnessed … There can be no excuse, the thing was open, unabashed and shameless.' Halswelle himself later wrote to the *Sporting Life* to clarify that he had not been struck any vigorous blows by Carpenter in the chest, but that Carpenter had 'bored me across quite two-thirds of the track and entirely stopped my running.'

The re-run on the final Saturday afternoon

'Then again he collapsed, kind hands saving him from a heavy fall. He was within a few yards of my seat. Amid stooping figures and grasping hands I caught a glimpse of the haggard yellow face, the glazed expressionless eyes, the lank black hair streaked across the brow ... It is horrible yet fascinating, this struggle between a set purpose and an utterly exhausted frame. The Italian's great performance can never be erased from our records of sport'

Sir Arthur Conan Doyle, describing the end of Dorando Pietri's Marathon in the *Daily Mail*

Opposite page

The start of the 1908 Marathon at Windsor Castle, 24 July 1908. It proved popular with London crowds, with an estimated 2 million people watching the race, which ended in the White City Stadium.

of the Athletics meeting was one of the London 1908 Games' most poignant moments. This time, admittedly after the horse had bolted, the British officials used thin rope to designate lanes for the final, a conciliatory gesture that failed to impress the protesting Americans. It was however, adopted for the Stockholm 1912 Games and all subsequent races. So matters came to a head, with the two remaining Americans withdrawing from the rerun of the 400m final. Bemused and embarrassed, Halswelle therefore competed the race on his own in a brisk but hardly world beating 50 seconds. For the only time in the history of the Olympic Games a competitor won a gold medal by virtue of a walkover. 'Halswelle that ends well', trumpeted more than one of the papers, but this was a long way from the truth.

No matter how you view the affair Halswelle, an upstanding officer and gentleman, was an entirely innocent party. Dismayed by the ruining of his cherished dream, he retired in disgust immediately after a farewell appearance at Ibrox a few weeks later. Seven years later, by now promoted to Captain, he was killed by a German sniper on the Western Front in the First World War.

A Very 'British' Loser

The most dramatic sporting story of the 1908 Olympic Games, a legend always associated with the London event, was undoubtedly the cruel luck that befell the Italian Dorando Pietri at the finishing line of the Marathon. His was, in fact, a very 'British' story – the plucky underdog who gains more glory and honour in defeat that he would have in victory. Those within the world of long distance running certainly recognised Pietri as a talented emerging runner who could figure in the shake-up, but for most he was a minor player in the battle with highly rated opponents from Britain and America. It was a story that the British public embraced and that ended with the Queen, possibly at the suggestion of Sir Arthur

Sir Arthur Conan Doyle, author of the Sherlock Holmes detective stories, reading at Undershaw, his Surrey home.

Conan Doyle, who wrote an emotional account of the race for the *Daily Mail*, donating a cup to Pietri the following day.

The story caused a press sensation, but that was not all. One of the defining moments of Olympic spirit was captured fully by the cameras of both the Charles Urban Trading Company, commissioned to film outside the Stadium, and Pathé News, which had procured an exclusive deal within the Stadium. Nearly half of the 10 minutes of surviving Pathé footage from the 1908 Games is centred on the Marathon, and the images tell the story fully. Pietri became beyond doubt the first global Olympic hero, even if his race had ended in agony and disqualification.

Racing competitively over such prodigious distances was still in its infancy, and the competitors were treated as objects of curiosity and wonder. Certainly the press, mindful of the excitement and controversies in the three Olympic Marathons thus far, didn't stint in the build-up. 'No athletic event in the history of Great Britain has aroused so much public enthusiasm,' wrote the not entirely objective Theodore Cook in the *Daily Telegraph*. 'The crowning day of the Games will be reached only next week when the Marathon race will be run over a distance of 26 miles [and 385 yards] starting from the walls of Windsor Castle and finishing in the Exhibition Grounds. Twenty-two different nations are represented in an amicable contest which reminds us that by slow but sure degrees civilisation is moving towards the friendly federation of mankind.' Afterwards the *New York Times* didn't hold back either. 'It was a spectacle the like of which none living had ever seen, and none who saw it expect ever to see repeated.'

In the event 55 runners from 16 countries actually made it to the start line at the East Terrace of Windsor Castle. Here HRH Princess Mary, Princess of Wales was present, with His Majesty still in high dudgeon after the flag-dipping incident from the Opening Ceremony. Friday 24 July dawned a bright day after heavy rain earlier in the week, but the heat was fierce and conditions sticky, far from ideal for long distance running. The Marathon was the most anticipated event and spectacle of the Games and there was a real fascination in seeing just how hard the human body could be driven, how fast mankind could go and how far it could endure. Crowds of Londoners came out to support the runners in the streets as they travelled from Windsor Castle through Slough and onwards to Uxbridge and the White City, where a 90,000 crowd was crammed into the Stadium. It was estimated that approaching two million spectators viewed the race at some stage,

'No athletic event in the history of Great Britain has aroused so much public enthusiasm'

Theodore Cook, reporting on the Marathon for the *Daily Telegraph*

'Firsts' of the 1908 Olympic Games

The distance of the Marathon was changed to 26 miles 385 yards so that the race could start under the Windsor Castle nursery and finish at the White City Stadium; this distance later became standardised for all Olympic Games.

Four figure skating events were included in the Games: men's and ladies' Singles, the men's Special Figures and the Pairs. They took place in October, several months after the rest of the Games.

The first African-American gold medallist was John Taylor, who won the 1600m medley relay for the USA.

Swimming events were hosted in the first purpose-built pool, at the new sporting complex White City, rather than the sea or rivers as in previous Games.

and the Metropolitan Police, fully expecting such numbers, had drafted in an extra 2,000 officers to help marshal the well-behaved crowds. West London was *en fête* for the must see, and must be seen at, event of the 1908 Games. Many fans on the roadside opted for a leisurely picnic and catch-up with friends, but the relentless Cook – apparently a man transformed when writing about the Marathon – breathlessly informed those who so desired that they could follow the race from more than one vantage point, 'Nor need the eager sightseer content himself with a single glimpse of the race. For example, having seen the runners pass him at Uxbridge he might snatch a train – if one prove convenient – as far as Harrow. If his appetite for excitement should happen to grow by what it feeds on, this enthusiastic spectator might get back into a train at Harrow, make a dash for Neasden, catch a tram at that point and have another view of the race at Harlesdon.'

The Marathon, an event not part of the ancient Olympic Games, had become more firmly established than ever as the centrepiece of London 1908. Its modern distance had generally been 25 miles, but combining a request to start the race under the nursery at Windsor Castle with the desire to finish proceedings in a packed White City saw the race distance extended by over a mile, to the now fixed distance of 26 miles 385 yards.

The route was much admired. As the Canadian manager Bill Sherring, winner of the Marathon at the 1906 Intercalated Games, commented to the *Daily Mail*: 'Never have I seen a better track than the one between Windsor and the Stadium. In no other country in the world could you find 26 miles of road with a better surface or a fairer course for all the runners.' In retrospect that decision to extend the

route was to cost Pietri his gold medal. Then again, if he had won in such routine fashion we would hardly still be writing about him today.

The slim unremarkable Italian, just 1.59m tall and coming from Correggio in the Province of Reggio Emilia, was the most unlikely of sporting heroes. He worked as a shop boy and errand runner in a confectionary shop and was entirely self-trained. Within the Athletics world he was considered an emerging talent – he had won long distance races in Paris and Rome – but he flopped at the Intercalated Games of 1906, retiring when in the lead due to stomach cramps and failing to complete the course. Just prior to the 1908 Olympic Games he had won a 40km race in Capri in the outstanding time of 2 hours 38 minutes, but the rather sniffy world of contemporary Anglo-Saxon Athletics considered the time 'suspect'. The winner would surely come from Great Britain, one of the Dominions or, inevitably, the Americans – the young T.P. (Thomas) Morrissey, runaway winner of the 1908 Boston Marathon, was apparently their best hope although some within the camp believed the more consistent Johnny Hayes would perform better under pressure.

The runners started to arrive at Windsor Station from 9am onwards. They headed straight for the Stationmaster's room where a team of doctors stood by to examine all competitors – nobody was allowed to run without a current medical certificate. The station's waiting rooms and cloakrooms also doubled up as dressing rooms. It was quite a logistical exercise and not without commercial opportunities. Scattered along the course at regular intervals were Oxo booths, where hot and cold Oxo drinks were readily available, along with fresh fruit, rice pudding and milk. Oxo also sponsored the official Marathon programme, featuring some rather over-the-top endorsements of their product from an array of Britain's Olympic stars.

As the start time approached the 55 runners, all wearing numbers to help with identification, were lined up four abreast. Both Great Britain and Canada fielded full teams of 12 runners each and it was generally accepted, even by the ferocious American manager James E. Sullivan, that a British competitor would probably win. The Canadian Tom Longboat (again the subject of a Sullivan complaint, which was dismissed) was another tipped for a medal, but he was to run erratically.

At 2.33pm Her Royal Highness indicated that proceedings may start and Lord Desborough fired the starting pistol from his motor car, from where he acted as the race referee. The runners swept through the sovereign gate into the crowd-lined streets. Adrenalin pumping hard, the first mile was covered in a blistering 5 minutes 1.4 seconds.

As the race settled down and the field spread out, dedicated team helpers and trainers on pushbikes accompanied their men, offering support and advice. They were also allowed to move up and down the race and report back with any tactical developments. Telephones had been installed at regular points along the race route and marshals phoned the positions of runners as they passed back to the White City Stadium. The running order was chalked up on a board so the large gathering crowd, also enjoying the Pole Vault final and a number of Swimming and Diving events, could follow proceedings.

Pietri, wearing 19 and perhaps better acquainted with the debilitating effects of running in hot humid weather, made a much more cautious start than many of the favourites. He started picking up pace in the second half of the race, however, and by 32km had moved into second place behind the highly rated Charles Hefferon, still a substantial four minutes

> **'Let the thousands who go to football matches in the winter; the thousands who watch cricket in the summer; the millions eager about all the games and exercises which all the year round form their greatest recreation – let them come forward now and contribute, in however small a measure, to the ideal which England represents'**
>
> From the *Daily Mail's* patriotic appeal for funds to stage the 1908 Games

ahead. The British-born runner came originally from Berkshire; his family emigrated to Canada and he then travelled to South Africa to fight in the Boer War. After hostilities he settled in South Africa and chose to represent his new country at the Olympic Games. The race appeared to be his but Hefferon 'cracked' dramatically after stopping briefly to accept a drink of champagne, offered by a member of the crowd in all innocence on such a hot day. Whether it was the cold drink itself or simply the act of stopping and losing rhythm, Hefferon was soon in serious trouble. He was passed by Pietri after 39km, at which stage the Italian appeared to be going well.

Back in the Stadium the excitement was mounting. Conan Doyle's account for the *Daily Mail* memorably captures the tension. 'We were waiting, eighty thousand of us, for the man to appear; waiting anxiously, eagerly with long turbulent swayings and heavings which mark the impatience of the multitude. Through yonder door he must come.

'Every eye in the great curved bank of humanity is fixed upon the gap. What blazoning will show upon that dust-stained jersey – the red maple leaf, the blue and yellow, the stars and stripes or the simple numbers of the Britons? Those figures on the board tell us nothing. Is it the man who has a dash in him at the end who may head the field. He must be very near now, speeding down the streets between the lines of shouting people. We can hear the growing murmur. Every eye is on the gap…'

A rocket was fired high into the sky outside the Stadium to signal the imminent arrival of the first runner. It had still been a supreme effort by Pietri to catch Hefferon, however, and his own 'crack' inside the Stadium was to provide the memorable denouement to the race. Initially on entering the packed Stadium – where the crowd was actually a 91,000 capacity not the 80,000 mentioned by Conan Doyle, and 20,000 would-be paying spectators had been turned away – he wanted to run the wrong way in his confusion. Then he fell, the first of five agonising falls, as he tried to make his way to the finishing line. Each time he was helped to his feet by officials and there is no doubting that this was contrary to the race laws, no matter where the sympathies of the huge crowd lie. Meanwhile the American runner Johnny Hayes had entered the Stadium and was gaining steadily.

Contrary to a longstanding rumour, one of those officials was not Sir Arthur Conan Doyle, although the substantial figure of Dr Michael Bulger, Chief Medical Officer at the Athletics track and a member of the Irish Athletics Association, does admittedly bear a striking resemblance to him. He features in many press pictures of the incident, as does Clerk to the course Jack Andrew, the official holding the megaphone who accompanied the race for the duration. Both officials were, of course, among those singled out for criticism by James E. Sullivan.

The *New York Times*, caught up in the unfolding drama, also offered a vivid account of the event: 'The colours and the number told the spectators that it was Dorando and his name was on every lip. He staggered along the cinder path like a man in a dream, his gait being neither a walk nor a run but simply a flounder with arms shaking and legs tottering. By devious ways he went on.'

'People had lost thought of his nationality and partisanship was forgotten. They rose in their seats and saw only this small man clad in red knickers tottering onwards with his head so bent forward that

> **'It was impossible to leave him there, for it looked as if he might die in the very presence of the Queen'**
>
> The official 1908 report reflects on Pietri's Marathon collapse

the chin rested on his chest.'

Recalling the final stages of the race Pietri himself later wrote: 'In my frenzy I could not see them [the spectators], but I heard them. I looked straight in front to search for something I could not see yet because the road made lots of turns. Suddenly, after another bend, my heart gave a jump, I saw a grey mass in front that seemed a bastion with its bridge beflagged. It was the stadium, and after that I remember very little.' He finally collapsed across the winner's line some 32 seconds ahead of Hayes before being rushed by stretcher to a medical room to be revived. The Italian flag was initially run up the winner's pole, an act again seen as provocative by the Americans, on this occasion rightly incensed. Pietri's disqualification – the Americans lodged an official complaint the moment he finished – may have been unpopular, but it was entirely within the rules. From the first moment Pietri fell, and was helped to his feet, he was technically disqualified.

Like many distance runners at the time, Johnny Hayes declined to drink anything during a race and – and this wasn't the norm – claimed to take to his bed for the two days before a marathon run. Of small stature and a year older than Pietri, he clearly prospered in the great heat of the day. By now an odd-job boy at the famous Bloomingdales store in New York, he later offered a novel explanation, namely that both his father and his grandfather had been bakers and that he had spent many hours as a youngster working in the family bakery in New York. Hayes was a confident character who had certainly travelled to London with genuine gold medal hopes. After the USA trials, in which he rather surprisingly finished second to Thomas Morrissey, he was talking himself up ahead of the departure for Britain. 'I just know I am going to win,' he said. 'I wish it were fifty

miles instead of twenty-six. The next time you fellows see me I will be wearing the laurel wreath.'

So the race was rightly awarded to Hayes and the Irish were celebrating again, as both Hayes' parents hailed from Nenagh in County Tipperary although Hayes himself was American-born and, unlike some of the 'Irish Whales', never a British and Irish citizen. The phlegmatic Hefferon was upgraded to second place and the silver medal although the South African refused to endorse the American appeal and always considered Pietri the moral victory of the race. Another American Joseph Forshaw took the bronze medal while the first British runner home was William Clarke, a distant 12th. Britain's humiliation in the showpiece event of the 1908 Olympic Games was total, but in a curious way it didn't seem to matter. Dorando was the toast of London and the name on everybody's lips.

The hero of the hour, accompanied by his brother and manager Ulpiano, recovered and made his weary way to his lodgings in Church Street. News of his disqualification arrived later that evening via Count Brunetta d'Usseaux, the Italian IOC member who arrived hotfoot from an Olympic banquet at the Holborn Restaurant where an ad hoc meeting of the appeals committee had confirmed that the Italian's disqualification must stand. It was a bitter pill for Pietri and initially the flowers of sympathy promptly sent by Lord Desborough were probably little consolation. That was to come the following day, when he woke to the extraordinary realisation that he had become a name and figure of world renown.

The following day, after the final session of Athletics, was prize-giving day for the sports: some 1,320 in all, including medals, trophies and cups, all given out to the accompanying sound of the Band of the Grenadier Guards playing 'See the Conquering Hero Comes'. The climax of this gala occasion came when Queen Alexandra asked for Dorando Pietri to come up to her box and presented him with a cup. So hastily had the gesture been organised that the

A smile that says it all, as Dorando Pietro of Italy carries his Gold Cup away from the Royal Box in 1908. It had been awarded to him by Queen Alexandra, who was impressed by his valiant struggle in the last stages of the Marathon.

cup was not inscribed, but Her Majesty handed the Italian a hand-written note, 'For P. Dorando [sic], In remembrance of the Marathon race, From Windsor to the stadium, From Queen Alexandra.'

Pietri was encouraged to embark on a lap of honour, which didn't best please the Americans who felt that their official race winner was not receiving sufficient acclaim. To rectify this, his colleagues placed Hayes on a table top and paraded him around the Stadium clutching the official Marathon trophy.

Whether the well-connected Conan Doyle really made a direct appeal to Queen Alexandra to suggest the Cup is not known, but he undoubtedly initiated

> 'This Cup is balm to my soul. I shall treasure it to the end of my life'
>
> Dorando Pietri after receiving a cup from Queen Alexandra despite disqualification from the Marathon

Johnny Hayes, the actual winner of the Marathon at the London 1908 Games, is paraded around White City by his teammates. The Americans were keen that his feat should not be overshadowed by Pietro's collapse.

small fry to what Pietri was about to earn on turning professional and racing in America.

Pietri's appeal to the British public – indeed the watching world, as the Pathé footage was shipped around the globe – was that of the small, frail common man, bravely taking on the world and losing but with honour and courage. With his almost comic scuttling running style, curly black hair and trademark moustache he, in retrospect, cuts a strangely Chaplinesque figure. And there's a thought. Chaplin himself was just 19 in 1908, living in his native London and setting out on his career in film and stage. As a keen sportsman and a compulsive watcher of the silent movies of the time, it is inconceivable that he wouldn't have followed the Dorando Pietri story closely in the Pathé booths, becoming aware of all the stunning images that captured the hearts of the world.

Two years later, Chaplin moved to America and soon after that his trademark 'Tramp' character – the ultimate heroic loser – emerged fully formed on the silent screen. The appeal and tug on the heartstrings was almost identical, the physical resemblance unmistakeable. Even if only subconsciously, you sense the two characters are not entirely unrelated.

For three years after his Marathon epic Pietri raced regularly, maximising his fame. Composer Irving Berlin even wrote the song 'Dorando' in his honour and it was in the USA, where his earning power was greatest, that he ran a succession of rematches with Jonny Hayes – the majority of which he won. On his first USA tour he won 17 of his 22 races over a large spectrum of distances. He ran his final Marathon in Buenos Aires in 1910, when he recorded a personal best of 2:38.42, and retired in 1911, at the age of 26, having made 200,000 lire in the previous three years. Sadly he proved a poor businessman; a hotel he built and ran in conjunction with his brother went bankrupt, which forced him to work in a car workshop in San Remo. There he died of heart attack in 1942, aged only 56.

a fundraising effort for Pietri via a letter in the *Daily Mail* that accompanied his race report. 'I am certain that many who saw his splendid effort in the stadium, an effort which ran him within an inch of his life,' he wrote, 'would like to feel that he carries away some souvenir from his admirers in England. I should be very glad to contribute £5 to such a fund if any of the authorities at the stadium would consent to organise it.' In the event the appeal quickly raised £308 10s – a considerable sum in those days, although

'To expect that every seat will be taken each day for a fortnight is absurd. Nowhere in the world could an athletic performance of any kind achieve such a feat as that'
The Times, 18 July 1908

Britain's Past Olympic Games

Above The 'flying housewife' from Holland, Fanny Blankers-Koen (far right) soars to glory in the 80m Hurdles at the London 1948 Olympics – one of the four gold medals that made her the superstar of the Games.

Above right Eugene Sandow, the 'father of bodybuilding', who coached Launceston Elliot to win the one hand lift at the Athens 1896 Games. Sandow, a firm supporter of the Olympic Movement, was the single biggest donor to the London 1908 Games.

Below It is 1908 and the White City Stadium is ready to stage the Olympic Games. A venue that became synonymous with the Marathon drama of Dorando Pietri who collapsed on his way to the finish line.

Below right In 1908, the events and results of the Games were relayed to the crowd by The City Toastmaster and his megaphone.

Above top Cycling in Herne Hill at the London 1948 Games. Mario Ghella leads Great Britain's Reg Harris in the first heat of the final of the 1000m sprint. The Italian progressed to win the gold medal.

Above The writer Sir Arthur Conan Doyle, whose reports from the Olympic Games in 1908 were widely read as London staged the Games for the first time.

Above right British swimmer Henry Taylor, winner of three gold medals at London 1908. His record three golds was equalled a century later by Chris Hoy.

Right Sybil 'Queenie' Newall, winner of the gold in the national round archery event at the London 1908 Games. Her success was a landmark occasion for the Games because she was 53 years and 275 days at the time. To this day she remains the oldest woman to win a gold medal.

Henry Taylor

Henry Taylor was the only British Olympian to win three gold medals at a single Games before Chris Hoy in 2008. A Lancashire lad from the Hollinwood area of Oldham, Taylor swam in the Hollinwood canal as a boy before moving on to the Chadderton Baths, where his exceptional talent soon became apparent. Wearing a revolutionary, hand woven silk swimming costume, especially made for him in Oldham and weighing less than an ounce, Taylor won gold in two individual events at the London 1908 Games, the 400m Freestyle and the 1500m Freestyle, as well as anchoring Great Britain to victory in the 4 x 200m Freestyle Relay. Taylor kept on swimming despite advancing years, winning relay bronze medals at two further Olympic Games, in Stockholm in 1912 and in Antwerp in 1920. He served on HMS *Vincent* and *Ramillies* in the First World War and was present at the battle of Jutland. After the war he fell on hard times, eventually becoming an attendant at Chadderton Baths where a plaque was erected in his honour and where some of the trophies he had to sell have now been collected for display. He died in 1951.

The Olympic Games in Full Spate

Away from the tumult and drama of the various athletics competitions, Britain reaped the benefit of being the host nation and fielding a large number of entrants. The country enjoyed a gratifyingly successful Games across the board, with pride of place going to swimmer Henry Taylor. He secured three gold medals in the unheated pool (in which the water became murkier and dirtier with each successive day as a filtration plant had not been installed). It was tough going all round for the swimmers, but Taylor was not concerned in the slightest. He used to train in icy canals and boating lakes and swim at his local pool at Chatterton Baths in Oldham on 'dirty water day', when the public would be allowed in free just before the water pool was drained and the water replaced. He won the 400m and 1500m in world record times and was a member of the British squad that won the 4 x 200m Relay in yet another world record. All six Swimming finals in London resulted in world record times – a remarkable achievement.

Britain also made a spectacular sweep of all five gold medals at the Boxing tournament. In the end the home nation won 14 of the 15 available medals, with the only threat to the clean sweep coming in the Middle Weight class. Here Johnny Douglas faced the formidable Australian Reginald 'Snowy' Baker in a fiery contest between two of the most extraordinary and popular competitors at the Olympic Games. Olympic finals then usually consisted of three rounds, but the pair could not be separated after a furious, even contest.

'The regatta at Henley was a splendid ending to perhaps the most splendid athletic meeting that had ever been seen in the world.'

Lord Desborough on the Rowing finale to the 1908 Olympic Games

A fourth round was duly ordered, after which Douglas was declared the winner.

Reginald Baker – inevitably known as Snowy on account of his shock of white hair – was the New South Wales 100m and 200m Swimming champion at the age of 13. He was also capped twice for the Wallabies Rugby Union team at scrum half, and even made himself available to the Wallabies if required for the 1908 Olympic Games final against England. At the 1908 Games, as well as taking the silver medal in the Boxing he finished fourth in the 4 x 200m Freestyle Relay and also took part in the men's Diving competition, where he was eliminated in the first round. After the First World War Baker became a considerable silent movie star in Hollywood, later becoming manager of a polo club where he taught actors such as Douglas Fairbanks Jr, Elizabeth Taylor, Shirley Temple, Greta Garbo and Rudolph Valentino how to ride, swim and, occasionally, shoot.

Johnny Douglas meanwhile was the epitome of a British all-rounder. He won three fights in a day to take his Olympic title in London, with a narrow victory in the final considered contentious by some. Contrary to a number of reports in the Australian press, however, it was not his father (Johnny H.Douglas, a well known figure in British Boxing circles), who refereed the contest. Douglas senior did present the medals afterwards, however, in his capacity as President of the Amateur Boxing Association.

The flood of British success continued at other venues as well. Britain won all four gold medals in the Rowing events held at Henley where only men were competing. It was a similar story in the Yachting events, where Britain took the four gold medals on offer. The opposition was variable, with a total of only 13 boats from five countries. In the 12m class, for example, only two British yachts were entered and the race was contested off Hunter's Quay in Glasgow, to save both boats having to sail south. The other three classes – the 6m, 7m and 8m – were all sailed in light winds off the coast of the Isle of Wight at Ryde, rather than at Cowes just along the Solent. The husband and wife team of Charles Rivett-Carnac and his wife, Frances, took the gold medal in the 7m event; not a surprising result, as their boat, *Heroine*, was the only one to make it to the start line.

There was also a British clean sweep in the six Tennis events – three indoors at the Queen's Club and three outdoors at Wimbledon. This was hardly surprising as the home nation boasted 22 of the 50 entrants, although with 10 competing nations the Tennis was one of the more international competitions. Arthur Gore won gold medals in the men's indoors Singles and Doubles, while Josiah Ritchie – always known as Major Ritchie although he had no military connections – took the main men's Singles event at Wimbledon to add to a silver in the men's Doubles and a bronze in the Indoors Singles.

Nor are recent successes on the Cycling track an entirely modern phenomenon. In 1908 Britain took five of the six gold medals on offer, with British success in the 660 yards, the 5,000m, 20km, 100km and Team Pursuit. Only in the tandem did they suffer defeat, the French breaking the British monopoly. Leading the way in the Cycling medals was Bennie Jones, a Wigan Collier who came close to equalling Henry Taylor's achievement of three gold medals. Jones, who also played two first team games for Manchester United, won gold medals in the 5,000m, the Team Pursuit and took silver in the 20km. Charles Kingsbury also won two gold medals, in the Team Pursuit and the 20km. He lost out on the chance of emulating Taylor when, having made the final of the

Johnny Douglas was a supreme British sportsman. At the London 1908 Olympic Games he won the Middle Weight title in the Boxing competition. Three years later he was captain of the England cricket team that won The Ashes series 4-1 in Australia.

> ### Best of British
> #### Johnny Douglas
> John William Henry Tyler Douglas, known as Johnny, was born in 1882 in Stoke Newington, London. A glamorous sporting figure and an all-round sportsman, he played football for England's amateur side and became an excellent Middle Weight boxer, taking gold at the 1908 Olympic Games despite all three of his bouts being held on the same day. After the Games he famously captained the full England cricket team in Australia in 1911, helping his side to a 4–1 series win with tight bowling and tenacious batting; his dogged occupation of the batting crease infuriated the Australian side and supporters. He was drowned with his father on a business trip to purchase timber in 1930, when the vessel in which they were travelling collided with its sister ship. The accident happened just four months after Douglas had retired as a competitive sportsman.

New Arrival: Hockey

The 1908 Olympic Games were the first to host a men's Hockey tournament, in which England, Ireland, Wales and Scotland competed separately. England won the gold medal and Ireland the silver, while Scotland and Wales (the losers of the semi-finals) each took bronze. The official report stops graciously after England took a 5–1 lead, but the eventual result was 8–1, with Reginald ('Reggie') Pridmore, killed in action during the First World War, scoring four goals. Hockey had a chequered early career, disappearing from the 1912 Games only to be re-introduced at Antwerp 1920, before being dropped again in 1924.

Sprint competition, the competitors engaged in a tactical standoff and exceeded the time limit, causing the race to be declared null and void.

The quality of these finals was certainly high. The 100km, for example, won for Britain by Charles Bartlett, saw France's Octave Lapize take the bronze medal. Lapize went on to win the Tour de France two years later and also to take three Paris–Roubaix titles. One of the most popular and charismatic French sportsmen of his generation, he died in the First World War while serving as a fighter pilot in the French Air Force.

Archery proved unexpectedly good value, basically comprising an Agincourt-style shoot-out between big teams from Britain and France, as Henry B. Richardson of the United States was the only other competitor. To the barely contained delight of the popular press, the winner of the main men's competition, the so-called 'Double York' competition, was William Dod. He was a direct descendent of Sir Anthony Dod, who had commanded the English archers at the Battle of Agincourt in 1415. You couldn't make it up. Better still, his dashing sister Lottie Dod, one of the most accomplished all-round sportswomen of this or any other era, took a silver medal in the women's competition. She had turned to Archery after a stellar Tennis career that included five Wimbledon singles titles, remaining to this day the youngest-ever holder of the women's singles title, which she won aged just 15 in 1887. Dod was also a former British ladies amateur golf champion, played hockey for England and was a frequent visitor to St Moritz, where she excelled at all the winter sports. Her all-round sporting talent knew almost no bounds, although in the 1908 Olympic Games she had to concede first place in the Archery event to the formidable 'Queenie' Newall from Rochdale, who ran out a comfortable winner in the National Round event. At 53 years old, Newall remains the oldest-ever female gold medallist at the Olympic Games.

The Shooting range at Bisley saw no less than 15 gold medals decided. The event proved one of the best attended and most representative of the entire Games; 14 nations fielded strong teams and six of those departed with gold medals. Britain fielded a huge team of 67 marksmen, and predictably topped the table with six gold medals and 21 medals in total. Much of the interest surrounded a phantom gold medal, however, which a British competitor won and then lost.

Great Britain was allowed to enter 12 competitors in the individual small bore event. The entry forms of George Barnes of the Twenty Two club went astray, so Philip Plater was allowed to compete in his place. At the last moment, however, Barnes' bona fide entrance forms were re-discovered, and he was allowed to rejoin, leaving Britain with 13 competitors rather than the permitted dozen.

On a long afternoon confusion soon reigned. The British officials, thinking that only 11 men had

Women competitors in the National Round Archery event of the London 1908 Games prepare at the White City Stadium. The gold medal was won by Sybil 'Queenie' Newall of Great Britain.

The historic tennis star Lottie Dod of Britain. She won Wimbledon on five occasions, including 1876 when she was only 15. Yet it was in Archery where she reached the podium at London 1908 to take the silver behind Sybil 'Queenie' Newall.

fired, called Plater forward. Despite murky windy conditions he promptly scored a world record 391 points – four points more than his nearest competitor, compatriot Arthur Carnell. Plater was declared the champion, but on tidying up the paperwork at the end of the day an official noticed that 13 British marksmen had fired that day. Days of agonising and negotiations followed before it was declared that strictly speaking Plater was ineligible, as Barnes had to be considered the 12th British competitor. Plater was therefore denied his gold medal and everybody moved up a position, resulting in the gold medal for Carnell and a bronze medal for Barnes, previously in fourth place. Later in the year, Plater was presented with a special gold medal and diploma by the BOA, but his world record performance goes unrecorded in the official Olympic records.

One of the curiosities of the 1908 Games was that it failed to include that most British game of golf, although the Golf tournament in St Louis four years earlier was one of the few events that could be hailed as an unqualified success. Over 80 entrants had competed, albeit mainly good American club players. The eventual winner was Canadian George Lyon, a former cricketer and Canadian Pole Vault champion who had taken to golf in his late 30s with marked success. A huge driver with a natural flair around the greens, Lyon was an extrovert given to doing handstands on the fairway when bored or waiting for his opponent. So much did Lyon enjoy the 1904 Olympic Games – especially beating Chandler Egan 3 and 2 in the final at St Louis' Glen Echo Country Club – that he was determined to defend his title in London, only to discover on arrival in Southampton that the Golf tournament had been cancelled. Desborough, with typical generosity, offered him the gold medal by default, but Lyon declined to accept.

Exactly what had happened has never been fully explained. It has even been suggested that lost letters in the post was the root of the dispute, but whatever the cause the Royal and Ancient Golf Club at St Andrew's, home of golf and the world governing body as far as rules and regulations are concerned, had not been informed of the Olympic Games tournament in advance. When plans for the Olympic Games were finally unveiled, the Royal and Ancient Golf Club were far from happy with a strange format that involved six rounds of golf in three days, with all the rounds counting towards the individual and team events. They expressed their disenchantment with the Olympic Golf event and the leading players, already under pressure because of a congested schedule of events that summer, quickly fell into line. Without them there could be no meaningful competition and Golf at the London 1908 Games was hurriedly cancelled.

Although a comparatively minor issue at the time it was, in retrospect, a far-reaching decision.

Just Not Cricket

In 1908 sporting sensitivities were acute, with Anglo-American rivalry extending well beyond Athletics events, and beyond the Olympic Games. Bart King, touring that year with the Philadelphians Cricket team, was a highly skilled swing bowler; even at the age of 35 he threatened to show the British how to play the game. On the tour King took 87 wickets in ten first class matches at just 11.01 runs apiece, topping the first class averages with a rate that was not bettered for 50 years.

Best of British

Madge Syers

Florence Madeleine 'Madge' Syers was a talented swimmer and rider who turned to ice skating. She met her future husband Edgar, one of Britain's top skaters, at the Prince's Skating Club in Knightsbridge. He tutored her in the continental style of skating, freer and less rigid than the traditional English style. They married in 1900 and often skated as a pair in international competitions. In 1903 Madge won the inaugural British Open Figure Skating championships, repeating the feat in 1904 by beating her coach and husband into second place. In 1908, when Figure Skating made an appearance in the Summer Olympic Games, Syers proved untouchable; all five judges placed her first in both the compulsory figures and free skating parts of the competition. She also entered the pairs event with Edgar, taking the bronze medal. Syers suffered from a weak heart throughout her competitive career and died in 1917, aged just 35.

Not only was the game of golf deprived of the fine spectacle of a tournament held at three excellent courses – Royal St George's, Prince's and Royal Cinque Ports had been earmarked for the event – but golf was then omitted from the Olympic Games altogether. The road not taken would have been an interesting one: Jack Nicklaus taking on Tony Jacklin on the last day of an Olympic tournament, for example, or Nick Faldo going toe to toe with Greg Norman for an Olympic Golf gold medal. Fortunately it was voted in 2009 to bring this great global sport back to the Rio de Janerio 2016 Games.

The Olympic Games in London did include a number of winter events, however, not least four Ice Skating competitions. Those were held at Prince's skating club in Knightsbridge on 28–29 October, a full 16 years before the first Winter Olympic Games was held at Chamonix. The competition included two of the biggest names that the sport has ever produced, with the 10 times world champion Ulrich Salchow from Sweden, after whom the Salchow jump was named, winning gold in the men's event. Britain took gold in the Ladies Singles, as it was called, thanks to the formidable Madge Syers. A feisty competitor, she had finished a narrow runner-up to Salchow at the 1902 World Championships when she exercised her right to compete against the men. The rules and regulations did not forbid it so Syers entered, and in the opinion of many should actually have won. At the 1908 Olympic Games, in addition to her gold medal, she won a bronze with her husband and coach Edgar Syers in the Pairs event.

The 1908 Games included four sports which never obtained medal status again at the Games: Lacrosse, Rackets, *Jeu de paume* (Real Tennis) and, by far the strangest of them all, Water Motorsports which we would now recognise as power boating. France entered one boat, the *Camille*, while Britain entered five power boats of varying size and reliability. Somehow they managed to manufacture three medal classes and won two titles in heavy conditions, while the gallant *Camille* also came away from Cowes with a gold medal. One interesting footnote to the odd appearance of this sport is that Isaac Thomas Thornycroft, winner of a gold medal in Classes B and C on board the *Gyrinus II*, also travelled to the Helsinki 1951 Games some 44 years later, at the age of 70. Rather sadly, as a reserve crew member for the British yachting team, he wasn't required to compete.

The Longer View

From the perspective of over a century, the Olympic Games of 1908 appears a seminal moment in modern Olympic history, and indeed in sport generally. The towering, purpose-built facilities at White City, the burgeoning international rivalry and the intense patriotism that such an emotional commitment can inspire were keynotes of these Games, which also revealed the manifest need for neutral judges and universally observed rules. The presence of a seemingly insatiable and not always objective media operating across the world, highlighting hero figures and truly inspiring individual stories – not necessarily those of victory – also has echoes in today's events. The Games of 1908 featured all of the above and much more besides.

No official medals table was compiled in 1908, but the relative tallies of individual nations preoccupied many unofficially during the Games. People are always going to keep count and judge themselves and others accordingly, and the Olympic Movement had to respond quickly to this. The IAAF emerged from these Games to regulate the core sport of Athletics. So, significantly, did the International Swimming Federation. A comparatively minor Olympic sport until the 1908 Games, Swimming finally took centre stage in a purpose-built pool at the Stadium. It has never looked back and become both a major Olympic and Paralympic sport. In 1908 six gold medals were contested; at the 2012 Games competitors will pursue 34 gold medals in Swimming, as well as a range of Diving, Synchronised Swimming and Water Polo events.

The 1908 Games were momentous and epic, if sometimes contentious. They were a wonderfully potent explosion of sporting ambition and rivalries – the moment that international sport lit the touchpaper and stood back to see what happened. Britain's adventurous and sporting Edwardian entrepreneurs demonstrated that they could rise to almost any challenge – except, of course, that of beating the USA in the Athletics events. Nobody, it seems, was indifferent, and a wide range of views emerged as the competition drew to a close. The satiric magazine *Bystander*, mocking the friction behind some of the events, expressed sardonic relief that at least 'for some reason or other we do not seem to have fallen foul of Germany', while the *Tatler* offered a gentler reprimand to British officialdom: 'We do think that the patriotic enthusiasm of the officials overcame their sense of responsibility … when an English competitor was winning they not only cheered him up the straight but showed the most unbounded enthusiasm after he had succeeded. We think it would have been more judicious to have left the cheering to the crowd.'

The tension had certainly made an impact, such that Casper Whitney, President of the American Olympic Committee and an influential editor of *Outing* magazine, felt it necessary to reassure Lord Desborough. 'I want to tell you that we Americans understand the highly coloured and sensational newspaper stories that correspondents have been sending over,' he wrote. 'We have in America the same fault finding, suspicious and bickering class that you have in England, but we know how much stock to take of the output and I suppose you in England also know.'

Nothing was ever quite same after the IV Olympiad. The 1908 Games shaped the international sporting world as we still know it to a large degree – no small achievement for an event conceived just two years earlier by a few amateur British sportsmen in Athens Bay. International sport and competition changed at a very fundamental level, as predicted by the Rev. Robert Stuart de Courcy Laffan at the last of the seven Olympic banquets. Rising to speak, the Honorary Secretary of the British Olympic Association urged those who attended the London Games to remember that 'they were at the beginning of the one of those great world movements which was going to develop long after all present have passed away.' History has proved his vision right.

Medal table from the 1908 Olympic Games				
Country	Gold	Silver	Bronze	Total
Great Britain	54	46	35	135
USA	22	12	12	46
Sweden	7	6	11	24
France	4	5	9	18
Germany	3	5	5	13
Hungary	3	4	2	9
Canada	2	3	10	15

Chapter 3
Gathering Strength

Gathering Strength

IF THE LONDON 1908 GAMES PROVIDED AN EARLY PEAK IN THE GAMES' DEVELOPMENT, THE DECADES IMMEDIATELY AFTERWARDS SAW A FINE-TUNING PROCESS. SUCCESSIVE OLYMPIC GAMES EFFECTIVELY ADOPTED THE BEST ELEMENTS OF LONDON 1908 AND DISCARDED THOSE THAT THEY DISLIKED. PIERRE DE COUBERTIN HIMSELF, HAVING MAINTAINED A DIPLOMATIC SILENCE THROUGHOUT THE 1908 GAMES, VOICED SOME INTERESTING RESERVATIONS THE FOLLOWING YEAR WHEN HE ADDRESSED THE IOC GENERAL COMMITTEE AFTER THEY HAD OPTED FOR STOCKHOLM TO HOST THE OLYMPIC GAMES IN 1912.

Previous page

The Great Britain Gymnastics team enter the Stadium at Stockholm 1912. A magnificent red brick structure, the Stadium is still an athletics venue today.

Opposite page

Harold Abrahams (right), who won a 100m gold medal at the Paris 1924 Games as told in the film Chariots of Fire, talking to German runner Otto Peltzer at Battersea Park, London in August 1929.

'Of all the countries in the world Sweden at the moment possesses the best conditions necessary for organising the Olympic Games in a way that will satisfy all the claims that athletics [sic] and our expectations may demand … The next Olympiads must not have such a character [as London 1908], they must not be so comprehensive. There was altogether too much in London. The Games must be kept more purely athletic … more dignified, more discreet and more in accordance with classic and artistic requirements, more intimate and above all less expensive.'

In the event, the three decades after London were a period of turmoil from which the Olympic Games was not exempt. The devastating impact of the First World War saw the Berlin 1916 Games cancelled, and those in Antwerp in 1920 took place in a city ravaged by war. Yet the Olympic ideal was reforged in these troubled years, defying practical difficulties on the ground, economic collapse and ideologies that sought to appropriate the event for their own ends. The Olympic Movement was to emerge stronger after the Second World War and to offer hope for a new and more peaceful age.

For Britain the period bridged by the end of the London 1908 Games and the start of the Second World War was to prove testing in medal terms. The Olympic Games had captured the imagination of countries all over the world, leaving Britain to confront an embarrassing reality of rapidly diminishing returns. The London 1908 total of 54 British gold medals was always artificially high, but by the 1930s it was slim pickings indeed: just four from the Los Angeles 1932 Games and four from the Berlin 1936 Games. Even at the Stockholm 1912 Games the overall total of 10 golds, third place in the table, was deceptive. In the Athletics arena, which as always took centre stage, Britain won just two golds, one silver and five bronze medals. If Britain had used the official points scoring system they had proposed for the London 1908 Games (three points for a gold, two for silver and one for bronze) their tally would have totalled 13 points, compared with the USA's 80, Sweden's 30 and Finland's 29. Not such a good idea after all.

Most clouds have a silver lining, however. Comparative decline meant that the athletes who did strike gold during this period became huge sporting heroes and national figures within Britain, and all the more treasured as a consequence. British competitors provided some of the more arresting stories of the time and their exploits are still compelling. Athletes such as Arnold Strode-Jackson, Harold Abrahams, Eric Liddell and Jack Beresford remain among the biggest and most evocative names in British Olympic history.

The Stockholm 1912 Games had their own distinctive character. They were smaller and more compact than those of London, which presumably pleased De Coubertin. In the event 2,407 competitors, including 48 women, contested 102 events in 12 sports, with these being positively the last Games at which a private individual could apply to compete. Stockholm 1912 was also the last Games in which the gold medals, introduced at Paris 1900, were actually gold (thereafter they were reduced to silver with gold leaf). Japan became the first Asian nation to compete and the 1912 Games were the only event to omit Boxing from the programme since its first appearance in 1904 (the Swedish hosts declining point blank to stage this tournament).

The centrepiece of the Stockholm 1912 Games was the beautiful red-bricked Olympic Stadium. It still exists, largely in its original format, and remains a much loved and fully functioning international Athletics venue, staging IAAF Diamond League fixtures every year. It was there that Strode-Jackson, the debonair Oxford Blue and most extraordinary of men, provided a rare Athletics highlight for Britain with his victory in the 1500m. The long-legged, beautifully balanced runner, nicknamed 'Jacko', had great natural talent and worked ferociously hard to give the impression he competed purely for fun in his spare time. Away from the public limelight he trained harder than most, although it is true that his final preparations for the eagerly awaited 1500m showdown in Stockholm involved a long-planned

Above The Opening Ceremony of the Stockholm 1912 Olympic Games held in the crowded Olympic Stadium on 5 May.

Right The exterior of the Olympic Stadium, designed by architect Torben Grut, where many of the events of the Stockholm 1912 Games were held. The Stadium was used again in 1956 for the Equestrian events of the Melbourne Games due to the problems associated with transporting horses all the way to Australia.

Practising for the Stockholm 1912 Games, the British trio (left to right) R.D. Clarke (who did not compete in the Stockholm 1912 Games), William Craig Moore and Arnold Strode-Jackson go through their paces. Strode-Jackson progressed to win the gold medal in the 1500m at the Games in 3:56.8. A late burst saw him beat American Abel Kiviat who was second in 3:56.9.

fishing and walking holiday in Norway. The strategy paid off, and in this relaxed state of mind he duly reeled in his opponents in a final then described as the race of the century.

Strode-Jackson was ably assisted in the race by the Philip Baker, a Cambridge student who later – as Philip Noel-Baker – became an MP and won the Nobel Peace Prize. A talented runner in his own right, Baker quickly concluded after a brief training session with Strode-Jackson that only one British runner was going to beat the Americans, and it wasn't himself. Mel Sheppard, who won three gold medals at the London 1908 Games, spearheaded the American challenge, and the US sent such a strong contingent that eventually seven of their runners qualified for the final. The opportunity for

'team tactics' – so controversial in the 400m in 1908 – was again evident.

'Four or five days before the race Jacko and I had a work-out together over three-quarters of a mile,' Baker recalled some years later. 'He was running so awfully well that I made up my mind that he was the probable winner whereas with a foot that wasn't wholly sound, without very long training I didn't think I had much of a chance myself. So I thought I'd better help him although I didn't tell him until we lined up at the start. He was very inexperienced really, he had never run a big race with a lot of starters and particularly a race of that class. As we were called up to the start I said, "Jacko, you stick close to me and I will see that we both get to the right place at the right time. And don't you try and do it, leave it to me."

The right place was just before the bell. We sprinted a little sooner than others and we managed to get Jacko in behind the leader [Abel] Kiviat who was the world record holder at the time.'

It was fairly plain sailing after that as Strode-Jackson destroyed the quality field down the home straight with a withering late burst. He took the blue riband event at the tender age of 21 and is still the youngest ever 1500m Olympic champion. His potential for future Games was immense, but the outbreak of the First World War changed everybody's plans. Strode-Jackson was soon to emerge as a dominant figure on the battlefield as well as the Athletics track. He was awarded the DSO and three bars for his bravery on the Western Front and was additionally mentioned in despatches on no less than six occasions – a quite remarkable testament to his courage and devotion to the troops under his command. Unsurprisingly he became the youngest ever Brigadier-General in the British Army.

Elsewhere the men's 4 x 100m Relay team of David Jacobs, Henry Macintosh, Victor d'Arcy and William Applegarth took gold, as did the men's Football team. Arsenal's amateur Gordon Hoare scored twice in the final as Great Britain defeated Denmark 4-2. Centre forward Vivian Woodward, also a gold medal winner in 1908 and a striker who scored 29 goals in 23 full internationals for England, was probably their stand-out player.

> 'We have lots of undiscovered talent. That is certain ... There must be many who are natural jumpers, sprinters and weight throwers. We have to find them'
>
> Conan Doyle in the *Daily Mail*

There was success for the men's Eights in the Rowing while William Kinnear took the Single Sculls. In the pool the men again took the Water Polo title, and the women's 4 x 100m Freestyle Relay squad of Isabella Moore, Jennie Fletcher, Annie Speirs and Irene Steer claimed a splendid win.

Such victories did not satisfy the press and public back home, however, who had basked in the torrent of success in the London 1908 Games. Expectations were unrealistically high and imperial Britain, albeit an empire in decline, did not respond well to coming a distant third. Lord Northcliffe, a hardnosed businessman and strong supporter of Britain's involvement in the Olympic Games, again started an appeal to raise funds. He first sought to raise £10,000, followed by a totally unrealistic £100,000, to prepare British competitors across the board for the

Below All ready for action, the British swimming team that won the gold medal in the 4 x 100m Freestyle Relay event at Stockholm 1912 – Isabella Moore, Jennie Fletcher, Annie Speirs and Irene Steer – pose for the camera.

1916 Olympic Games. Northcliffe also asked the ever-willing Conan Doyle to strike the patriotic drum by contributing a number of articles for the *Daily Mail*. Conan Doyle's most powerful call to arms, however, came in the introduction of a book he wrote on field events at this time. His analysis was succinct, and much of what he wrote was being repeated, with slight variations, 70 or 80 years later.

'The present time is a very critical one for British athletic sport,' he noted. 'It is abundantly clear that in international competitions there are only two possible courses for this country to follow, the one being to cease to compete and the other to take the matter more seriously and to adopt those scientific methods which are used by athletes in other nations.' He acknowledged the dislike of 'overspecialisation' in some amateur quarters, but believed a dignified withdrawal was not a viable option. To him this struck an attitude of malingering defeatism, as well as being unfair to Britain's considerable sporting talent.

'There remains then only one alternative, which is to take the matter more earnestly and work not only by the light of nature but by the light of science. We have lots of undiscovered talent. That is certain. It is not one in a hundred of us who ever happens to have our attention drawn strongly to athletic sports. Along the odd 99 there must be many who are natural jumpers, sprinters and weight throwers. We have to find them … If we are beaten because we are the worse athletes we must smile and congratulate the better man. But at least let us make sure that our best men have been found and brought to the field.'

All eyes now turned towards Berlin. A splendid new stadium, the Deutsches Stadion, was built at Grunewald Racecourse and, despite the war, German preparations for the Olympic Games continued well into 1915. Only then was it reluctantly conceded that there was no foreseeable end to hostilities, and that there would in any case be no inclination for anybody to travel to Germany and compete.

The Olympic Games were finally reconstituted in 1920. This time they were held at Antwerp in Belgium, a remarkable effort by a country that had suffered so much during the war. Originally Budapest had been selected for the 1920 Games, but as part of the Austro-Hungarian Empire that had sided with the Germans this was considered unthinkable, so they were switched to Antwerp. Neither Germany nor Austria was allowed to compete, and facilities were inevitably very limited. Swimming and Diving events took place in an old moat, female athletes stayed in the YMCA and their male colleagues in schools and army barracks. The Americans, many of whom had had a very trying voyage to Antwerp aboard the US army transport ship *Princess Matoika*, complained of their rat-infested accommodation and one member of their team, Triple Jumper Dan Ahearn, was banned for trying to seek alternative lodgings. About 200 members of the American team signed a petition to their own officials demanding

On route to glory, American athletes wave flags and take photographs as they set sail for the Antwerp 1920 Games. It was the first Olympic Games after the First World War and it proved to be a good one for the USA. They won 41 golds, topping the medal table, while Great Britain won 15 golds.

The finish of the men's 5000m final of the Stockholm 1912 Games, showing Finland's Hannes Kolehmainen crossing the line to take the gold medal, followed by France's Jean Bouin.

Medal table from the 1912 Olympic Games				
Country	Gold	Silver	Bronze	Total
USA	25	18	19	62
Sweden	20	24	17	61
Great Britain	10	15	16	41
Finland	9	8	8	25
France	7	4	3	14
Germany	5	11	7	23
South Africa	4	2	0	6

better accommodation and Ahearn's reinstatement. In the end Ahearn was allowed to compete, but the accommodations stayed the same.

Many athletes had died in the four years of conflict and the shadow of loss hung heavy over the Games. Powerful and poignant stories emerged, such as that of Finnish bricklayer Johan 'Hannes' Kolehmainen who had taken the gold medal and set a new world record with a time of 14:36.6 seconds at the men's 5000m in the Stockholm 1912 Games. His victory was achieved by the narrowest of margins over French rival Jean Bouin and Britain's George Hutson, who took silver and bronze respectively. In 1920 Kolehmainen returned as a Marathon runner, only to discover that he was now the sole survivor.

Hutson had been killed at the battle of the Marne in September 1914, and Bouin died in action near Xivray, on the Meuse, a fortnight later. After the War an all purpose sports stadium was built in Paris, in his honour, and to this day is the home of Rugby team Stade Francais. Kolehmainen went on to take Marathon gold at Antwerp 1920, with the memory of absent friends no doubt never far from his mind.

After the horrors of war, however, there was a distinct attempt to make a new start. Doves were released to signify peace, the distinctive Olympic Flag with the five interlocking Olympic Rings was also flown for the first time and the Olympic Oath was introduced. Harmony was not everywhere, of course – Paul Radmilovic's winning goal for Britain

VIIe OLYMPIADE
ANVERS (BELGIQUE)
AOÛT-SEPTEMBRE 1920

Paavo Nurmi

Paavo Nurmi was born in 1897 at Turku on the southwest coast of Finland. One of the three 'Flying Finns', he brought Finland great Athletic success in the early Olympic Games and was the best middle and long distance runner in the world in the 1920s. Nurmi took a total of nine gold and three silver medals from the 12 events in which he competed at Olympic Games between 1920 and 1928. He was the most successful individual athlete of the 1924 Games, in which he won five gold medals from five events – no mean feat, as the 1500m and 5000m had a gap of only 26 minutes between finals. A dispute over travel expenses and amateur/ professional status led to him being barred from competing in the 1932 Olympic Games, and despite pleas from all the other Marathon competitors the ban remained. Nurmi lit the Olympic Flame at Helsinki 1952. He died in 1973 and received a state funeral.

Medal table from the 1920 Olympic Games

Country	Gold	Silver	Bronze	Total
USA	41	27	27	95
Sweden	17	18	24	59
Great Britain	15	15	13	43
Finland	14	9	9	32
Belgium	13	11	10	34
Norway	13	10	9	32
Italy	13	5	5	23

Finland's Paavo Nurmi was one of the greatest distance runners of all time. He won nine Olympic gold medals between Antwerp 1920 and Amsterdam 1928. His best Games was Paris 1924, where he won five golds – including the 1500m and 5000m crowns.

against his Belgian hosts in the Water Polo caused a minor riot among spectators at the final, and left the British squad requiring a police escort off the premises as tempers flared. He had won two previous gold medals with the British Water Polo team in Olympic Games spanning 1908 to 1920, as well as another gold as one of the 4 x 200m Freestyle Relay team.

As far as the wider world was concerned, the Antwerp 1920 Games were all about the emergence of Paavo Nurmi; he spearheaded a remarkable phalanx of Finnish distance runners and went on to win nine Olympic gold medals in his career. In the Antwerp 1920 Games Nurmi contented himself with the 10,000m, the Individual Cross Country and the Team Cross Country. In medal terms, Britain just about held its own on this occasion. Albert Hill was certainly one of the athletes of the 1920 Games, and Max Woosnam one of the great characters.

Hill, from Tooting in south London, first made an impression as a distance runner in 1910 when he won the 4 miles competition at the AAA Championships. He disappeared off the radar for a long while, only to re-emerge after the First World War, having served in the Royal Flying Corps. Hill had re-invented himself as an 800m–1500m specialist. Coached by the famous Sam Mussabini, whose speciality was originally the sprints, he suddenly started producing the form of his career at the age of 31. The British selectors were initially reluctant, but their faith was repaid with an extraordinary double gold in the 800m and 1500m at Antwerp 1920, a feat that was to prove beyond even Sebastian Coe and Steve Ovett 60 years later. In the 1500m the durable Noel-Baker, the British team captain having added his wife's name to his own after marrying in 1915, again played a splendid team hand in support of Hill, this time hanging on to receive a silver medal. Hill, who later went on to coach world mile record holder Sydney Wooderson, also took silver in the 3000m Team Race.

Britain's Albert Hill is congratulated after winning the 1500m gold medal at the Antwerp 1920 Games. Hill also won the 800m. No Briton was able to repeat this amazing middle-distance feat until Kelly Holmes did the double at the Athens 2004 Games.

And so to the Paris 1924 Olympic Games, the last organised under the auspices of De Coubertin. He was determined to make up for a slightly disappointing, low-key event in 1900, when he felt his home city had not lived up to his expectations. The Paris 1924 Olympic Games were to prove notably newsworthy for Britain. Several stories resonated with the general public, most significantly that of Eric Liddell. He was no great stylist rather like Emil Zátopek three decades later, he was an ungainly runner. As his British colleague and the 100m gold medallist Harold Abrahams observed, 'He had probably the worst style of any great athlete that's ever been seen but he put his whole being into his running.' His technique did catch on, however.

Cartoons of *Wilson of the Wizard*, who was Britain's most popular comic book hero before the arrival of *Roy of the Rovers*, show Wilson throwing his head back in exactly the same manner as Liddell used to. Imitation is the sincerest form of praise.

Liddle was born in China to a missionary couple and indeed the Chinese still claim him as their first Olympic gold medal winner. An all round sporting talent, he played on the wing for the Scotland Rugby XV before switching full-time to Athletics in 1923. He had been aiming for an Olympic 100m title – an event at which he held the British record – until discovering that the 100m final would be held on a Sunday. His strong religious convictions prevented him from running on the Sabbath and so, a full six months before the Games, and not on the eve of competition as depicted in the film, he concentrated on the 200m, in which he was to win a bronze medal, and, on the 400m. He made dramatic improvements in the latter event, culminating in his gold medal winning, world record breaking time of 47.8 seconds in the final.

Liddell clutched a note as he made his way to the Stadium for the final. It had been signed by members of the British team and was handed to him, at the team hotel in rue de la République, by the team masseur who had attended him throughout the Games. 'He that honours me, I will honour', it read, a quote adapted from the Book of Samuel ('Them that honour me, I will honour'). Liddell also rather startled his opponents by walking up to each of them in their lanes and shaking hands before the race, something that hadn't been seen before.

The Eric Liddell story went around the world at the time. It later inspired the 1981 British film *Chariots of Fire*, which used the Oval Sports Centre, Bebington,

'Only think of two things. The report of the pistol and the tape. When you hear the one, just run like hell until you break the other'

The note from coach Sam Mussabini that Harold Abrahams kept with him at the Paris 1924 Olympic Games

'I run the first 200 as hard as I can ... then, for the second 200, with God's help, I run harder'

Eric Liddell, athlete and missionary

for the Colombes Olympic Stadium and Liverpool Town Hall for the British Embassy in Paris; the famous scene showing athletes running on the beach was filmed at West Sands, St Andrews Scotland.

Liddell's achievement was not the only British success of the Paris 1924 Games. Harold Abrahams, son of a Lithuanian Jew and another prominent character in *Chariots of Fire*, won the 100m despite being left horribly behind at the start, losing up to three metres on his nearest competitors. Cambridge student Douglas Lowe fought his way to another hard earned gold in the 800m. Harry Mallin and Harry Mitchell won the men's Middle Weight and Light Heavy Weight Boxing titles respectively. It was also a defining moment for British Swimming as Lucy Morton became the first British woman to win an Olympic Swimming title, taking gold in the 200m Breaststroke. She had long been a world-class pioneer swimmer, but her Olympic opportunities had been thwarted, first by the cancellation of the 1916 Olympic Games, then by the omission of any women's Breaststroke and Backstroke events in the Antwerp 1920 Games. At the age of 26 she was a 'veteran' when she lined up in Paris seeking Olympic glory, but she overcame the American Agnes Geraghty for a remarkable upset that set the seal on her successful career. The fastest qualifier, Mietje Baron of Holland, was disqualified in the semi-finals because she touched the wall with only one hand.

Rowing saw the emergence of Jack Beresford. One of Britain's Olympic greats, he was eventually to win three gold medals and two silvers in four

England's Harold Abrahams, the Paris 1924 Games 100m champion, at the AAA Championships at Stamford Bridge, London, after winning the 100 yards. His place in Olympic history was assured - and he became known to a new generation because of the film *Chariots of Fire*.

separate Rowing events spanning five Games. The Steve Redgrave of his era, Beresford was an infinitely versatile oarsman. From being an outstanding rower and star rugby player at Bedford School, he switched full time to rowing after the First World War in which

Jack Beresford, the Steve Redgrave of his day, won five consecutive Olympic Games Rowing medals between 1920 and 1936 and remains one of the greatest heores of the sport. He won three golds – in 1924, 1932 and 1936 – and two silvers and was preparing for his sixth Games when war broke out in 1939.

Best of British

Jack Beresford

Rower Jack Beresford, the son of an Olympic silver medallist in the sport, was born in 1899 and educated at Bedford School. He served in the Liverpool Scottish Regiment during the First World War, during which a leg wound ended his rugby career. He enjoyed success in several Rowing competitions, including an exceptionally tight finish in the Antwerp 1920 Games where he lost to John B Kelly Sr to take the silver medal. Beresford won the Wingfield Sculls (the amateur sculling championship of the Thames) on seven consecutive occasions, and was a member of the Eights boat that won a silver medal in the Amsterdam 1928 Olympic Games. Beresford won three Olympic gold medals, in the Single Sculls at the Paris 1924 Games, the Coxless Fours at the Los Angeles 1932 Games and the Double Sculls at Berlin 1936 – beating the German crew in the last in a late surge at only 200m from the line. Beresford was elected a Steward of Henley Royal Regatta in 1946 and served on the Organising Committee of the London 1948 Games. He was made a CBE in 1960 and was President of the Thames Rowing Club until his death in 1977.

he wounded a leg while serving for the Liverpool Scottish Regiment in France. Beresford proved to be a brilliant natural sculler who started blazing a trail almost immediately. At the Antwerp 1920 Olympic Games he had contested a closely fought battle in the Single Sculls with American John 'Jack' Kelly, was thefather of the future Hollywood actress Grace Kelly, which was decided in the American's favour by inches. Now, four years later, Beresford finally landed the first of his three Olympic golds by defeating William Gilmore in the Single Sculls. He went on to win a silver in the Eights at Amsterdam 1928, a gold in the Coxless Fours at Los Angeles

1932 and another gold in the Doubles Sculls with Dick Southwood at the Berlin Games in 1936. Beresford fully intended defending his Double Sculls title in the 1940 Games, at the age of 41, when the Second World War forced their cancellation.

Elsewhere 1924 is largely remembered for the emergence in the swimming pool of Romanian-born Johnny Weissmuller. Born to German parents who emigrated to America when Weissmuller was seven months old, he won three gold medals for the USA in the Paris 1924 Olympic Games. Weissmuller went on to win another two golds in Amsterdam four years later before embarking on a successful career in

'... he was not, I believe, naturally a great athlete. But he was from the beginning a tremendous fighter'

Harold Abrahams on David Burghley, gold medallist in the 400m Hurdles at Amsterdam 1928.

Left Britain's Douglas Lowe shows the agony in his glory as he stretches on the line to win the 800m at the Amsterdam 1928 Olympic Games in a championship-record time of 1:51.8. It was a magnificent performance as he retained his title he had won four years earlier at Paris 1924 and is the only Briton to have won the Olympic 800m crown twice.

Bottom A 220-yards hurdles race at London's Stamford Bridge in 1927 featuring (nearest to the camera) J.E. Schurman and David Burghley. A year later in Amsterdam, David Burghley won the 400m Hurdles title. He played a greater part in Britain's history of the Games when he became Chairman of the Organising Committee for the London 1948 Games.

Hollywood became his destination, but the Olympic Games was a huge part of the life of future Tarzan, the American Johnny Weissmuller. He won five gold Swimming gold medals, three at Paris 1924 and two in Amsterdam 1928. He is seen here in an iconic pose with Maureen O'Sullivan, who played Jane.

acting. He went on to become arguably Hollywood's most famous Tarzan.

If the Paris 1924 Olympic Games were headline-grabbing for Britain, the 1928 Games in Amsterdam proved something of an anti-climax. Britain left with only three gold medals to celebrate, a sign that the country, one of the founding fathers of the Games, seemed unable to tap the nation's full athletic and sporting potential. The reasons are

not immediately apparent. Demographically you could argue that many potential male competitors who might have been at the peak of their careers in 1928 would have been lost to the First World War, but that would apply equally to many nations in continental Europe. In the event Germany, Finland, Sweden, Italy, Switzerland, France, Holland and Hungary all ranked above Britain in the medal table, as well as Canada and the USA. Conan Doyle's predictions were beginning to ring horribly true. Certainly the Games were evolving. The 400m track at the Olympisch Stadion in Amsterdam was to become standard, replacing the 500m track of the Paris 1924 Games. The Olympic Flame was introduced for the first time in Amsterdam, as was the tradition of Greece leading the parade and the Host Nation entering the Stadium last. Germany was allowed back into the Games having been barred from two Olympiads since the First World War, and Coca-Cola appeared as a sponsor for the first time, a nod to burgeoning commercial potential around the event.

For the British team the Amsterdam 1928 Games were a struggle, plain and simple. There was a gold medal for the Coxless Four at the Rowing venue at Sloten, but that and the two golds won on the Athletics track were the only genuine highlights. At the Olympisch Stadion Douglas Lowe's classy retaining of his 800m title stood out, along with a gold medal in the 400m Hurdles for David Burghley – who later, as Lord Burghley, did so much to shape the London 1948 Games.

Abrahams, non-participating captain of the British team in 1928 after a broken leg ended his career,

Medal table from the 1924 Olympic Games

Country	Gold	Silver	Bronze	Total
USA	45	27	27	99
Finland	14	13	10	37
France	13	14	10	37
Great Britain	9	13	12	34
Italy	8	3	5	16
Switzerland	7	8	10	25
Norway	5	2	3	10

'Even as a kid I didn't tense up. Not even the Olympics bothered me'

Johnny Weissmuller, future Tarzan, on the secret of his success

Medal table from the 1928 Olympic Games

Country	Gold	Silver	Bronze	Total
USA	23	18	16	57
Germany	10	7	14	31
Finland	8	8	9	25
Italy	7	5	7	19
Switzerland	7	4	4	15
France	6	9	5	20
Netherlands	5	10	4	19
Great Britain (10th position)	3	10	7	20

Between The Wars

Above The British Eight at the Amsterdam 1928 Games, where they won the silver medal, losing to the USA.

Above right At the Paris 1924 Games, Britain's Douglas Lowe (left), the 800m gold medallist, is congratulated by Paul Martin, who took silver.

Right A scene from *Chariots of Fire*, the 1981 British film that told the story of Harold Abrahams and Eric Liddell at the Paris 1924 Games.

Below British Olympians on *Empress of Britain* at Southampton, following their return from the Los Angeles 1932 Games, where the team won four gold medals.

Left Britain's Harold Abrahams (second left) crosses the line to win the 100m from American Jackson Scholz (second right) and New Zealander Arthur Porritt at the Paris 1924 Games.

Above Helen Wills stretches for the ball as partner Hazel Wightman looks on during the Doubles final at the Paris 1924 Games, where they defeated British pair Phyllis Covell and Kathleen 'Kitty' McKane.

Below left Alf Baxter, of Great Britain, who won a series of national weightlifting titles, competes at Amsterdam 1928, the only occasion the Netherlands has staged the Olympic Games.

Below British swimmer Lucy Morton wins the women's 200m Breaststroke at Tourelles, near Paris, during the Paris 1924 Games. Her victory came in 3:33.2 ahead of American Agnes Geraghty.

'... the slower journey by boat probably gave us a chance to do some training en route ... certainly wherever the transcontinental train stopped ... we had an opportunity to get out and take at least ten or fifteen minutes' exercise'

British Olympic gold medallist Tommy Hampson, on his journey to Los Angeles in 1932

'Firsts' Of The 1928 Olympic Games

The 1928 Games was the first to feature a lighted Olympic Flame during the event, although the Torch Relay did not appear until 1936.

A 16-day schedule, now standard, was used for the first time; previously events had spanned much longer periods.

The Opening Ceremony's parade of nations started with Greece, the country with the longest Olympic association, and ended with the host country. This has become the customary format for the Ceremony in subsequent Games.

Coca Cola became a sponsor of the Games for the first time.

Germany was allowed to participate for the first time since the First World War.

India won its first Hockey gold, the start of a run of six consecutive titles.

had distinct memories for both great champions. 'Lowe would himself I think say that he was lucky to win in 1924 because he was still up at Cambridge and a comparative novice, but by 1928 he had become a polished athlete with a great knowledge of tactics and in that final, when he did a new Olympic record, the outstanding memory is how he dominated the whole field. He seemed to be shepherding them into running the way he wanted to run from about third or fourth position.

'Burghley's was an amazing performance because, although one of the greatest athletes we have ever had, he was not, I believe, naturally a great athlete – but he was from the beginning a tremendous fighter. When I saw Burghley just get through the semi-final of the 400m Hurdles I wouldn't have given you anything for his chances in the final; but he won that final decisively against world record holders simply because he had enormous courage when he wasn't 100 per cent fit.'

It was a similar story of honest endeavour meeting mainly with frustration at the Los Angeles 1932 Olympic Games. Britain took a team of 108 competitors to California, but came home with only four gold medals. Coinciding with the world economic depression, this represented a fine, committed effort from Britain to get such a large team to the other side of the world; overall only half the number of athletes who attended the Amsterdam 1928 Olympic Games from around the world travelled to Los Angeles. Exceptions to Britain's disappointment were the Rowers, holding their heads high with golds in the men's Coxless Pairs and the Coxless Fours, but efforts in Athletics were rewarded with just two gold medals: Tommy Hampson in the 800m and Tommy Green in the 50km Race Walk.

Hampson was a late developer who didn't take up running seriously until his final year at Oxford. He arrived as one of the favourites in Los Angeles following his remarkable success in the 880 yards at the 1930 British Empire Games, later to be restyled

as the Commonwealth Games in Hamilton, Canada. He didn't let anybody down in Los Angeles either, defeating the challenge of Canada's Alex Wilson to win the 800m final in a world record time of 1:49.7 seconds, becoming the first man in history to break through the 1:50 barrier. He later added a silver medal in the 4 x 400m Relay, in which David Burghley also ran, and retired soon after the Olympic Games.

Hampson's account of his race remains a powerful read:

'Phil Edwards [of Canada] went off at a tremendous rate and covered his first 200m in just outside 24 seconds. I know that he was running too fast, but nevertheless I was in a little doubt as to whether I should let him go so far ahead. He covered the first 400m in about 52.5 seconds and I was about 12–15 yards behind, following him with quite a bunch of four or five others. We gradually closed the gaps as we went around the third bend and into the back straight, and it was at the top of the back straight that I decided to make my effort to get on Edward's shoulder. No sooner had I started that than Alex Wilson came dashing past me and got in close behind Edwards and overtook him. I had to make a split decision whether I would take the risk of running an extra four or five yards by trying to go around the outside of Edwards around that bend or ... to save that extra little bit of energy for a final finishing onslaught on Wilson down that the finishing straight. I happened to choose the second course, but Wilson had a 7–8 yards lead when we came to that final 80-yard stretch and I shall always remember the terrific effort of getting up to home, overhauling him and passing him just in time to feel the worsted break across my chest.'

British 110m Hurdler Donald Finlay became the first athlete in Olympic history to win a medal after judges examined evidence from the recently invented photo-finish equipment to overturn the original result. Originally the bronze medal had been awarded to Jack Keller of the USA, but after the ceremony the

Britain's Donald Finlay followed his bronze medal at Los Angeles 1932 with a silver in the 110m Hurdles at Berlin 1936. In the latter race he came behind the spectacularly-named Forrest 'Spec' Towns of the USA. Not until Colin Jackson made the podium by finishing second at Seoul 1988 did a Briton follow Finlay's lead.

decision was overturned; Keller himself went to the Olympic Village to find Finlay and gave him the medal. That same Olympian spirit was shown by Briton Judy Guinness, favourite to win a gold medal at the Fencing in the women's Individual Foil. Guinness noticed that the judges had not recorded two 'touches' by her opponent, Ellen Preis of Austria. She sportingly reported them herself, a decision that was to cost her the gold medal; she eventually took silver.

Although participating numbers were down, the

Medal table from the 1932 Olympic Games

Country	Gold	Silver	Bronze	Total
USA	41	31	30	102
Italy	12	12	12	36
France	10	5	4	19
Sweden	9	5	8	22
Japan	7	7	4	18
Hungary	6	4	5	15
Finland	5	8	12	25
Great Britain (8th position)	4	7	5	16

Below A picture that tells a story of its own from the Berlin 1936 Games. Nazi flags form a backdrop to the Olympic Torch at the start of one of the most dramatic Games in history.

Los Angeles 1932 Olympic Games had a big feel once competitors got there. Over 100,000 spectators attended the Opening Ceremony and the big Athletics days. Hampson described the running surface as 'silk' and there was a marked rise in standards of both facilities and performances, with an amazing 18 world records being broken. These were also the first Games to return a substantial profit of £1 million.

The 1936 Olympic Games that followed in Berlin were to be unique: a high water mark in terms of size, profile and controversy. They were the first Olympic Games to feature live television coverage: 21 huge screens were erected around Greater Berlin, allowing an estimated 150,000 locals to watch the action as it happened. News footage was also quickly distributed, to be shown at cinemas throughout Germany and beyond. At the Olympic Stadium itself up to 110,000 paying fans packed in for the big event. The Olympic Games had officially become a global phenomenon.

The IOC commissioned an official film, *Olympia*, to be directed by Leni Riefenstahl who had infamously produced and directed a film for the Nazis of the 1934 Nuremberg party rally. (*Triumph of the Will* is believed by some to have been a dress rehearsal for the staging and filming of the Games). Although known to be friendly with Hitler, a big admirer of her work, and under pressure from Goebbels and other spin-doctors, Riefenstahl, who spent 18 months editing the footage, produced a

remarkable film nonetheless. Three different versions were cut in German, English and French, and in the end *Olympia* celebrates the universal human spirit and diversity as much as the 1936 Games.

Although her segments on Hitler are undoubtedly idolatry, so too is Riefenstahl's treatment of Jesse Owens and other athletes. Her techniques, decades ahead of her time, set the template for forms of coverage we still enjoy. It was Riefenstahl who perfected the techniques of using slow motion, composing new music to accompany a specific action sequence, putting cameras on rails to follow the athletes, placing cameramen in little foxholes and trenches at ground level to get a different perspective and sending a roaming camera into the throng to get crowd reaction shots. At the Diving event she filmed the competitors from above the board, below the board, alongside them on the board and under the water, resulting in what is still one of the most stunning sporting sequences ever composed. Regardless of the race and nationality of those involved, she always looked for the human story behind the triumph or failure, with a versatility and range far beyond that of the written press. In fairness the press at the 1936 Games were on a tight rein. Only accredited German photographers were allowed to attend the Games, the net result being that only images pleasing to the Nazi authorities were offered for use by foreign media. The British media, like that of other countries, found itself muzzled.

The full scale of Hitler's horrific plans for Jews had not yet become apparent as the Berlin 1936 Olympic Games approached, but his aggressive, unambiguously anti-Jewish stance had already alarmed some sections of society. W.P. Crozier, the distinguished editor of the *Manchester Guardian*, addressed the issue in an editorial written for the edition of 7 December 1935:

'There will be a handful of German Jewish athletes at the Berlin Games. They will be there in order to conciliate foreign opinion; they will be there also because if they were not there Britain and the United States would be absent and the Games would fail. But the Olympic Games, by their charter, assemble athletes of all nations "on an equal footing", and German Jewish athletes in their own country are not equals; they are inferiors, almost untouchables. The German delegates at Athens in 1934 declared that only German citizenship was required of German athletes for the Games, but the Jews are no longer German citizens.

'The chosen handful is paraded before foreign eyes, food for the credulous … the Nazi party has injected the political poison of its anti-Semitism to the principle of human equality on which the Games are based, on which they have so far been conducted, and without which they are spiritually dead. How can this country approve and confirm this perversion of a noble principle by joining the Berlin Games? Must it not, for its self-respect, withdraw?'

There was a genuine dilemma. The British Olympic Association briefly debated whether to participate or not in 1935, but there was no real appetite to withdraw from those in authority. Nationwide a mood of appeasement with Germany held sway, at least with those in control of national destiny. Philip Noel-Baker, captain of the British Olympic team in 1920 and 1924 and now an MP, was one notable voice of protest. In a letter to the *Manchester Guardian* he insisted that the Nazis 'had injected politics into all sports and the situation … is a laughing stock to those who understand what sportsmanship involves'.

Calls for a boycott in Britain quickly fizzled out. Less than 20 years after the end of the First World War, people were partly in denial over Hitler, wanting to hope for the best and above all preserve the peace. There was a more serious debate in the USA, with the AOC having a formal vote on the issue. The AOC President Avery Brundage argued long and hard for participation, however, and American competitors were eventually given the

---

First of the Berlin 1936 Olympic Games

Live television coverage of the Olympic Games took place for the first time in 1936. Over 70 hours of footage was broadcast, using equipment from the German company Telefunken and Berlin's Paul Nipkow television station for transmission. It was received by special viewing rooms in Berlin and nearby Potsdam, as well as by a few private television sets.

The first Torch Relay brought the Olympic Flame to the Olympic Stadium from Olympia in Greece.

Basketball was introduced to the Olympic programme, and was played outside on a dirt court in driving rain.

Diving blocks were brought in for the Freestyle event (swimmers had previously dived from pool walls).

green light. Ultimately the number of participating countries, 49, was to prove a record for the Games to date. Only Spain, under a left-wing popular front government, and Ireland boycotted the Berlin 1936 Olympic Games because of Nazi Germany's unacceptably anti-Semitic overtones. At one stage an alternative event, for those wishing to disassociate themselves from Berlin 1936, was planned in Barcelona, but fell by the wayside with the onset of the Spanish Civil War in July 1936.

Those anti-Semitic overtones were brought into stark focus in Britain by the experience of Gretel Bergmann, later Bergmann-Lambert. Born into a Jewish family at Laupheim, her case received much publicity when she sought refuge in Britain for three years before the Berlin 1936 Olympic Games. She had set a German High Jump record in 1931 when competing for the Ulmer FV 1894 club, but was expelled from the club following the Nazis' rise to power in 1933. By April that year she had arrived in Britain and the following year she won the British high jump championship with a leap of 1.55m, Afterwich she started to make plans to compete for Britain at Berlin 1936.

In January 1936, however, her family in Germany were threatened with reprisals if she failed to return. Bergmann was 'encouraged' to travel back to Germany – significantly at the time when the AOC was seriously considering whether to boycott the Games. Nazi officials calculated that the return of Bergmann might hint at a slightly more liberal approach, but it didn't last long. In June 1936 Bergmann equalled the German record with a jump of 1.60m at the German championships, but two weeks later the authorities expunged her record from the books and she was removed from the German Olympic squad for 'under-performance'. She was replaced by Dora Ratjen who was later revealed to be a man with intersexual characteristics who had been raised as a girl.

Bergmann found German Jews facing a desperate situation on her return to Germany. 'Jews were not allowed in restaurants, in movies, in whatever,' she later told the US Holocaust Memorial Museum. 'Even though I was a member of the German Olympic women's team, I was not allowed in a stadium. I couldn't practice.' She returned to Britain before emigrating to the USA in 1937, where she settled in New York. In 1999 she finally returned to Germany to visit the Stadium in Laupheim, from where she had once been banned. Now it was dedicated to her: 'I was not going to participate, but then I was told they were naming the facilities for me so that when young people ask "Who was Gretel Bergmann?" they will be told my story and the story of those times. I felt it was important to remember and I agreed to return to a place I swore I would never go again. But I had stopped talking German and didn't even try when I was there. They provided a translator.' In 2009 her German High Jump record was restored to the record books.

Britain, although travelling with a large team of 208 competitors, again endured a mediocre medal haul. These were difficult times as the rest of the world poured resources into their Olympic sports. Jack Beresford, ever reliable, won another Rowing medal in his fifth consecutive Games, this time a gold with Dick Southwood in the Double Sculls. There was also an Athletics gold in the men's 4 x 400m Relay at the Stadium when Godfrey Rampling, father of the future Hollywood actress Charlotte Rampling, helped the squad to a memorable success. Harold Whitlock, an expert motor mechanic who used to fine-tune racing cars for record attempts at the old Brooklands circuit, also took gold in the 50km Race Walk.

The Sailing events were held in the Fjord of Kiel on the Baltic Sea. The British 6m crew took gold while in the O-Jolle class helmsman Peter Scott took bronze behind Daan Kagchelland of the Netherlands and Werner Krogmann of Germany. Scott was the son of Robert Falcon Scott and later became a noted conservationist and founder of the Wildfowl and Wetlands Trust. Scott had started the final in equal second place, but had a disastrous last race in which he failed to finish. Scott later also became British gliding champion.

The undoubted international star of Berlin 1936 was Jesse Owens, who dominated an Olympic Games designed by the Nazi regime to promote Aryan supremacy. On his return to the USA after the Games Owens stopped off at London, to be mobbed by press and public alike. One of the greatest athletes in history, he has been described by coaches down the years as the athlete with the most perfect combination of strength, speed and suppleness. Propaganda failed beside this embodiment of the Olympic spirit. Owens' deeds transcended nationality; his story was the one that transfixed the British public and every sports fan around the world. In 1955 Owens was officially honoured by his nation, President Dwight Eisenhower naming him as an ambassador of sports for the USA.

'I wanted no part of politics. I wasn't in Berlin to compete against any one athlete. The purpose of the Olympics was to do your best'

Jesse Owens on the 1936 Olympic Games

Jesse Owens wrote himself into Olympic history in at Berlin 1936 by winning four gold medals and sending a message to the world. The American is pictured at the start of the 200m, which he won in 20.7 seconds – a world record. He won three other gold medals, in the 100m, 4 x 100m Relay and Long Jump.

Friends and rivals, Jesse Owens talks to Germany's Lutz Long. The pair had an amazing duel in the Long Jump at the Berlin 1936 Games, with Owens taking gold and Long winning silver. In July 1943, Long was killed in action during the Second World War.

James Cleveland Owens became Jesse early in his life; a primary school teacher misunderstood 'J.C. Owens' at roll call and enrolled him as Jesse. An absolutely phenomenal natural talent, Owens blazed an early trail. While a student at Ohio State he broke three world records and equalled a fourth at a Big Ten Meeting at Ann Arbor on 25 May 1935 – all in the space of 45 minutes and with a bad back. Just before the meeting started he had asked his coach if he could withdraw. Owens equalled the world record in the 100 yards (9.4 seconds) and broke the world record in the Long Jump (8.13m) with his one leap. He went on to win the straight 220 yards in 20.3 seconds and the 220 yards Low Hurdles in 22.6 seconds. In fact you could claim he broke five world records, because in both the 220 yard events he simultaneously set world records for the respective 200m events.

It was much the same story at the Olympic Games in Berlin a year later where he roared to victory in the

> ### 'Friendships born on the field of athletic strife are the real gold of competition'
>
> **Jesse Owens, speaking of fellow athlete Lutz Long, with whom he competed at Berlin 1936**

100m, 200m, Long Jump and 4 x 100m Relay. Only in the Long Jump were there any dramas, and a friendly rivalry sprang up to become the defining moment of the 1936 Games.

Owens was struggling badly in qualification. Believing everybody was still warming up he ran through his first jump, and was shocked to see a no-jump signalled. With his second jump he was six inches over the board; that was signalled a no-jump as well. At this point Lutz Long of Germany, Europe's best jumper and Owens' closest rival, drew him to one side and advised him to calm down, move his run-up mark back a foot and play safe with his final jump. Owens took the advice on board, although he almost played it too safe, surpassing the automatic qualifying mark of 7.16m by just 1cm. Long then had a titanic battle in the final with a much relieved Owens. The latter prevailed when he posted the second longest jump in history (8.06m) to take gold. Long acclaimed Owens as the victor and the two athletes paraded around the Stadium together – not for the first time an Olympic loser rightfully shared the glory.

The two friends stayed in regular touch for seven years until Long's letters stopped. Owens discovered that his former rival had been killed at the battle of St Pietro in 1943. Thereafter Owens kept in touch with Long's son until his own death in 1980. The unlikely friendship between Owens and Long, the black grandson of an American slave and the blonde German epitome of Aryan youth, sent out the strongest message from the 1936 Games and is the story that endures to this day. 'Friendships born on the field of athletic strife are the real gold of competition,' insisted Owens. 'Awards become corroded, friends gather no dust.'

The Closing Ceremony of the Berlin 1936 Games, which took place on 16 August. In the foreground, the Olympic Flame still burns; around it, the crowd unanimously performs the Nazi salute.

Briefly the Berlin 1936 Olympic Games seemed to leave politics in its wake, but not for long. Two days after the Games Captain Wolfgang Fürstner, who had run the Olympic Village in the early stages of the Games before being replaced overnight by Werner von Gilsa, committed suicide; he had been dismissed from military service because of his Jewish ancestry. The world was about to spiral out of control again and Olympic sport was to be shelved for 12 long years, until the London 1948 Games breathed life back into the Olympic Movement.

Medal table from the 1936 Olympic Games				
Country	Gold	Silver	Bronze	Total
Germany	28	25	29	82
USA	24	20	12	56
Hungary	9	1	5	15
Italy	8	9	5	22
Finland	7	6	6	19
France	7	6	6	19
Japan	6	4	8	18
Great Britain (10th position)	4	7	3	14

Cancelled Games

The Olympic Games of 1916, scheduled to be in Berlin, were cancelled due to the outbreak of the First World War in August 1914. Work on a prestigious new stadium to host the Games, the Deutsches Stadion, had begun in Berlin in 1912. The structure was dedicated in June 1913, in front of 60,000 people and 10,000 live pigeons, released to celebrate the occasion. No-one believed the war would last for several years, but two years later it was clear the hostilities were far from over and the Games were cancelled. Global conflict also put an end to the proposed 1940 Olympic Games, due to be held in Tokyo, and it was not until 1964 that the Games came to Japan.

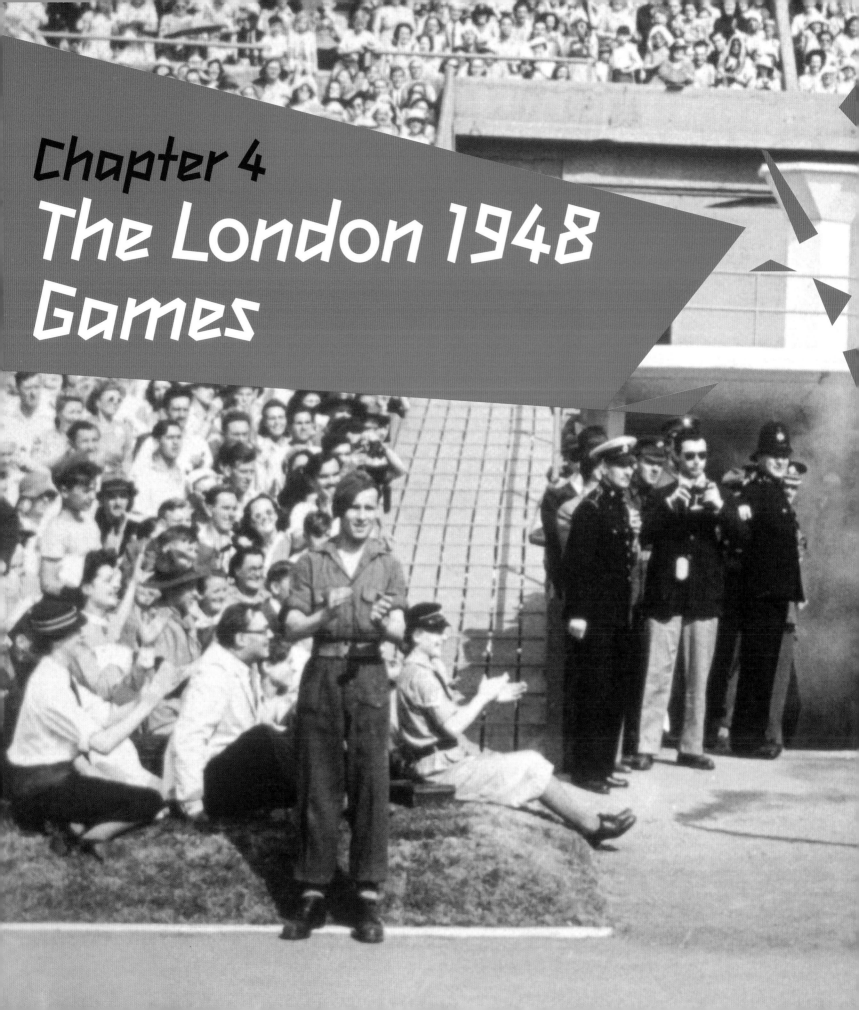

Chapter 4
The London 1948 Games

The London 1948 Games

IN JUNE 1939, WITH THE WORLD HURTLING TOWARDS ANOTHER GLOBAL CONFLICT, THE IOC VOTED TO DECIDE THE VENUE FOR THE 1944 OLYMPIC GAMES. LONDON FOUGHT OFF THE CLAIMS OF ROME, DETROIT, BUDAPEST, LAUSANNE, HELSINKI, MONTREAL AND ATHENS TO SECURE THE VOTE. SIX LONG YEARS LATER, HOWEVER – AFTER THE 1944 GAMES HAD BEEN CANCELLED – WITH THE END TO HOSTILITIES MERCIFULLY IN SIGHT, MUCH OF EUROPE LAY IN RUINS. THE IOC QUITE SENSIBLY SET ABOUT STARTING A NEW BIDDING PROCESS TO FIND THE HOST CITY FOR THE 1948 GAMES. ALL PREVIOUS BETS WERE OFF.

'After all those dark days of the war, the bombing, the killing, the starvation, the revival of the Olympics was as if the sun had come out ... I went into the Olympic Village and suddenly there were no more frontiers, no more barriers. Just the people meeting together. It was wonderfully warm. Men and women who had just lost five years of life were back again'

Emil Zátopek

Very few nations or cities in war-ravaged Europe were in a position to contemplate staging the event. In America the President of the American Olympic Committee (AOC), Avery Brundage, who was also Vice President of the IOC, initially offered the opinion that only an American city, untouched by conflict, could realistically contemplate staging an Olympic Games. Many agreed with him, and as if on cue Baltimore, Minneapolis, Philadelphia and Los Angeles all immediately announced their candidature, along with Lausanne from neutral Switzerland. Arguably they had the infrastructure, facilities and resources to take on the Games and see it through.

In London, officials of the British Olympic Authority (BOA) viewed things very differently. They objected that their great city had helped out the Olympic Movement in 1908 and had won the vote for the 1944 Games fair and square. Britain had stood alone in the war for a critical period; did it not deserve first crack at a peacetime Olympic Games? King George VI was keen as well, sensing the challenge of holding the Olympic Games would galvanise Britain. He believed the Games offered the perfect opportunity to restore morale in the weary country and to signal a return to 'normality' across the globe. Quickly the momentum for a new British bid started to build. In October 1945 Lord Burghley, now chairman of the

BOA met with the President of the IOC in Stockholm to discuss London's possible selection. As the official report for the 1948 Games observes, 'an investigating committee was set up by the British Olympic Council [sic] to work out in some detail the possibility of holding the Games. After several meetings they recommended to the Council that the Lord Mayor of London should be invited to apply for the allocation of the Olympic Games of 1948.'

Sigfrid Edström, the President of the IOC, had always been in favour of Britain staging the 1948 Games. He was also keen that the first Games after the war be slightly different – a commemoration of those who had perished so recently. The priority was simply to get as many nations as possible gathered under the same roof, and to let the unique atmosphere of the Olympic Games inspire the youth of the world again. Brundage was quickly convinced by Edström's enthusiasm for London and changed his position.

Britain's determination also struck a chord with IOC candidates generally. There was a widespread feeling that London, a symbol of democracy and freedom throughout the years of conflict, would be the most fitting venue for the first post-war world gathering. In practical terms it would certainly be the easiest for most hard-pressed nations to travel to. The IOC duly organised a postal vote in March 1946, with London emerging as the overwhelming choice.

Slowly, the so-called Austerity Games began to take shape. Germany and Japan were not permitted to compete and Russia, although it had begun competing internationally in other sports, chose not to travel. They did send a large team of observers, however, to make notes at all the events.

London's candidature wasn't entirely without its critics at home. The London *Evening Standard* delivered a critical editorial, complaining that, 'a people which has had its housing programme and food imports cut … may be forgiven for thinking that a full year of expensive preparation for the reception of an army of foreign athletes verges on the border of excessive'. Generally, however, the British public seemed glad to have something positive to focus on.

The BOA formed an Organising Committee. Three or four of its members were very much 'usual suspects': Lord Burghley, for example (Eton, Cambridge, an Olympic gold medallist from 1928 and a former MP) was a natural choice as Chairman of the Organising Committee, while Colonel Evan Hunter OBE proved an unsung hero as Secretary, a role in which he had served the BOA since 1925. Hunter, a career soldier who had fought in both world wars, had organised the British Empire Games at the White City Stadium, London, in August 1934 and took a sanguine and relaxed view of affairs. Nothing could faze him. New Zealander Arthur Porritt, a 100m bronze medallist in Athletics at the Paris 1924 Olympic Games, had settled in London where he became surgeon to the Royal Household. He was placed in charge of Olympic Medical Services while Harold Abrahams, who beat Porritt at the 1924 Games, was appointed Treasurer to the Games Committee. It was a rock solid team combining experience and influence. However, history shows that in delivering something as big as the Olympic Games you also need somebody who thinks outside the box, an entrepreneur who sees the bigger picture, and 1948 was to be no exception.

The maverick this time was another brilliant self-made entrepreneur, Sir Arthur Elvin. He had rescued Wembley Stadium from insolvency in 1927, becoming the Managing Director of Wembley Ltd. He found various ways of making it pay – mainly through greyhound racing, the formation of a speedway team and staging Rugby League Cup finals. He also established two successful ice hockey teams, the Wembley Lions and the Wembley Monarchs, at the Empire Pool.

Although no new venues were to be built and expenditure was to be kept to a minimum, Wembley needed approximately £90,000 (over two million pounds in today's money) for essential repairs and the installation of a 400m cinder running track. The government were not prepared to spend such money, while its citizens still endured strict rationing and large areas of Britain were being rebuilt. The all-powerful Elvin soon managed to persuade his Wembley Stadium Management Board to put up the money, offset against future ticket sales. It was the key moment in deciding whether the Games would take place, and King George VI showed his gratitude in 1947 by rewarding Elvin with a knighthood.

Elvin really was an extraordinarily adroit mover behind the scenes. Somehow he persuaded Arthur J. Rank to pay £25,000 for exclusive film rights to make the official film of the 1948 Games. This amounted to three per cent of the total budget and was an early indication of the Olympic Games's commercial potential. Rank, the shrewdest of businessmen himself, had also done his sums: he knew he could make it pay as well. Unlike the Leni Riefenstahl masterpiece *Olympia*, which appeared 18 months after the Berlin 1936 Games, Rank's people had the official Technicolor film, *The Glory of Sport*, showing in all his cinemas two weeks after the end of the Games. Rank also had separate crews filming in black and white to turn around twice weekly news packages to show in his cinemas before the regular feature.

Elvin was a tough practical operator, but he was

London 1948 Venues

Wembley Empire Stadium
Wembley Empire Pool
Wembley Palace of Engineering
Empress Hall, Earl's Court
Harringay Arena, Harringay
Royal Regatta Course, Henley-on Thames
Herne Hill Velodrome, Herne Hill
Windsor Great Park
Central Stadium, Military Headquarters, Aldershot
Tweseldown Racecourse
Arsenal Stadium, Highbury
Selhurst Park
Craven Cottage, Fulham
Lynn Road Stadium, Ilford
Griffin Park, Brentford
Champion Hill, Dulwich
Green Pond Road Stadium, Walthamstow
White Hart Lane, Tottenham
Lyons' Sports Club, Sudbury
Guinness Sports Club, Park Royal
Polytechnic Sports Ground, Chiswick
National Rifle Association Ranges, Bisley
Finchley Lido, Finchley
Torbay,
Fratton Park, Portsmouth
Goldstone Ground, Brighton
Royal Military Academy

Opposite page

Fans enjoy the Athletics action at a full Wembley Stadium during the London 1948 Games. There hardly seems a spare seat, and notice how there is no roof over the far straight of the famous venue.

victory awarded the British sprinters was the first time the British crowd had the opportunity to cheer a triumph by their countrymen. But the Britons disagreed with the judges. They did not want to win even one victory that way. They gave their loudest cheer to the disqualified Americans … that is sportsmanship at its best.' It was a far cry from the antagonism of the London 1908 Games, a reflection of changing attitudes that 40 years had wrought. Two world wars had forged a deeper relationship, and a new and proper perspective had been rediscovered.

Austerity for All

With no choice but to 'downsize', the London 1948 Olympic Games made a virtue of its austerity and celebrated the fact that the Games were being held at all that year. Everything was done on a shoestring. Morally, not a penny could be wasted in a country bankrupted by years of conflict. It says much that all the competing nations bought into this approach, with shared struggle and hardship fostering a unique atmosphere.

It was decided early on that no new stadia or other facilities were to be built. This was to prove a problem for Britain heading into the 1950s, but it was accepted in 1948 as the price of stepping forward straight after the war. A comparatively modest budget of around £730,000 was put aside for essential renovations, the restoration of existing facilities and the housing and feeding of nearly 6,000 competitors and officials, plus associated media. In the event some £732, 648 was spent on the 1948 Games. With receipts totalling £761,688, a pre-tax profit of more than £29,000 was returned.

The 3,714 male competitors and additional coaches and management were housed at three RAF camps in Uxbridge, West Drayton and Richmond. Female competitors stayed in various London college buildings. Linen and blankets were provided, but all concerned were asked to bring their own towels. Many countries on the near continent rallied around

Above Building work takes place at Wembley before the start of the London 1948 Games with the laying of the track. The Stadium was to prove one of the great homes for Olympic Athletics' feats with the multi-medal glory of Dutch superstar Fanny Blankers-Koen.

also a sports fan. His enthusiasm shone through when he was quoted in the *News of the World* on the eve of competition, 'Cannot everyone in the world see that even in far-away Moscow it is better that men should run and jump against each other rather than to blow each other to pieces on the battlefield? The approach is quite different from the 1936 Berlin Games. We want to see the best men win, no matter where they come from and who they represent.'

Such an approach was genuine and reflected in the responses of spectators and organisers alike. Just staging the Games seemed reward enough for Britain, evidenced on the last but one day of the Athletics when the 4 x 100m Relay squad appeared to have won Britain's first gold medal of the Games. The USA had actually won the race by five yards, but they were mysteriously disqualified for a faulty baton change. The British quartet thus accepted the gold medals on the podium in front of a very subdued home crowd before the decision was officially reversed three days later. Impressed, the *New York Times* reported the following day that: 'The judicial to help feed the assembled athletes. The Dutch authorities, for example, sent over 100 tonnes of fresh fruit and vegetables in twice weekly shipments for general use, while the Danish government donated 160,000 eggs. Czechoslovakia contributed 20,000 bottles of mineral water, and the British Trawlers Federation came up trumps by transporting 20 tonnes of kippers and herring to London. Austria, Switzerland and Ireland also contributed to the general kitty, and all competing countries were invited to bring as many of their own supplies as possible.

The USA team were re-supplied on an almost daily basis with foodstuffs flown into USAF bases in Britain, while the fortunate Argentinians arrived with a large contingent of frozen steak. Gradually a good-natured barter system began to develop at the team bases; the Italians, for instance, offered pasta and wine in return for the Argentinians' steaks. In the end there was so much to go round that many foodstuffs became surplus to requirements; they were distributed to nearby hospitals. To save money, some of the London-based members of the British team stayed in their homes or with friends. Maureen Gardner, who went on to win silver in the 80m Hurdles, caught the Tube into Wembley every day from her base with friends in Snaresbrook.

Dame Mary Glen-Haig, later an IOC member for Britain, recalled queuing with competitors for a meal one evening when a smell wafted down from the French dormitories. 'The smell was too much for us,' she recalled. 'We went down to the cellars and found a way through to next door where we joined a queue of French girls in their dining room; they were eating beefsteak and chips. That was the best meal I had.' There were very few official banquets,

> 'It was very austere because it was just after the war and the rationing was still on. There was no Olympic Village. We - the Cycling team - lived in a private house, and my mother came down and she was the cook, preparing all the food for us. We had Spam fritters and toad-in-the-hole'
>
> Tommy Godwin, British cyclist who won two bronze medals

in contrast to the gastronomic delights surrounding the London 1908 Games, but the Lord Mayor, Sir Frederick Wells, did host a dinner for selected VIPs at Mansion House after the Opening Ceremony. The fare, although tasty, did not compare with that served up 40 years earlier. Now dignitaries were offered a simple menu: cream of vegetable soup and roast Australian lamb with potatoes, asparagus and beans, followed by fruit tart or cheese and biscuits.

The competing nations also assisted with the venues themselves. Finland and Sweden, for example, donated large quantities of timber to replace rotting seats and floors. Switzerland sent over expensive specialist gymnastics equipment and German POWs were pressed into service to help build Olympic Way, the walk up to Wembley Stadium. This was opened on 6 July, less than a month before the start of the Olympic Games.

To maximise revenue at a difficult time, Wembley maintained its greyhound racing schedule until a fortnight before the Games, after which 800 tonnes of cinder were delivered to the stadium and an athletics track laid down seemingly overnight. It was a brief interlude: two weeks after the Games had finished it was business as usual for the greyhound fans. At the Empire Pool, meanwhile, a workforce had to climb all over the windows to scrape off the blackout paint used in the war, and a makeshift boxing ring was built over the swimming pool once the programme in the pool had been completed.

Small-scale sponsorship and advertising helped to defray a few of the costs. For a minimum of £250 commercial enterprises could buy the right to display the Olympic Rings on any of their advertising. Coca-Cola, Brylcreem, Guinness, Sloan's Liniment, Quaker

---

Best of British

Men's 4 x 100m Relay team

The British team were an eclectic quartet spearheaded by legendary Welsh rugby wing Ken Jones. Jones won 44 Wales caps in total, as well as a silver relay medal at the 1954 European Championships and a bronze in the 220 yard sprint at the Commonwealth Games in Vancouver that year. Joining Jones was rugby international Jack Gregory, who played for Bristol before switching to Huddersfield RL. Jack Archer was another good rugby player, who had been European 100m champion in 1946. The quartet was completed by the extravagantly gifted Alastair McCorquodale, who could run like the wind but was always a cricketer at heart. The quartet's silver medal behind the USA was not without drama. Although crossing the line behind the USA they were announced as the winners because a judge had called a 'faulty' baton exchange between Barney Ewell and Lorenzo Wright. Nobody in the Stadium, including the British team and management, could see anything wrong with the exchange and it was a subdued British quartet that accepted the gold medals, the home crowd making a point of cheering the USA team when their disqualification was announced. Three days later, after studying the film taken by the J. Arthur Rank cameramen, the decision was reversed. The Americans got their gold medals in the post two months later.

Best of British

Lord Burghley (athlete of earlier Games and organiser of this one)

David Burghley (1905–81), eir to the 5th Marquess of Exeter, was a notable British athlete who famously ran around the Great Court at Trinity College, Cambridge while the clock struck 12. Although he went out in the first round of the 110m Hurdles at the Paris 1924 Games, he had great success at the British AAA championships between 1926 and 1932. At the Amsterdam 1928 Games he won the 400m Hurdles in a competition record time of 53.4 seconds – the first non-American to win the event. Four years later in Los Angeles he was part of the British team that won silver in the 4 x 400m Relay. In the ravages of the Second World War Burghley achieved perhaps his greatest triumph: organising the London 1948 Games in just two short years. He also served as a member of the IOC for 48 years.

Oats, Ovaltine, Martell brandy, Gillette razors and Nescafé all took advantage of this and featured them prominently on billboards. Lloyds Bank, who had provided a mobile banking kiosk at the London 1908 Games, came on board as a sponsor in 1948; 62 years later, as Lloyds TSB, they became one of the first domestic commercial sponsors of the London 2012 Games. The watch manufacturers Omega, renowned for their precision timing, were also heavily involved; they retain their connections with the Games to this day. Billy Butlin donated a week's free accommodation and entertainment to the British squad in a holiday camp at Clacton before the Games, and the BBC were charged a fee of 1,000 Guineas (£1,050) for the television rights to the event. The London 1948 Games may have been run on a shoestring, but they hinted strongly at the great commercial potential of future Games.

Normal Service is Resumed

Thursday 29 July, the opening day of the 1948 Games, dawned clear and very hot. The temperature was eventually to rise to over 34°C, reportedly the hottest day in Britain since 1911. It was distinctly uncomfortable for VIPs in their finery, spectators roasting in the sun, marching bands in their tunics and parading competitors, but, despite starting 20 minutes late, the Opening Ceremony went off without any major mishap. The main casualties of the heat came from among the 7,000 pigeons due to be released as part of the ceremony, many of whom expired in their cages.

Pre-publicity in the newspapers for the London 1948 Olympic Games had been a little underwhelming. Some of it was sceptical and carping in tone. Sporting hearts and minds seemed to be concentrated on the fortunes of the all-conquering Australian cricket team who, under the captaincy of Sir Donald Bradman, were to complete an unbeaten tour of 34 matches that summer. Just two days before the Olympic Games opened, Australia

had famously scored 404 for three on the final day of the Fourth Test at Headingley in Yorkshire to clinch an historic win, with Bradman scoring an unbeaten 173. Over 158,000 fans watched the five days' play, still a record Test Match attendance in England. Cricket had deep roots of allegiance, though. Would the hard-pressed paying customer turn out in such numbers for the Olympic Games?

Foreign correspondents covering the Olympic Games back in London wrote articles commenting that it felt like a sideshow in comparison. Everything seemed a little low key and half-hearted, and there were complaints that there was virtually no advertising or posters in London promoting the event.

Such reservations proved ill founded, however. Come the day, with the eyes of the world on London and Britain, 85,000 paying spectators, many of them in difficult circumstances financially, flocked to Wembley. The huge stadium was rarely less than 90 per cent full for the duration of the Games, despite a disappointing deterioration in the weather. In total 670,000 spectators attended events at Wembley, and other venues also reported excellent attendances.

The organisers kept the Opening Ceremony simple and relatively short, which the 4,000 or so parading competitors from 59 nations must have appreciated. Even then most of them were kept waiting for nearly three hours behind the stadium, the well prepared having brought a picnic with them to pass the time. The Guards Band played and marched in their inimitable fashion and the parade of nations went off without an obvious hitch. Behind the scenes there had been a major panic, however, when the Union Jack flag for the British team went missing at the last minute.

A young Roger Bannister, helping out with the organisation, remembered he had a flag in his car. He sprinted off to the public car park to retrieve it, eventually found his car – and then realised he had left the key back at the stadium. The clock was ticking so, after explaining the situation to a

THE IMPORTANT THING IN
THE OLYMPIC GAMES IS NOT
WINNING BUT TAKING PART.
THE ESSENTIAL THING IN
LIFE IS NOT CONQUERING
BUT FIGHTING WELL.

BARON de COUBERTIN

watching policeman, he broke his car window with a brick, grabbed the flag and then ran full pelt to where the British team were gathering. A good man in a tight spot.

King George VI opened proceedings, and the surviving pigeons were released. Many promptly proceeded to do what pigeons do, to the amusement of spectators and the discomfort of those lined up underneath them. A 21-gun salute was followed by a rousing rendition of the Hallelujah Chorus, then British hurdler Donald Finlay stepped forward to swear the Olympic Oath on behalf of all the competitors. 'We swear that we will take part in the Olympic Games in loyal competition, respecting the regulations which govern them, and desirous of participating in them in the true spirit of sportsmanship, for the honour of our country and for the glory of sport.' Lord Burghley then addressed the King and all those gathered with a powerful endorsement of the Games' role in the post-war world: 'Your Majesty, the hour has struck … London represents a warm flame of hope for a better understanding in the world which has burned so low.' His achievement in bringing together a record 59 nations, represented by 4,104 athletes (3,714 men and 390 women) in 22 sports disciplines, was indeed no mean feat. Yet he was confident it would be worth all the work.

The Ceremony concluded with the massed bands accompanying the National Anthem, and then the shoestring Games were up and running. The occasion seemed to strike a chord with even sceptical observers. In the words of the much-admired James Cameron at the *Daily Express*, 'Even the tired men and cynics, wearied for years by false symbols and phoney goodwill talk, said: "This must mean something. Not much, not the Millennium, but something." You cannot usher 59 nations into an arena, make them mingle in a split minute schedule, give them a common salutation, without something profitable emerging, big or little as it may be. The cheer-leaders may be labouring after a vain thing, but yesterday's Opening Ceremony gave one that momentary excitement, that perennial glimpse of co-operation, that passing feeling that men might one day succeed where States and Governments always fail.'

> **'Your Majesty: The hour has struck. A visionary dream has today become a glorious reality. At the end of the worldwide struggle in 1945, many institutions and associations were found to have withered and only the strongest had survived. How, many wondered, had the great Olympic Movement prospered?'**
>
> Lord Burghley at the Opening Ceremony

Lighting the Flame

The London 1948 Olympic Games was one of the last occasions when the Olympic Torch was carried into the Olympic Stadium by someone other than a notable former competitor – and even in 1948 the choice of Torchbearer caused something of a stir. John Mark, who performed the role admirably, was a useful 400m and 800m runner; he had gained a Cambridge Athletics Blue and narrowly missed out on a Rugby Blue after dislocating his shoulder. But he was virtually unknown to the sporting public in 1948, and there were several seemingly more obvious candidates. Wing Commander Donald Finlay DFC, AFC, the man who took the Olympic Oath, would have been the choice of most. A dashing and distinguished RAF ace, he had won a bronze medal in the 110m Hurdles at Los Angeles 1932 and a silver in the same event at Berlin four years later, but he was eventually ruled out by the authorities because of his very obvious military connections. A new start was needed after the war, with no looking back. Finlay, now a sprightly 39, still competed in the 110m Hurdles the following day, but unfortunately crashed to the ground when he had his heat well won.

Two other highly distinguished athletes also ranked far above Mark in profile and public popularity. They were the former half mile and mile world record holder Sydney Wooderson, the popular solicitor's clerk, and Godfrey Brown, the Olympic gold medallist in the men's 4 x 400m Relay from the 1936 Games. Yet neither runner was a physically striking or imposing individual – both wore spectacles and cut curiously unathletic figures for such outstanding performers. The BOA Organising Committee, with Lord Burghley taking the lead on this matter, took a very deliberate decision to choose a young, good-looking, male athlete instead.

Public perception was now all-important. The Olympic Games had become a huge media event, and after a 12-year hiatus it was again attracting the eyes of the world. It was deemed vital to send out a vibrant positive message from a country still in the depths of rationing and post-war reconstruction – so Mark, now studying at St Mary's after graduating from Cambridge, received the surprise call. The height of his athletics achievements was probably fourth place in the AAA 440 yards race in 1947, but this was part of the point. The Organising Committee minutes, which do not record the background to the decision, note agreement on 24 June 1948 that an approach should be made to Mark, 'subject to him not being included in the British team'. A few days later Mark failed to advance beyond the heats of the 440 yards at the AAA Championships, and three weeks before the opening he accepted the invitation to be Britain's Torchbearer.

> '... it was the proudest moment of my life to be chosen to light the Olympic Flame, and I will never ever forget the day I carried the Torch around the Wembley track'
>
> John Mark, who lit the 1948 Flame

Everything was meticulously rehearsed. A contemporary, Dr Claude Harvard, recalled in Mark's obituary in the *British Medical Journal* that in the weeks leading up to the Games a white Rolls Royce, almost certainly belonging to Sir Arthur Elvin, used regularly to turn up at St Mary's and whisk Mark away for a couple of hours. Unknown to his fellow students, Mark was rehearsing for his big day, first at Motspur Park and then at Wembley itself. Another young athlete, Angus Scott, who was to run in the 400m Hurdles at the Helsinki 1952 Olympic Games, was installed as Mark's first reserve and also took part in the practices.

The sun shone brightly on 29 July and Mark made exactly the impact the organisers had planned. As Philip Noel-Baker, like Mark a former President of the Cambridge University Athletic Club, recalled, 'Tall and handsome like a young Greek God he stood for a moment in the sunshine, held the Torch aloft to salute the concourse, then ran in perfect rhythm around the track, saluted again and lit the Flame in the bowl where day and night it burned until the Games were done.'

One of the most enduring images of London 1948 is still John Mark carrying the Torch and lighting the Flame – a golden British youth on a sun-kissed afternoon. He may not have been very representative of Britain in 1948, but as an image for the future it had immense resonance. Harvard recalls the reaction of incredulous fellow students at St Mary's, who teased Mark for keeping the secret. 'When they saw him they used to light their cigarette lighters and run

> 'I wish happiness and the renewing of old and the making of new friendships, may they take from Britain happy memories that will be a source of joy to them throughout their lives'
>
> Prime Minister Clement Attlee's speech to welcome the nations

The scoreboard reads:

> THE IMPORTANT THING IN
> THE OLYMPIC GAMES IS NOT
> WINNING BUT TAKING PART.
> THE ESSENTIAL THING IN
> LIFE IS NOT CONQUERING
> BUT FIGHTING WELL.

John Mark, a medical student and former president of Cambridge University Athletic Club, carries the Olympic Torch into Wembley Stadium in the Opening Ceremony of the 1948 Games. His Torch contained extra magnesium to blaze brightly even in brilliant sunlight.

around him in a circle. When they said he looked like a Greek god it was right, he did.'

The reality behind the icon was a modest and retiring man, a million miles away from the Hollywood persona bestowed upon him. After qualifying at St Mary's, Mark happily settled down to lifelong GP duties in Liss in Hampshire. Rugby became his main sporting interest and he played locally until his late 30s, when he suffered one shoulder dislocation too many and decided it really was time to retire from sport. His legacy, a golden, stage-managed moment, lives on, a powerful

compensation for Britain's failure to win an Athletics gold medal at the 1948 Games.

Although Britain's medal haul was to prove disappointing, there were many compelling moments at the 1948 Games. The venues and facilities, despite the absence of new stadia, rose splendidly to the occasion: mighty Wembley Stadium, with a capacity of 80,000 even after the construction of a cinder track, housed the Athletics as well as the Football and Hockey finals, and the Equestrian Jumping. The nearby Empire Pool, with scope for 8,000 spectators, hosted the Aquatics events and

Boxing finals. Herne Hill Velodrome was used for the Track Cycling, the Harringay Arena for Basketball, Henley for the Rowing and Torquay, known as the English Riviera, for the yachting. The term 'yachting' is possibly unfamiliar these days having been changed to 'sailing' in 1996. The Cycling Road Race was held at Windsor Great Park, while the pool matches of the Football competition were distributed through a number of stadia in London and the south-east: Highbury, Selhurst Park, Craven Cottage, White Hart Lane, Lynn Road Stadium in Ilford, Griffin Park in Brentford, Green Pond Road in Walthamstow, Champion Hill in Dulwich and Fratton Park and Goldstone Ground from Portsmouth and Brighton respectively.

The 'flying housewife'

The dominating figure of the Olympic 1948 Games, and one of the most iconic sportswomen in history, was Fanny Blankers-Koen. A 30-year-old Dutch housewife and mother of two, her practical, no-nonsense approach to life and sport seemed to

capture the essence of the London Games. Certainly the British crowd took to her even though in three finals – 110m, 200m and 80m Hurdles – she beat British athletes into second place.

Blankers-Koen was the best female athlete in the world long before the 1948 Games, but the Second World War had denied her the biggest stage until now. She switched to Athletics from Swimming at the age of 16, competing as a teenager in the Berlin 1936 Games in both the High Jump and 4 x 100m Relay. However her specialist event, the 800m, was then considered too demanding for women and did not feature in the 1948 Games programme.

In 1938 Blankers-Koen had set a world record for the 100 yards, and even during the war years she managed to set a clutch of world records – in the 100m, Long Jump, High Jump, 100 yards and the 80m Hurdles. She had also married her coach, Jan Blankers, a former Olympic Triple Jumper who

Top left Mexican springboard diver Rosa Pardo at the Wembley Empire Pool, in training for the London 1948 Games. The venue was transformed for the Aquatics competition.

Top right Fanny Blankers-Koen, far right, surges to victory in the 80m Hurdles. The 'flying housewife' from the Netherlands became the superstar of London 1948 as she won four gold medals in Athletics – her other triumphs were in the 100m, 200m and 4 x 100m Relay.

'All I've done is run fast. I don't see why people should make much fuss about that'

Fanny Blankers-Koen

finished ninth at the Amsterdam 1928 Games, giving birth to her first child in 1941 and flouting convention by continuing her track career. At the end of the war, only six weeks after the birth of her second child, she took gold in the 80m Hurdles and 4 x 100m Relay at the European Championships. She fell badly during the qualifying rounds of the High Jump, however, thus failing to make it through to the final.

At one stage she intended to enter six events at the 1948 Games, but the schedule, although technically allowing it, was in reality too tight. Eventually she dropped the two jumps that also carried the threat of injury. Just ahead of the Games the British team manager, Jack Crump, famously predicted that Blankers-Koen 'was too old to make the grade' – not one of his better judgement calls.

Blankers-Koen opened her account in the 100m, comfortably beating Britain's Dorothy Manley in a relatively straightforward final. Then came possibly the most hyped clash of the Games in the 80m Hurdles. She ran against Britain's pin-up girl Maureen Gardner, a 19-year-old former ballet prodigy who was, as you might expect, a superb technician over the hurdles. Gardner got the best of starts, leaving Blankers-Koen three yards adrift after the worst start in her career, but the Dutchwoman found a burst of speed midway through the race. The two girls crossed the line together, inseparable to the naked eye. Blankers-Koen feared the worst when a Guards Band nearby struck up the British National Anthem, but that was only to announce the arrival of George VI and Queen Elizabeth in the stadium. Technology came to the rescue, the photo finish clearly demonstrating that she had won by about three inches.

The following day Blankers-Koen had to be persuaded by husband, Jan, to continue her quest for four gold medals. Overcoming the pull of home and children, she continued on her unbeatable way again, winning the 200m by a record distance and then (arriving late at the stadium after a morning of

West End shopping) anchoring the Dutch team to the 4x 100m Relay title. On her arrival in Amsterdam a few days later, Blankers-Koen was greeted by a horse-drawn carriage to parade her around the city. She arrived home to discover that her neighbours had clubbed together to present her with a bicycle.

Blankers-Koen's success after the 1948 Games meant that lecture tours of Australia and USA soon followed. She became a role model for many women, especially athletes seeking to juggle motherhood and elite sport, and went on to win another two gold medals and a silver at the 1950 European Championships. In 1999 the IOC voted her the female athlete of the century.

From 'Desert Rats' to Golden Rowers

Rowing was to prove the golden sport for Britain in 1948. 'Desert Rats' William 'Ran' Laurie and John 'Jack' Wilson won the host nation's first gold medal of the 1948 Games in the Coxless Pairs – a remarkable feat for a crew that first rowed in the outstanding Cambridge Blues boats in 1934, 1935 and 1936. Both took leave from their jobs in the Sudan Political Service and swiftly earned selection for the national team; although both were then considered 'old' at 35, they were immensely skilled, lifelong rowers with a passionate desire for an Olympic gold medal. It was a heady combination, honed by the training camp at which they received full rations and were able to train on the water every day.

The opening day of the regatta, Thursday 5 August, was cold and wet although a following wind made for fast times. The stretch of river at Henley could be tricky, narrow and prone to cross winds, so only three boats would be allowed to compete in the final. The organisers thus arranged a qualifying round and semi-final before the gold medal race-off, a situation that suited the more experienced and consistent crews.

Laurie, usually a man of iron constitution, had

been up all night with a stomach bug, but he somehow made it on to the water. Together with Wilson, they qualified for the semi-finals with the second fastest time behind the Austrians although they were hard-pressed by the Italians for much of their heat. The three semi-final races were on the Saturday, again wet and gusty, and the British pair rowed smoothly, well within themselves, to win their race – although they qualified for the final as only the third fastest crew.

The Kalt brothers from Switzerland, who had eliminated both Australia and Austria in their semi-final, started as clear favourites, while the Italians Bruno Boni and Felice Fanetti appeared to be getting stronger with every race. finals day on Monday dawned sunny and bright but with a vicious cross wind, the curse of oarsmen worldwide. Laurie and Wilson were secretly delighted, however, as such conditions suited their superior boat craft. The dynamic Swiss boat lead all the way to the 1,000m mark, but thereafter Britain caught up, drew level and forged ahead to take the gold medal. 'A thoroughly

satisfactory race, it was the best row we ever had,' was Laurie's verdict.

Richard Burnell, about to win a gold medal himself later in the afternoon, also doubled up as *The Times*' rowing correspondent. Inspired by the colour and understated emotion of the Victory Ceremony on the banks of the Thames, Burnell celebrated the occasion in vivid prose: 'Tired legs straightened as those lithe figures stood to attention in honour of their country. The poignant simplicity of the brief ceremony was enhanced by the colours which surrounded it. The brilliant green of the grass, the white flag staffs, the blazers of the men and frocks of the women, the white canvas of the grandstand and the scarlet, blue, green, yellow and white of the ensigns of the nations outlined against the green of the hillside made for an unforgettable picture.'

The Odd Couple

The second gold medal that Britain won on the Thames that sunny Monday afternoon came from the unlikely alliance of Richard Burnell and Bert Bushnell

Below Henley, the venue for the Royal Regatta, was used for the Rowing events at the London 1948 Games. It proved a good setting for the host nation: of the three gold medals that Britain won at the Games, two were for Rowing and one was for yachting.

Above British duo Dickie Burnell and Bert Bushnell (on left of picture) move towards the finish at Henley-on-Thames, soon to become Olympic champions in the Double Sculls. They beat Denmark and Uruguay.

in the Double Sculls. Although it would be difficult to imagine two athletes more disparate in character and physique, it all came together perfectly in the boat.

Richard Desborough Burnell – always known as 'Dickie' – was born to row. His father, Charles Burnell (Eton and Magdalen), rowed in four successive Oxford wins at the University Boat Race and was an outstanding member of Britain's gold medal winning Eight at the London 1908 Games. His son followed in his footsteps, both educationally and in sport, and they are to this day the only father and son combination in Rowing history to both win Olympic gold medals. Just to complete a notable hat-trick, Dickie Burnell's future father-in-law, Stanley Garton,

was also a gold medal winner with the British Eight at the Stockholm 1912 Olympic Games.

At 1.93m and just under 95kg, Burnell was a powerhouse in any boat – a force of nature with an oar in his hands. After serving in Northern Europe during the war he resumed his rowing career. Burnell even wrote the Rowing section of the official 1948 Olympic Games Report, including an account of his own gold medal with Bushnell. Typically this victory received merely an acknowledgment that he and Bushnell 'won safely' from the Danes, which hardly did justice to the occasion or their efforts.

His partner Bushnell had very different roots. He grew up by the river, learned to row at Maidenhead

Rowing Club and spent most of his time on the Thames in one form of boat or another. He was an expert waterman in an all-round sense who recognised all the moods of the river and how to handle a boat in any conditions. Bright enough to win a place at Henley Grammar School, Bushnell left school at 14 to join the Thornycroft marine engineering company in Southampton, where he worked on torpedo boats. He also participated in the Dunkirk evacuation of 1940, when every conceivable small boat on the south coast of Britain was pressed into service to get 300,000 British soldiers home.

Bushnell was slim, tough and wiry; bespectacled, he was in the habit of wearing a strange looking but highly practical skull cap that kept the wind and sun off his head during long hours on the river. The contrast with Burnell's Adonis-like figure couldn't be greater, yet – once Bushnell had cleverly re-rigged the boat to ensure they could both 'reach' together – the pairing worked well. Burnell was the engine while Bushnell was essentially the helmsman and technician. Each had a deep respect for the other's qualities, which didn't stop some lively banter; as Burnell accurately observed, 'Our respective weak points cancelled each other out and our strong points were complementary'. They were not an established pair, but were thrown together at a very late stage, starting from scratch less than six weeks before the Games.

Burnell never harboured any serious ambitions to compete in the Single Sculls, conscious that he didn't possess the requisite skills, but Bushnell most certainly did. He won the Diamond Sculls final at Henley in 1947 and reached the final again in 1948, when he lost to the outstanding Australian

All smiles, and no wonder, from rower Bert Bushnell after he became one of Britain's heroes at the London 1948 Games by winning gold in the Double Sculls event with Dickie Burnell.

Mervyn Wood. To his chagrin, Bushnell was overlooked by the British selectors in favour of Tony Rowe who had lost to Wood in an earlier round. In reality, however, it was a blessing in disguise. Nobody was going to defeat Wood in the 1948 Games; he was untouchable. In tandem with Burnell, however, Bushnell had a fighting chance of gaining a gold medal in the Double Sculls.

'We only had a month's preparation, so I went training barmy and we sculled three times a day,' recalled Bushnell. 'We had no training machines – we had to be on the water. Before Dickie arrived from London each morning I would run three miles up White Hill and three miles back. Food was rationed, but I was friendly with Grace Kelly's brother Jack who had food flown in from America. Merv Wood used to get food from Australia, so I would invite them both to supper and they would bring steaks with them for us to cook.'

Bushnell always claimed he was the captain on the bridge and that Dickie was the engine room, an ironic role reversal given their social backgrounds. However, the ultra-confident Burnell did make one crucial tactical call on behalf of the pair. He took a look at the draw and insisted that they should deliberately lose their first round race to France; this meant they would have to qualify via the repêchage system, but would

'You talk about magnificence. There wasn't any. After the racing [at Henley] the oarsmen had a dinner, threw bread rolls at each other and then went home'

Bert Bushnell, who, with Dickie Burnell. won the Rowing Double Sculls gold for Britain

enable them to avoid the powerful Denmark in the semi-finals (critical, as only the winners of each semi-final would progress to the final). Burnell, with his wide, up-to-date knowledge of the sport, rightly considered Denmark their strongest rivals. He wanted to hit them with everything they had just the once, when it really counted.

'Dickie decided we should lose the first heat so as not to meet the Danes – Ebbe Parsner and Aage Larsen – in the semi-final,' recalled Bushnell. 'I wouldn't have had the nerve to do that. We could have won, but we didn't, and so we came into the semis through the repêchage, avoiding the Danes.' Burnell's ploy succeeded. On the day of the final, Britain completed a fine day on the river, which also included a silver medal for the men's Eight, when the duo came home by two lengths.

One Swallow Makes a Summer

A third and final gold medal for Britain at the 1948 Games was gained in the Yachting regatta down at Torquay. Here Stewart Morris and David Bond emerged as winners of an ultra-competitive Swallow fleet – a truly nail-biting affair. Not only did they have to recover from a disastrous start in the final race, which left them in last position, although they did recover to eventually come home fourth, but also they had to contest a disqualification, with an Italian judge claiming that their poor start had also been illegal.

Morris, a hugely respected figure within the sport, was having none of that. He immediately called on his fellow competitors and rivals to give evidence to the jury that nothing against the regulations had occurred. After half an hour's deliberations the disqualification was overturned, and Morris and Bond could celebrate their gold medal.

It was a deeply satisfying moment for Morris, who had been at the forefront of dinghy sailing for nearly two decades. He had regularly defeated Peter Scott in previous years, but missed out on selection

for the Berlin 1936 Olympic Games. Over a decade later he was still sailing as well as ever and was eventually to win the prestigious International 14 Prince of Wales Cup, the Holy Grail of the sport at the time, on no less than 12 occasions.

Torquay was the one place where the 'Austerity Olympics' let its hair down a little. As well as being a fine sailing venue, ideal for the smaller fleets competing in the Olympic Games of the day, the local town council was also determined to re-establish Torquay, along with neighbours Brixham and Paignton, as premier holiday destinations. Together they pushed the boat out, so to speak. Local produce was more easily obtainable than in London, and officials ensured there were banquets and entertainment for the competitors and visitors most nights. This was especially so during a three-day break in the middle of the regatta, during which the entire bay seemed en fête.

As a spectator event it proved popular, despite some unseasonal weather at times. The spectacle was impressive, with British battleships such as George V anchored just outside the bay along with the aircraft carrier HMS Victorious. The French sent the destroyer Deasiz along and Prince Olaf of Norway attended for the duration in the Royal yacht Norge. Closer inshore HMS Anson and HMS Tremadoc Bay provided administrative and communication bases for the regatta.

There was even an Olympic Torch Relay, effectively paid for by Torbay Council. The BOA had originally baulked at the extra cost of sending the Relay over such a distance over 320km separated Torquay and Wembley but Torquay Council footed the £115 bill for 100 extra Torches and organised the Relay. It took just over 26 hours and enthusiastic locals gave it a rousing welcome. At 3am, when the Torch went through the village of Chard, it was reported that a crowd of 3,000 witnessed the occasion – rather demolishing the suggestion of some commentators that the Olympic Games were

Best of British
Stewart Morris and David Bond

An interesting character, Stewart Morris was awarded an OBE for his part in the Normandy landings when he served as a Commander in the Royal Naval Volunteer Reserve. He is also credited with devising the standard defence system for British aircraft carriers during the war. Morris was 39 when he entered the London 1948 Games, bringing his vast experience as helmsman to the competition. Some 13 years younger than Morris, David Bond acted as crew on their Swallow class keelboat, Swift. Bond had served as an aircraftsman in the RAF during the war, after which he worked for the British Aircraft Corporation. He later returned to his native Cornwall and became a yacht builder.

Above Yachts round the buoy on the final day of the Swallow class yachting event at Torbay at the London 1948 Games. From left to right, USA's *Margaret*, Sweden's *Change*, Holland's *St Margrite*, Britain's *Swift*, Norway's Nora and Brazil's *Andorinha*.

Left The Finnish crew who came sixth in the Dragon class in their yacht *Vinha* (left to right): Niilo Orama, Rainer Packalen and Aatos Hirvisalo. The gold medal was won by Norway.

Guttmann and the Early Paralympic/Stoke Mandeville Games

Born in 1899 into an Orthodox Jewish family in the small town of Tost in Silesia, Germany, Ludwig Guttmann worked in a hospital in Konigshutte when, in 1917, he encountered soldiers returning from the Western Front with serious disabilities. He completed his medical degree at the University of Freiburg and later became director of the Jewish hospital in Breslau. Life in Nazi Germany became increasingly impossible and, with the help of influential patients, Guttmann moved to Oxford in 1939. Here, his exceptional abilities were quickly recognised with an appointment at the groundbreaking Nuffield Department of Neurosurgery. In 1944 he surprised his academic colleagues by accepting an offer from the wartime government to found the National Spinal Injuries Centre at Stoke Mandeville Hospital in Buckinghamshire. Guttmann probably owed his appointment to Brigadier Heroge Riddoch, the leading neurologist at the London Hospital and a former field doctor during the First World War, who had been impressed by a number of Guttmann's papers at the Nuffield. If so, Riddoch chose well.

Opposite page

A Dutch Archery team practising from their wheelchairs before they competed in the 2nd International Stoke Mandeville Games in 1953. Five years earlier the first Stoke Mandeville Games for the Paralysed took place involving Second World War veterans with spinal cord injuries.

something of a non-event to people outside the London area who could not afford to attend and were unable to catch the BBC's television coverage.

The opening day of competition on Tuesday 3 August certainly impressed *The Times*' reporter, who responded in lyrical style: 'One had an area of wonderful beauty whose waters, if not wine dark, were foam flecked and sunlit and sparkling with all shades of blue and green. On this shining expanse were five clusters of white sail, each the centre of a struggle of inexpressible intensity.'

The Stoke Mandeville Games

Britain has made a large and lasting contribution over the centuries to many sports, Olympic and non-Olympic. Yet perhaps the nation's greatest achievement is the 'invention' and constant championing of sport for athletes with a disability. This concept, fine-tuned into what we now call the Paralympic Games, has become in its own right the second biggest multi-sports gathering in the world (behind only the Olympic Games themselves). All this arose from a specialist hospital in Stoke Mandeville near Aylesbury, Buckinghamshire, and the pioneering work that Sir Ludwig Guttmann and his staff did there over 60 years ago. In tribute to them one of London 2012's two mascots is called Mandeville. The other mascot is named Wenlock after Much Wenlock, the Shropshire village where the Wenlock Olympian Games were the inspiration for the modern Olympic Games.

Ludwig Guttmann was an exceptional and driven individual, not always easy to work with for those not on the same wavelength. He emigrated to Britain from Breslau in Germany in 1939, and in 1944 he founded the experimental National Spinal Injuries Centre at Stoke Mandeville Hospital. This was an increasingly important area of medicine and rehabilitation – many thousands of servicemen had returned from the Seconds World War with disabling and life-changing injuries. The position offered

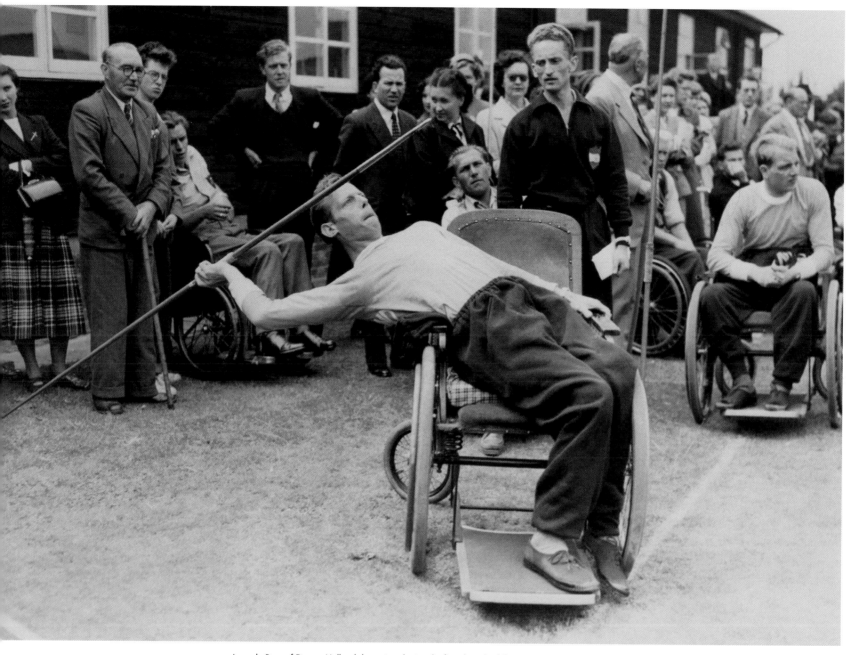

Joep de Beer of Doorn, Holland, leans into the javelin from his wheelchair on 2 August 1954 during the 3rd International Stoke Mandeville Games. Winners were awarded trophies in this forerunner of the Paralympic Games.

Guttmann an opportunity to put into practice his belief that sport, as a method of therapy, could prove invaluable in treating those with serious and traumatic spinal injuries. It helped not only to rebuild a patient's upper body strength but also, just as importantly, to re-create their self-confidence and morale.

Initially the sports were straightforward. Darts, skittles, snooker and punch ball were all featured, but Guttmann always sought to expand the range. Team games were an avenue he badly wanted to pursue, and gradually he and his staff worked out how to stage a game of wheelchair netball, eventually refined into wheelchair basketball. During this start-up period much of the credit for devising the actual sports and making them work in practice must go to the head of the Physiotherapy Department, Charlie Atkinson. He joined Stoke Mandeville straight from the army and proved to be a tower of strength.

Such activity at Stoke Mandeville went on largely unnoticed until Guttmann, with a fine sense of timing, chose Wednesday 28 July – the day before the grand Opening Ceremony of the London 1948 Olympic Games, 56km away at Wembley – to stage his first Stoke Mandeville Games for the Paralysed. He invited press and a few local dignitaries to a modest affair featuring a friendly archery competition between 16 competitors (14 former servicemen and two former servicewomen). They were divided into two teams, representing the Stoke Mandeville Hospital and the Garter Home for Injured War Veterans in Richmond, south-west London. The occasion was also used to celebrate the official handing over of a specially adapted bus for athletes with a disability, which had been donated by the British Legion and London Transport. The atmosphere may have been that of a small village fete, but the significance of the occasion for the future was immense.

The selection of archery as the highlighted sport on the first afternoon was no coincidence. Guttmann had long considered it the showpiece sport for what he was trying to achieve, firstly for its physical benefits (the development of arms, shoulders and core muscle strength along with an enhanced sense of balance) and secondly for the potential it offered his disabled athletes to succeed. The latter quickly became apparent as some of the star disabled pupils started not only to match the performance of non-disabled guests, but also to beat them on a regular basis. This was exactly what Guttmann desired. Non-disabled archers started travelling to Stoke Mandeville for regular competitions – and Stoke

Mandeville competitors happily piled into their new coach to travel hundreds of miles for return fixtures. As a way of reintegrating patients into 'normal' society, the scheme could scarcely be improved. Atkinson and his staff also invented the entirely new game of Dartchery, in which archers shot at a massive dartboard and scored in exactly the same way as in darts.

From small acorns do mighty oak trees grow. A year later, in July 1949, six spinal units from around the country, this time with 37 competitors, gathered for the day. A team netball competition was added to the archery, with the teams on this occasion being Stoke Mandeville, a Stoke Mandeville Old Boys' team of former patients (now living back at home), Chaseley, Lyme Green, the Star and Garter Home and the Polish Hospital in Penley. Already Guttmann was courting those who counted. Among the guests were the Minister of Pensions, the Permanent Secretary for Pensions and the Director of HM Medical Services.

And on it went. In 1950 there were 10 teams and an estimated 60 competitors – records for these early days are incomplete. A javelin event was added to the existing sports, and Dick Thompson from Hexham proved to be the star turn with a best throw of 46ft 1in. Then his personal best, he improved it to 56ft 4in the following year, while by the end of his career he had pushed it out to 67ft 10in. His achievement was underlined when Guttmann invited non-disabled javelin throwers of repute to try their hand at throwing from a wheelchair. More often than not Thompson was the winner.

Guttmann's former patients played a key role in developing the Stoke Mandeville Games at this stage. As their recoveries progressed they were transferred to other units and they took their sports skills with them, so spreading the word. Staff from Stoke Mandeville also learned from the work of Guttmann and Atkinson, and then took their knowledge across the world. Guttmann himself also travelled extensively, lecturing on the physical and psychological benefits of competitive sport. Society was changing, as the widespread shock at war injuries was replaced by new attitudes to all forms of disability. This combined with a new awareness of the potential of athletes with disabilities to achieve expertise and fitness in a range of sports.

Guttmann's idea of disability sports for those suffering from paraplegia was innovative, but the concept of competitive gatherings for those with less severe disabilities was well established. The Disabled Drivers motor club had been founded back in 1922, the British Society of One-Armed Golfers in 1922 and the Silent Games for Deaf Athletes was first held in Paris in 1924, shortly after the Olympic Games. Guttmann's genius was to apply an existing idea to seriously disabled individuals. Development of a new range of sulpha drugs had also significantly improved the prospects of those with traumatic spinal injuries,

enabling them to start to look beyond mere survival.

By 1952, just four years after the London 1948 Olympic Games and eight years after Guttmann's appointment as head of the new unit, Stoke Mandeville had become the world leader in the treatment of spinal injuries. It was also beginning to open its doors to non-service personnel. Many specialists from around the world came to visit or were posted on short secondments in order to observe, learn and then take the expertise back to their own countries. One such was Colonel J.S. Keyser, Medical Director of the Doorn Centre in the Netherlands, and in 1952 he decided to bring a small team of four paralysed Dutch war veterans to the 1952 Stoke Mandeville Games, accompanied by a physiotherapist and a nursing sister. The Stoke Mandeville Games were going international; ever more popular, they had to allocate a full weekend to the competitions as gradually snooker, table tennis,

> **'We're so busy in this bloody place we haven't got time to be ill'**
>
> A patient at Stoke Mandeville describes life under Guttmann's regime

A Wheelchair Basketball match between the USA and the Netherlands at the 4th International Stoke Mandeville Games in 1955. The American team is seen here scoring in front of a large number of spectators.

A kneeling boy aims to shoot a lit cigarette from the mouth of a man at the 2nd International Stoke Mandeville Games, held at the grounds of the National Spinal Injuries Centre in 1953.

swimming and fencing were added to the schedule. These were still pioneering days, with transport a major hurdle for anybody with a serious spinal injury, but the Stoke Mandeville bus proved its worth as it rattled down to Tilbury Docks in Essex to pick up the Dutch party. A year later a benefactor donated an upgraded version with a hydraulic lift at the rear. It was immediately passed into service to ferry a party of Canadian competitors from Heathrow Airport to the Stoke Mandeville Games.

The trips became reciprocal, and around this time Stoke Mandeville sent a team to contest a number of sports against their French equivalents in France. Atkinson, quoted in Joan Scutton's book on Stoke Mandeville, takes up the story. His account provides a perfect insight as to why and how the Paralympic Games were to become so universally popular and successful:

'It was in the De Coubertin Stadium in Paris and a French paraplegic team and ours were to play a match, following a display and competition of top class able-bodied basketball players. To have to follow such a brilliant display filled us with misgivings … it was with mixed feelings that the French referee and I filed into the arena to start the game. There was a deathly hush during the first few minutes and then a tremendous roar filled the stadium as the crowd cheered their French team, with the French

'If I ever did one good thing in my medical career it was to introduce sport into the rehabilitation of disabled people'

Dr Ludwig Guttmann, founder of the Paralympic Games

THE IMPORTANT THING IN THE OLYMPIC GAMES IS NOT WINNING BUT TAKING PART. THE ESSENTIAL THING IN LIFE IS NOT CONQUERING BUT FIGHTING WELL

BRITISH OLYMPIC ASSOCIATION
OFFICIAL REPORT
OF THE LONDON
OLYMPIC
GAMES 1948
OOO
PUBLISHED BY WORLD SPORTS
THE OFFICIAL MAGAZINE OF THE BRITISH OLYMPIC ASSOCIATION
PRICE FIVE SHILLINGS

AUGUST
7
Sat., August 7, 1948
at 3 pm
ATHLETICS

SOUTH GRAND
STAND 10s. 6d
Entrance 42
ROW   SEAT
26   9

EMPIRE STADIUM WEMBLEY
XIVTH OLYMPIAD
LONDON
1948
This Session will be preceded at 2.10 pm
by a Gymnastic Display by The Svenska
Gymnastikforbundet
(TO BE RETAINED)

WM. SKELTON & SON, LTD., LONDON, W.8, ENGLAND

referee and me being called all the usual names when we decided a foul against the other team. It was amazing. The crowd had forgotten that these were people in wheelchairs and were just watching two teams of basketball players.'

London Calling

The 1948 Games might have been termed the Austerity Olympics, but the press and media operation was on a massive scale. After six years of conflict there was a real thirst for updated and, if possible, live information – delivering the story was key to the Games' success. It was also to be part of its legacy; after London 1948 the media landscape of the Olympic Games had totally changed.

The most obvious innovation at the 1948 Games was the live television coverage from the BBC. It was admittedly limited in terms of range, with reception being confined mainly to viewers in London and the south-east, although curiously a number of people wrote in to report they were receiving perfect pictures in Jersey. Estimates vary, but it is generally conceded that no more than 80,000 households in the London area had television sets at the time of the Games – still an increase of 500 per cent from just two years earlier.

Initially the BBC had scheduled 50 hours of coverage but, reacting to a surge in public interest and the momentum of the event itself, it started cutting into other programmes or cancelling them altogether. Eventually it broadcast a grand total of 69 hours and 29 minutes of live action, in addition to their regular news bulletin updates. Technically this was testing in the extreme. Live outside broadcasts were limited not

> 'We were so thrilled to be saying "the war is over, look what we're doing, we're picking up and starting all over again"'
>
> USA Basketball team captain Robert Jackson Robinson

limited to Wembley; they came from the Yachting in Torquay, the Cycling at Herne Hill, the Shooting at Bisley and various Football grounds in the south-east. Twelve mobile recording cars were available, but journalists were expected to travel to the events by public transport.

Sir Arthur Elvin, well aware of the necessity to look after and nurture the media, donated the Palace of Art to the BBC. They duly based their television and radio operations there for the Games, with 30 recording studios and 11 edit suites. An information room was also provided for journalists containing 'the official Olympic Games teleprinter service'. At Wembley alone the BBC installed 15 commentary boxes and 16 open commentary positions, with a further 15 commentary positions at the Empire Pool. All were to be fully employed in covering an event without precedent in television history; as the *Radio Times* of 23 July 1948 noted, 'the broadcasting and televising of the London Olympiad will be the biggest operation of its kind that the BBC has ever undertaken'. The Senior Superintendent Engineer, a Mr Hotine, emphasised the technical challenge in the BBC *Yearbook* for 1949; covering the Games, he acknowledged, had presented 'a planning and operational problem which had never been encountered before in the history of any broadcasting organisation in the world.'

Wynford Vaughan-Thomas was the star turn in the BBC's radio team, at a time when the 'wireless' was firmly established as the main medium of mass communication. Radio coverage virtually took care of

Previous page

Top A BBC camera films the proceedings at Wembley Stadium as King George VI takes the march past of just over 4,000 athletes representing 59 countries, at the Opening Ceremony of the London 1948 Games.

Bottom left The official report of the London 1948 Games, produced by the British Olympic Association and featuring the Olympic Torch on the cover.

Bottom right An admission ticket for the Athletics events, held at Wembley Stadium on 7 August 1948. The tickets had pictograms on them for each Olympic sport – the first time pictograms were used at the Games.

Opposite page

On 21 August 1948, a week after the Games ended, the *Illustrated London News* featured the Closing Ceremony of the Olympic Games at Wembley Stadium. Just three years after the end of the Second World War, amid crippling bomb damage and rationing, London had staged one of the most successful Games to date.

BBC Commentators at the 1948 Games

After a rigorous selection process, the Radio Times of 23 July 1948 listed the television commentators of the London Games as follows:

Opening and Closing Ceremonies: Richard Dimbleby and Michael Henderson

Athletics: Roy Moor, Pat Lansberg, and Jack Crump

Swimming: Fred Milton, John Webb

Boxing: Peter Wilson and Dudley Lister

Football: James Jewell

Hockey: Michael Henderson

Equestrian: Col. Allenby and Peter Dimmock

itself, a continuation of the excellent service to the 11 million British households possessing radio sets. The popularity of the BBC World Service meant that the radio operation was virtually around the clock.

The dawn of live sports coverage on television can be dated precisely to the 1948 Games. BBC executives were initially dubious, believing that it could never replace 'being there' – but it nevertheless changed the way sport was covered forever. The BBC TV commentary team was an eclectic mix as you could ever envisage, but it hadn't just been thrown together, despite occasional appearances to the contrary. The team had actually been carefully constructed, reflecting a very real appreciation that television was 'different'.

Ian Orr-Ewing, Outside Broadcast Manager for the BBC at the 1948 Games, wrote at some length about this in the *Radio Times* just before the Opening Ceremony on Thursday 29 July. In many ways he was trying to prepare a new audience for what they were about to receive, and there is just a hint of managing expectations in his address. 'During the last year, large numbers of commentators have been tested in an endeavour to select the best possible team for our Olympic Games programmes,' he explained. 'Regular viewers will understand that television commentary demands a technique different from that which has been established for sound broadcasting; a television commentator is not merely describing what he can see but is explaining the picture in the light of his expert knowledge.' Aspiring commentators, he assured readers, had been extensively tested 'to plumb the depths of the aspirant's knowledge; a silent film has been used to test his voice, quickness of reaction, sense of drama and general aptitude for television commentary.'

In the end, Orr-Ewing had come up with an interesting bunch. Peter Wilson was a hardnosed Fleet Street sports writer who majored in Boxing and wasn't averse to criticising both the Olympic Games and its organisers. In his memoirs he described the 1948

Games as his least favourite of the eight he covered because of the lack of fine new stadia to serve the British public over the next two or three decades.

Richard Dimbleby, already a broadcasting heavyweight, came to the fore during the Opening and Closing Ceremonies. Unflappable and authoritative, he set the bar very high indeed for those following in his footsteps over the years. Michael Henderson, a silky smooth former Oxford Rugby Blue who served with the Desert Rats in the war, could turn his hand to anything, while Bill Allenby, nephew of Field Marshall Viscount Allenby, looked after anything Equestrian. Harry Littlewood was an all-rounder, but focused on Gymnastics, Swimming and Athletics, and Dudley Lister was another tried and tested Boxing commentator. Boxing had always had a huge radio following, and the BBC assumed television would be no different. Last but not least was Peter Dimmock, a flying instructor in the war who had joined the BBC in 1946, primarily as a outside broadcasts producer. He was to emerge as the organisation's most innovative presenter/ producer in the decades that followed.

As for the written press, some 2,000 journalists from around the world were accredited. They worked from Wembley Civic Hall, where Lord Rothermere, son of the generous benefactor from 1908, contributed the £7,000 needed to convert the building. He set up a canteen and bar, with special permission to serve drinks until 11.30pm, and installed a telephone exchange. For domestic calls there were banks of phones, but only four international lines could be installed, with overseas correspondents often needing to book calls days in advance. Telegrams were still the main form of communication and reporting, and teams of Boy Scouts were on hand all day to run journalists' copy to the telegram centre. The Scout Movement received £50 for their efforts over the fortnight. Some enterprising Scouts were also tipped individually to keep a correspondent's place in the phone queue.

THE ILLUSTRATED LONDON NEWS

The World Copyright of all the Editorial Matter, both Illustrations and Letterpress, is Strictly Reserved in Great Britain, the British Dominions and Colonies, Europe, and the United States of America.

SATURDAY, AUGUST 21, 1948.

THE CLOSE, AT WEMBLEY STADIUM, OF THE 14TH, AND MOST SUCCESSFUL, MODERN OLYMPIAD; MR. EDSTRÖM HAS HANDED THE OLYMPIC FLAG TO THE LORD MAYOR OF LONDON AND THE FANFARE IS ABOUT TO SOUND.

The 14th Modern Olympiad closed on August 14. The white Tribune of Honour was placed before the Royal Box (occupied by the Duke of Edinburgh, the Duchess of Kent, Princess Juliana of the Netherlands and Prince Bernhard) and the flags of the fifty-eight competing nations arranged behind it. Mr. J. Sigfrid Edström, President of the International Olympic Committee, speaking from the Tribune, referred to the ties of brotherhood and friendship formed between the 6000 athletes who had fought nobly and with honour. After announcing the end of the Games, he handed to the Lord Mayor of London, Sir Frederick Wells, for safe keeping until it goes to Helsinki in 1952, the Olympic flag of embroidered satin. A fanfare of trumpets and a salute of guns sounded, and the choir (centre background, behind the massed bands of the Guards) sang the Olympic hymn while the flag in the arena was lowered and the flame extinguished before the march out began. The Games not only set up a record for attendance and receipts (estimated at £500,000), but have been remarkable for the excellence of the organisation and absence of incidents.

Italy's Mario Ghella leads Britain's Reg Harris in the first heat of the Cycling Sprint on 9 August 1948. Ghella won and progressed to take gold with Harris taking silver in both this event and the Tandem with Alan Bannister.

Photographic rights were sold to the Olympic Photo Association, composed of all the leading agencies, but only eight photographers were allowed into Wembley Stadium at any one time. Part of the agreement for the agencies was also that all their pictures should be available as prints to the public to buy the next day. A roaring trade was done at the Palace of Engineering where every morning each new 'crop' was displayed. When the dust finally settled R.E. Church of the Olympic Press Committee reported with pride that, 'more space was given to the Games than any other single event since the end of the war' – a remarkable achievement that testified to the enduring British enthusiasm for the Olympic Games.

Fond Farewells

On the evening of the Closing Ceremony the BOA threw its first and only party for athletes and competitors at the Hurlingham Club in south-west London, a splendid venue in which to relax after all the work. With everybody accommodated in various locations around Greater London and transport around the city not the easiest, there had been less opportunity to socialise than at some previous Games and many later ones. Yet circumstances dictated that the 1948 Games would be very different from the outset, and all involved seemed to accept that.

There was much for the Pimms-sipping competitors to discuss. The general verdict was that Britain had delivered in the most extraordinary fashion against huge odds; the nation's reputation for being brilliant at improvising seemed never more deserved. This process continued right to the end; equipment was sold off to the highest bidders as the organisers continued the process of making the Games pay for themselves.

At Torquay the specially constructed Firefly dinghies were sold at £135 each, while down at Harringay basketballs went at 30 shillings apiece and surplus wood donated by Sweden and Finland was sold off. A £280 cheque from the Argentinian delegation bounced, but their expenses were settled by the BOA. A more serious overspend of £9,000 by Torquay, which had thrown itself whole-heartedly into the spirit of the Games, included a number of unavoidable costs as the only major venue outside of London. It too was written off by the BOA. Eventually, a profit of £29,420 was declared which, after tax, was handed over to the IOC – grateful not for the first time for Britain's valiant efforts.

In terms of medals won, three golds possibly appeared a disappointing return for Britain when compared with countries that had suffered similarly in the war. A total haul of 23 medals would have looked much healthier if some of the 14 silvers – notably Reg Harris in Track Cycling, Maureen Gardner in the 80m Hurdles and boxers John Wright and Donald Scott – had been converted into gold. Nonetheless it was a decent effort by the hosts, and on a par with Britain's showing in the Games immediately preceding the Second World War. Internationally, the extraordinary Blankers-Koen was the story, although there was also considerable interest in Hungarian marksman and Army officer Károly Takács. He had lost his right hand when a grenade accidentally went off in 1938, but he switched to using his left and won the gold medal in the 25m Rapid Fire Pistol event – an early example of someone we would now consider to be a Paralympian competing on equal terms.

Left The gold medal winner of the Decathlon, American Bob Mathias, stands on the podium during the victory ceremony with teammate Floyd Simmons, who took bronze, and silver medallist Ignace Heinrich of France.

'I'll start shaving, I guess'

Bob Mathias, 17, of the USA, after becoming the youngest ever Olympic track and field gold medallist

The most individual medals were won by Veikko Huhtanen of Finland, who took three golds, a silver and a bronze in the men's Gymnastics. Youth also had its place in the sun when American Bob Mathias, aged just 17, took the Decathlon gold in sensational style – when asked how he might celebrate his momentous victory, he mentioned that he might start shaving. In the Football tournament the British team was managed by Matt (later Sir Matt) Busby. Even his influence could not prevent a 3-5 defeat against Denmark in the bronze medal match, however, while Sweden took the gold with a 3-1 victory over Yugoslavia in the Wembley final. The Swedish front line of Gunnar

Best of British

Reg Harris

Three months before the London 1948 Games, Reg Harris was favourite to win three gold medals in the Cycling – the Sprint, the Tandem and the 1000m Time Trial or 'Kilo'. But then fate took a hand. Racing on the road he crashed heavily and fractured two vertebrae. Then a month or so before the Olympic Games he fractured his elbow and had to complete his training with his arm in plaster – not that this particularly bothered Harris, who was a tank driver in North Africa during the war before he was invalided home after escaping his burning vehicle. Then came a third blow. The schedule for the Cycling was announced and it did not allow him to compete in the Kilo, so he withdrew from contention and Tommy Godwin was selected (Godwin was ultimately to win the bronze medal). So Harris concentrated on the two pure sprint events at the open-air Herne Hill Velodrome. In the men's individual Sprint, he was outfoxed by Mario Ghella, the Italian taking the series 2-0 to win gold. A couple of days later, Harris teamed up with Alan Bannister in the men's Tandem and again came off second best to an Italian team, Renato Perona and Ferdinando Teruzzi winning 2-1.

Previous Olympic Games In London

Above Competitors in the men's 3000m Steeplechase battle for victory in Wembley Stadium, August 1948. In the lead is Roger Chesneau of France, but Tore Sjostrand of Sweden eventually won the gold medal.

Above right Guardsmen parade round the perimeter of the track inside Wembley Stadium during the Opening Ceremony of the 1948 Olympic Games.

Below The dramatic final of the 100m, 31 July 1948. Harrison Dillard (left) of the USA took gold and fellow-American Barney Ewell (right) silver. Fourth place went to Alasdair McCorquodale (centre) of Great Britain.

Right The oldest-ever winner of a track and field medal, 48-year-old Tebbs Lloyd-Johnson, took bronze for Great Britain in the 50km Road Walk, 31 July 1948.

Above left American Harry Porter clears the bar in the High Jump at the 1908 Olympic Games. He also set an Olympic record height of 1.905 metres.

Above right Women archers take aim in the National Round (60 yards) at the 1908 London Olympic Games. The gold medal was won for Great Britain by Sybil 'Queenie' Newall.

Below left One of only two men to win three Olympic Boxing titles, Hungarian Laszlo Papp sizes up the opposition at London in 1948. He won a gold medal in the Middle Weight class in 1948 and in the Light Middle Weight class in 1952 and 1956.

Below right Marathon runners in the 1908 Olympic Games follow the route between Windsor Castle and the White City Stadium. The race became famous for the collapse and subsequent disqualification of Italian runner Dorando Pietri.

Right A view of the Closing Ceremony of the London 1948 Games, which took place on 14 August at Wembley Stadium.

Opposite page A souvenir edition of the *Illustrated London News* includes a montage of some of the record-breaking athletes of the London 1948 Games who helped to bring the Olympic Games into a new age after the Second World War.

'The Games cannot enforce the peace to which all humanity aspires but they give the opportunity to the youth of the world to find out that all men on earth are brothers. In the troubled times in which we live the Games of 1948 were a bold adventure. They have succeeded beyond all hopes; they stand out as something virile, clean and noble'

IOC President Mr Sigfrid Edström at the Closing Ceremony

Medal table from the 1948 Olympic Games

Country	Gold	Silver	Bronze	Total
USA	38	27	19	84
Sweden	16	11	16	43
France	10	6	13	29
Hungary	10	5	11	26
Italy	8	11	8	27
Finland	6	7	5	18
Czechoslovakia	6	2	3	11
Great Britain (12th position)	3	14	6	23

Gren, Gunnar Nordahl and Nils Liedholm proved unstoppable; they later signed en masse for AC Milan, where they were nicknamed Gre–No–Li.

A dramatic finish of the Marathon had aroused echoes of the London 1908 Games. Once again the first man to enter the stadium, on this occasion Etienne Gailly of Belgium, became exhausted and was nearly unable to carry on running. While he was struggling Argentinian athlete Delfo Cabrera and Thomas Richards of Britain passed him, with Cabrera winning the gold and Richards taking the silver. Gailly managed to recover enough to cross the line in third place to take bronze.

Within a few days of the Olympic Games ending, attention focused on the manager of the Czechoslovakian gymnastics team. Marie Provaznikova, at the age of 57, sought political refuge in England before emigrating to the USA. Another competitor subsequently to make the headlines away from actual competition was USA weightlifter Toshiyuki 'Harold' Sakata from Hawaii, who took a silver medal in the Light Heavyweight division. He was later to achieve international fame and recognition as the fearsome 'Oddjob' in the James Bond film *Goldfinger*.

Earlier on the final day, at the Closing Ceremony itself, the IOC President Sigfrid Edström observed that the Games, 'give the opportunity to the youth of the world to find out that all men on earth are brothers. In the troubled times in which we live the Games of 1948 were a bold adventure. They have succeeded beyond all hopes; they stand out as something virile, clean and noble. At the stadium the flag that inks the continents has been lowered, the Flame is out. But the Olympic spirit lingers and it leaves us a vision and a hope.'

The *Daily Telegraph* gave a similar verdict the following day. It was a balanced assessment, regretting the lack of success in Athletics even as it celebrated 'those Olympic trophies we won last week on the river and on the seas'. In praising national resourcefulness in the face of 'obvious material difficulties', however, the article acknowledged that Britain's achievement was deeper and longer lasting than a simple medal haul. The paper's final declaration that 'the experience of reviving the Games within three years of a world convulsion, and of making London the host city, has fulfilled the hopes of those who greatly dared' offered a fitting and powerful epitaph to an extraordinary Games.

SOME BROKEN RECORDS.

M. THOMPSON (U.S.A.)
ting the Shot—56 ft.
2 ins.

THY TYLER (Great
in) New record for
Jump—5 ft. 6⅛ ins.

CONSOLINO (Italy)
wing the Discus

MAUREEN GARDNER (Great Britain) created joint Olympic record with Fanny Blankers-Koen (Holland), 11·2 secs., in the 80-Metres Hurdles.

ANN CURTIS (America), 23-year-old holder of thirty-nine national and three world records who set up a new Olympic record of 5 mins. 17·8 secs. for 400-Metres Swimming, Free-style.

J. F. MIKAELSSON (Sweden), easy winner of 10,000-Metres Walk, in spite of fierce competition. New record, 45 mins. 13·2 secs.

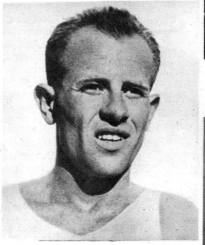

EMILE ZATOPEK (Czechoslovakia), of extraordinary style and unusual tactics, established new 10,000-Metres Olympic record—29 mins. 59·6 secs.

NELL VAN VLIET (Holland), 200-Metres Breast-stroke, 2 mins. 57·2 secs.

KAREN HARUP (Denmark), 100 - Metres Back-stroke, 1 min. 14·4 secs.

M. G. WHITFIELD (U.S.A.), 800-Metres— 1 min. 49·2 secs.

WILLIAM SMITH (U.S.A.), 400-Metres Swimming.

Chapter 5
Post-war Blues

Post-war Blues

AFTER THE SUCCESS OF STAGING THE LONDON 1948 OLYMPIC GAMES, BRITAIN APPEARED RATHER DRAINED, EMOTIONALLY AND FINANCIALLY, IN THE YEARS THAT FOLLOWED. IN HELSINKI FOUR YEARS LATER THE BRITISH TEAM EXPERIENCED ITS POOREST GAMES TO DATE, GAINING JUST ONE GOLD, TWO SILVERS AND EIGHT BRONZES. THEY FINISHED A LOWLY 17TH IN THE MEDAL TABLE, BEHIND COUNTRIES SUCH AS TURKEY, DENMARK AND JAMAICA – A PREVIOUSLY UNTHINKABLE PROSPECT.

Previous page

Members of the British women's 4 x 100m Relay team – (from left to right) Janet Simpson, Mary Rand, Daphne Arden and Dorothy Hyman – set off from London Airport to Buckingham Palace to meet the Queen after winning bronze at the Tokyo 1964 Games.

Norbert Schemansky of the USA poses at the Helsinki 1952 Games where he won the gold medal in the Middle Heavy Weight (82.5–90kg) category of the Weightlifting.

Opposite page

Detail of an official poster from the Tokyo 1964 Games by Yusaku Kamekura. Astonishingly, this was the first Olympic Games poster to employ photography. The background has been blacked out to intensify focus on the athletes.

It was not hard to discover why. Rationing was still biting hard in Britain, reaching a peak in 1952 and continuing in some form until 1954. Facilities and resources for Olympic sports were scarce, and the lack of new stadia for the London 1948 Games did not help the situation. On top of that a huge new player, the Soviet Union, finally made its entrance on to the Olympic stage in 1952. After biding its time and preparing assiduously in the background for many decades, the Soviet Union won a spectacular 71 medals at the Helsinki 1952 Games, 22 of them gold. The dominance of the Soviet Union, and the growing strength of countries in the Soviet bloc, brought Cold War rivalry to a sporting arena as well as a political one. The Soviet Union and its satellites placed great emphasis upon international sporting success, and the financial resources they poured into Olympic events significantly changed the tenor of the Games over the next three or four decades. Certainly the emergence of this driving force did little to improve Britain's medal prospects.

The change in dynamic left Britain in a quandary. American pre-eminence at the Olympic Games had long been a demographic fact of life, given their wealth and population. Competing countries had grown to accept that to an extent, contenting themselves with scoring occasional notable victories against the odds. Yet now an increasing proportion of the rest of the world was beginning to direct most of their best athletes into Olympic events, and to back them with state money and training facilities. Before London 1908, individuals had been able to compete at the Olympic Games without being assigned to a particular country. Now, in a harsher post-war world, considerable international prestige was invested in a nation's performance at the Games.

There were cultural factors too. Britain may have been one of the founding fathers of the modern Olympic Games, but Olympic sports were not a national obsession – they were rather an important part of a bigger picture. Britain's extraordinarily varied sporting scene was centred around largely non-Olympic sports, such as cricket, rugby, golf, motor-racing, horse racing and tennis (which lost its Olympic status after the Paris 1924 Games, only being restored as a full Olympic event at Seoul 1988). Football remained the national game, and although it was an Olympic sport the FIFA World Cup was, and remains, football's premier event. Up until the Munich 1972 Games, Britain either competed in the Olympic Football tournament or the qualifying rounds, but when the FA scrapped the distinction between amateur and professional players in 1974 no more British Olympic teams were entered. Most of the limited resources available were therefore poured into non-Olympic sports and the national 'talent'

Thousands of carrier pigeons fly over the Olympic Stadium at the Helsinki 1952 Games. They were released during the Opening Ceremony to convey the news of the Games to other countries around the world.

gravitated towards them. The situation was reflected in daily media coverage, dominated by non-Olympic sports yet prone to expressions of anguish every four years if a medal haul did not meet expectations. To some extent, this predictable cycle continues to this day, broken by the individual brilliance of some exceptional athletes across a range of events.

Helsinki 1952

Nevertheless Britain's low medal tally in the Helsinki 1952 Olympic Games was disappointing in the extreme. At least the final day saw the Games end on a golden note, with Britain's solitary success coming right at the death in the last event of all: the Equestrian Team Jumping competition. Not surprisingly the story captured the imagination of a nation with an enduring love of horses.

Colonel Harry Llewellyn – 'Harry the Horse' as he was christened by the British press – and his legendary mount Foxhunter were acclaimed as the 'heroes' of the hour, jumping clear in the second round to secure the gold medal. This was only half the story, however, as they had earlier been the villains of the piece. A miserable first round effort incurred 16.75 faults that nearly scuppered all Britain's hopes and left them languishing in sixth place going into the final round of jumps. Llewellyn himself was always at pains to point out the contributions of his colleagues. Wilfred White, a Cheshire farmer who had finished fourth in the individual event after a jump-off for gold, was the strong man of the team with just eight faults in his two rounds. Major Duggie Stewart also incurred less faults than Llewellyn, with

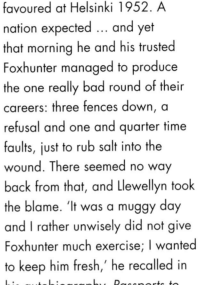

'When he entered the ring he was raring to go ... there was no question of him being tired because I was at him the whole time'

Colonel Harry Llewellyn describes Foxhunter, the horse who helped him to win the Team Jumping gold for Britain at Helsinki 1952

16 faults over his two rounds.

The final day thus started appallingly for Llewellyn, Britain's premier jumper. He had won a bronze medal in the Team Jumping four years previously in London, and the British were strongly favoured at Helsinki 1952. A nation expected ... and yet that morning he and his trusted Foxhunter managed to produce the one really bad round of their careers: three fences down, a refusal and one and quarter time faults, just to rub salt into the wound. There seemed no way back from that, and Llewellyn took the blame. 'It was a muggy day and I rather unwisely did not give Foxhunter much exercise; I wanted to keep him fresh,' he recalled in his autobiography, *Passports to Life*. 'My feeling in those days was that he jumped better when fresh, but there is a great difference between being fresh and not warmed up enough

Best of British

Harry Llewellyn and Foxhunter

Born in Aberdare, South Wales, Harry Llewellyn (1911–99) was educated at Oundle School and Trinity College, Cambridge before joining the army. In the 1930s he was a regular steeplechaser, coming second in the Grand National in 1936 and fourth in 1937. After the Second World War, in which he served as senior liaison officer to Field Marshal Montgomery, Llewellyn scoured the country looking for the best possible horse, settling on a Norfolk-bred golden bay gelding called Foxhunter. Together they won 78 competitions in five years including a Team Jumping bronze medal at the London 1948 Games and the prestigious George V Gold Cup on three occasions. The duo were members of no less than 12 winning GB teams in the Nations Cup. Both were characters. When the pair led the British team to victory at the 1949 Nations Cup in Geneva, Foxhunter amused the crowd by munching the flowers decorating the hat worn by a Swiss general's wife as she presented the prizes. Foxhunter died in 1959; some 40 years later Llewellyn's own ashes were scattered near the spot where his beloved horse was buried.

Left Flying his way through the air to glory in Helsinki, Colonel Harry Llewellyn on Foxhunter. Along with Duggie Stewart and Wilfred White, Llewellyn won the Equestrian Team Jumping event – Britain's only gold medal of the Helsinki 1952 Games.

Below A parade of the medal winners after the Team Jumping event at the Helsinki 1952 Games, where Britain won the gold medal. The British trio of (fourth from the left) Colonel Harry Llewellyn, Wilfred White and Duggie Stewart are either side of the team from Chile who finished second and the USA who were third.

and I am afraid I was guilty of the latter. Our round was disastrous ... I decided I would go back and rest myself and my shattered nerves. I think that my greatest ever triumph was that I did actually manage to sleep for an hour.'

In the second round White (on Nizefela) and Stewart (on Aherlow) continued their fine form with just four faults apiece. This saw Britain move into third place behind Chile and USA as Llewellyn and Foxhunter entered the arena. The horse was now fully engaged and full of spirit, as Llewellyn later observed, and his dramatic, faultless final round earned the team the gold medal.

Llewellyn and Foxhunter, a golden bay gelding, were, in truth, a formidable combination, serving in no less than 12 victorious British teams in the Nations Cup. Llewellyn often found himself upstaged in the public's affections by Foxhunter, who he described affectionately as a 'bit of a show off'. The horse certainly emerged as the real hero of the Games and when he died in 1959 his remains were ceremonially buried on the Blorenge Mountain, high above Abergavenny in Gwent where he and his owner often used to ride.

Elsewhere success was in short supply. Sheila Lerwill won Britain's best Athletics medal of the

Games by taking silver in the High Jump. She had set a world record of 1.72m the previous year, beating the phenomenal Fanny Blankers-Koen's record of 1.71 from 1943, but had to settle for second place in the Helsinki 1952 Games behind Esther Brand of South Africa. Charles Currey also won a well-deserved silver in the Finn class at the Yachting off the coast of Harmaja. He had been prevented from competing in the London 1948 Games after a fellow competitor had claimed he wasn't an amateur and that he worked as a boatbuilder at the Fairey yard in Hampshire, which produced the Firefly dinghy. In 1952, Currey made sure there was no repetition of these charges, by insisting that the four British Finns were made at a different boatyard. Currey was a striking and innovative individual; he fine-tuned and perfected Peter Scott's raw idea of using a trapeze in small dinghy sailing to improve speed, and was also involved in the development and construction of the new Firefly boats. In the Second World War, still less than a decade ago, he had commanded a Motor Torpedo Boat (MTB) and delivered various covert operations personnel to locations on the North French coast and Channel Islands.

The Football tournament at Helsinki 1952 was dominated by Soviet bloc nations, most significantly Hungary who went on to take the gold medal. This truly remarkable team was the product of nationalised sport in Hungary, run by Mihály Farkas, the Minister of Defence. The leading domestic club Kispest was merged with the army team Honvéd, who thus acquired future international legends Ferenc Puskás and József Bozsik. Other stars were transferred from clubs across the country to create a striking array of talent, placed under the control of top coach Gusztáv Sebes. A brilliant generation of players united to present a new footballing ideology to the Olympic Games. It earned them the name 'Magical Magyars' long before Johann Cruyff and the concept of 'Total Football' had emerged from the Netherlands.

The legendary Hungarian football superstar Ferenc Puskás, a member of the 'Magical Magyars', one of the greatest Football teams in history, who won the Olympic title at Helsinki 1952 when they beat Yugoslavia 2-0 in the final.

Hungary's progress through the tournament was dramatic. After beating Italy 3-0, they scored seven goals against Turkey in the Quarter-final and a further six against Sweden in the semi-final. In the Swedish match Puskás opened the scoring in the first minute whilst Sándor Kocsis got the second and Nándor Hidegkuti, a midfield phenomenon from MTK police club, struck three goals in four minutes in the second half. The final, against Germany's conquerors Yugoslavia, had rumbling political undercurrents as Yugoslavia's outspoken Marshall Tito was no friend of the Soviet bloc. So charged was the encounter that the Budapest government only approved a live radio

Emil Zátopek

One of the greatest long-distance runners of all-time, Emil Zátopek (1922–2000) started running as a teenager in Czecholovakia. In his 20s he was running for his country at the London 1948 Games, winning gold in the 10,000m and silver in the 5000m. Four years later in Helsinki he retained his title in the 10,000m and took gold in the 5000m and Marathon, breaking the Olympic records in all three events. Zátopek's running style was very distinctive. His face would often contort with the effort, his head would rock from side to side and his breathing could sound tortured, earning him the nickname 'the Czech Locomotive'. Despite this peculiar style, in his 15-year career, Zátopek set 18 world records.

'I was unable to walk for a whole week after that, so much did the race take out of me. But it was the most pleasure and exhaustion I have ever known'

Emil Zátopek

Opposite page

The track events at the Helsinki 1952 were dominated by one man, the remarkable Czechoslovakian star Emil Zátopek, here leading the pack at the Games where he won the 5000m, 10,000m and the Marathon.

broadcast on 2 August 1952, the very morning of the match.

The Olympic final, watched by a crowd of almost 60,000, proved a tense affair. This was particularly so for Hungarian supporters, huddled at home over radio sets, for whom the team was a powerful symbol of national pride. Puskás unusually missed a penalty in the first half, awarded by the English referee Arthur Ellis, but he redeemed himself by scoring in the 70th minute to put the Hungarians ahead. It remained tight, however, with the talented Yugoslav team threatening to score until Zoltán Czibor, another former Ferencváros FC player, secured the gold medal with a second goal two minutes from time. Public rejoicing in Hungary lasted for a week. The players received new cars, admittedly only East German Wartburgs, as rewards for their efforts. They were also invited to play England at Wembley the following year by Stanley Rous, secretary of the Football Association, who had been at the Olympic final. His admiration was well founded; England, only once beaten at home, were comprehensively defeated six goals to three. Ironically several heroes of the 1952 Games, including Puskás, Kocsis and Czibor, were later to defect to the West following the suppressed uprising of 1956 (when Honvéd had been abroad on tour). Kocsis and Czibor joined Barcelona and Puskás went on to sign for Real Madrid, but the years of the 'Magical Magyars' were over.

The Olympic Torch was carried into Helsinki's Olympic Stadium by 55-year-old Paavo Nurmi, the legendary runner known as the 'Flying Finn'. Nurmi had won an astonishing nine gold and three

'If you want to run, run a mile. If you want to experience a different life, run a marathon'.

Emil Zátopek, who amazingly won the 5000m, 10,000m and Marathon in Helsinki

silver medals in the Antwerp 1920, Paris 1924 and Amsterdam 1928 Games. The track sensation of Helsinki 1952 proved to be the 'Czech locomotive' Emil Zátopek, who achieved an astonishing three gold medals in just eight days. His first success was in the 10,000m, an event he had also won at the London 1948 Games, where he broke the Olympic record he had himself set in London by over 40 seconds. He went on to win gold in the 5000m, setting another Olympic record after an extraordinarily fast final lap of 57.5 seconds. Zátopek, who was famous for his facial grimaces and swaying running style, deemed 'inefficient' by experts of the day, moved relentlessly up the field from fourth to first, while British medal hope Christopher Chataway tripped on the kerb when running in second place and eventually finishing fifth. Zátopek's wife, Dana Zátopková, an outstanding Javelin thrower with the Czech team, also took gold, securing victory only a few moments after her husband's 5000m success.

Zátopek's most remarkable feat was arguably in the men's Marathon, an event in which he had never previously competed and which he entered at the last minute. Once again he set a new Olympic record, defeating Jim Peters, the British world record holder and a favourite for the title, by simply accelerating away after a ferocious first 15km. Peters dropped out four-fifths of the way through the race, and Zátopek went on to knock an astounding six minutes off the Olympic record. The redoubtable Czech, who undertook punishing training routines in all weathers and ran in heavy boots rather than training shoes, retired in 1957 after finishing sixth in the Marathon at Melbourne

Medal table from the 1952 Olympic Games

Country	Gold	Silver	Bronze	Total
USA	40	19	16	75
USSR	22	29	19	70
Hungary	16	10	16	42
Sweden	10	12	10	32
Italy	8	9	4	21
Czechoslovakia	7	3	3	13
France	6	6	6	18
Great Britain (17th position)	1	2	8	11

1956 an event he entered despite having had a hernia operation only six weeks earlier. He is now recognised as his country's greatest athlete, and was awarded the Pierre de Coubertin Medal in December 2000, shortly after his death.

The cause of disability sport was to receive a remarkable boost from two competitors at the 1952 Olympic Games. Károly Takács, the Hungarian pistol shooter who had re-learned to shoot with his left hand following an accident to his right, had been a dramatic gold medal winner four years earlier in London (setting a new world record in the process). He repeated his success at Helsinki 1952, again taking gold in the Rapid Fire Pistol event against able-bodied opposition.

Another disabled athlete, Lis Hartel of Denmark, also showed her ability to compete on equal terms in the Dressage – an event opened up for the first time at Helsinki 1952 to civilians and women. Hartel, Danish dressage champion in 1943 and 1944, contracted polio later in 1944 while pregnant with her second child. She defied medical opinion and started to ride again, despite being paralysed below the knees; her arms and hands were also partially affected. In 1947 Hartel was again competing in dressage events, and was selected for the Olympic team in 1952. She had to be lifted on and off her mount, her favourite horse Jubilee, but once mounted proved a formidable competitor. She went on to take a superb silver medal in the Individual event and became the first female Olympic competitor to share a podium with men. Four years later, again with Jubilee, she won another Olympic Dressage silver medal, this time in Stockholm where the Equestrian events were held for the Melbourne 1956 Olympic Games.

Hartel's achievements, drive and charisma made her a role model for others suffering the after-effects of polio. She raised funds for their treatment through dressage exhibitions and inspired the development of therapeutic riding schools. A centre for the disabled

The first known physically disabled athlete to compete in an Olympic Games, Károly Takács's shooting hand was mutilated by a faulty grenade. The Hungarian made an astonishing comeback, however, winning Olympic gold with his other hand in the 25m rapid fire pistol event at London 1948 and Helsinki 1952.

in Doorn in Netherlands, the Lis Hartel Foundation, is named after her in recognition of her work.

Melbourne 1956

Britain enjoyed a considerably happier time at the Melbourne 1956 Olympic Games, the first to be held in the southern hemisphere. They were also the first Games to be significantly affected by boycotts – the downside of the event's rapidly growing influence and prestige. Egypt, Iraq and Lebanon withdrew in protest over intervention in Suez, while the Netherlands, Spain and Switzerland all declined to attend following the Soviet invasion of Hungary (although the Hungarians themselves made a point

Australian athlete Ron Clarke, holder of the junior mile record, carries the Olympic Torch into the Stadium during the Opening Ceremony of the Melbourne 1956 Games.

of competing). The political shadow remained, however, and a tense, tempestuous Water Polo match between the Soviet Union and Hungary led to some angry clashes. One Hungarian player was led from the swimming pool, and the match was eventually abandoned with Hungary, leading 4-0, being declared the winners. At the end of the Games no less than 45 members of the Hungarian delegation chose to seek political asylum in Australia.

Britain's gold medals were gathered from across the board in Athletics, Boxing, Swimming, Fencing and Equestrian – a remarkably varied haul. Chris Brasher's triumph in the 3000m Steeplechase probably had the most impact, however. It was Britain's first Athletics gold of any kind since 1936.

Brasher was an extraordinary man, with an enviable range of talents. As a runner, however,

he seemed destined to be overshadowed by Sir Roger Bannister, for whom he made the pace on a number of mile world record attempts. These included the ultimately successful race at Iffley Road in May 1954 when Brasher took Bannister and Chris Chataway through the first two and a half laps at the required pace. Chris Chataway, who then took up the pacemaker role, also went on to forge his own outstandingly successful athletics career, breaking the 5000m record later that year. But Brasher appeared to experts and casual observers alike to be the dogged plodder who, by sheer determination and passion for his sport, transformed himself into a very decent international class athlete. The idea that he alone of the three would gain an Olympic gold medal seemed extraordinary – yet so it turned out.

Brasher, with his precise analytical mind, saw

things differently. After finishing a distant 11th in the 3000m Steeplechase at Helsinki 1952, he upped his training enormously. The 1956 Games would represent his last chance at a medal; he would not pursue his athletics career beyond that event. So he made plans to compete in Melbourne and to win the gold medal there. He didn't want the pinnacle of his athletics career to be merely serving as Roger Bannister's pacemaker.

Brasher dedicated himself to training. He ordered especially lightweight leather spikes (weighing under 110g), which the manufacturer warned him would probably collapse after a maximum of four races. A lifelong wearer of glasses, he ordered up a pair of contact lenses just in case it rained, not

impossible in Melbourne. Feeling that the British team were leaving too late for proper acclimatisation to the first Games in the southern hemisphere, he travelled to Australia six weeks ahead of the Games. An intensive training and racing schedule saw him record a personal best of 4:06 for the mile in Geelong by way of preparation.

Despite his improvement Brasher still only ranked third among the British steeplechasers; both John Disley and Eric Shirley were considered to be far more likely medal prospects. Brasher qualified comfortably enough, fourth of five qualifiers in the second heat. Going into the final on a wave of confidence he had a very definite plan – attack with 300m to go – and that's exactly what he did. As he

Right One of the true stars of British distance running, Chris Brasher, won the 3000m Steeplechase gold in controversial circumstances at the Melbourne 1956 Games. Brasher had an amazing career. In 1954 he acted as pacemaker to Roger Bannister when the latter ran the first sub-four-minute mile; then, in 1981, Brasher founded the London Marathon.

executed his plan Brasher's elbow did unarguably make momentary contact with Norway's Ernst Larsen, but that was forgotten as he powered on down the back straight and then in to the home straight, unopposed and fully 14m ahead of the field. Victory was clinical and utterly convincing

Except that when the stadium PA announcer called the 1 2 3, Brasher's name was missing. He had been disqualified by a judge despite the fact that Larsen had raised no objection and that Heinz Laufer, now promoted to the bronze medal position, stated repeatedly that he would not accept the bronze medal if the result was allowed to stand.

Three hours later, with the stadium empty, the appeal jury finally restored Brasher as the winner and the Victory Ceremony was rearranged for the next day. Brasher, meanwhile, after living like a monk for over a year, embarked on a massive celebratory binge. He finished off with a riotous lunch with the British press before, in his own words, he staggered onto the winner's podium smelling like a brewery. In the stands Bannister and Chataway looked on, delighted for their erstwhile pacemaker. He had come a long way. Brasher's teammates, Disley and Shirley, came in sixth and eighth respectively.

There were several other Athletics successes for Britain at the Melbourne 1956 Olympic Games. Derek Johnson, an Oxford medical student, took silver in the 800m, losing to American Tom Courtney by only 0.11 seconds with Courtney collapsing from exhaustion after the race. Gordon Pirie also won silver in the 5000m, in which teammate Derek Ibbotson gained a bronze. Pirie ran from the front of the chasing pack after Vladimir Kuts of the Soviet Union pulled clear, and had to fight off a strong challenge from Ibbotson for second place. Thelma Hopkins won a silver medal in the women's High Jump. She ended in a tie with Mariya Pisareva of the Soviet Union, both women losing out only to American Mildred McDaniel who set a new world record height to take gold. A very versatile and

talented athlete who lived and trained in Northern Ireland, Hopkins followed in the footsteps of Dorothy Tyler and Sheila Lerwill to continue Britain's success in this event.

It was also a good Olympic Games for British teamwork, especially in Stockholm, where Equestrian events were held to avoid quarantine restrictions and the prohibitive costs of transporting horses to Australia. Here Britain's powerful Eventing team (consisting of Bertie Hill, Laurence Rook, and Frank Weldon) came away with the gold medal. Weldon, again on his mount Kilbarry, took bronze in the Individual Eventing, while Wilfred White, one of the heroes of the 1952 Games, joined with Pat Smythe and Peter Robeson to win a Team Jumping bronze.

There were also successes in team events in Melbourne. In the Athletics, the women's 4 x 100m Relay won silver and the men's 4 x 400m Relay a bronze, while in Cycling Britain won silver and bronze in the men's Team Road Race and the 4000m Team Pursuit respectively. In Yachting, which took place in Port Phillip Bay, Britain received a well-deserved silver in the men's 5.5m class; a rare spot of bad weather saw the dismasting of the boats from the Soviet Union and South Africa in the same event.

In Fencing Gillian Sheen won a gold medal for Britain in the women's Individual Foil, and Judy Grinham's victory in the 100m Backstroke made her the first Briton to win an Olympic Swimming gold since Lucy Morton at the Paris 1924 Olympic Games. Another British swimmer, Margaret Edwards, took bronze. The highly talented Grinham broke the world record in the process with a time of 1:12.09; two years later she won both the European and Commonwealth titles, broke the world record again and then promptly retired on her 20th birthday to get married.

Other notable British performances occurred in the Boxing ring, where Thomas Nicholls took silver in the men's Feather Weight division and both Terry Spinks and Dick McTaggart won golds. Spinks, from

'I looked so young
I didn't get served
in a pub. I couldn't
buy a drink.'

Terry Spinks, recalling winning Boxing gold
in the Fly Weight class at the 1956 Olympic
Games

Above Terry Spinks, who won Fly Weight
gold for Britain at the Melbourne 1956
Games when he beat Romanian Mircea
Dobrescu. Spinks progressed to become
the British Feather Weight champion.

Right Britain's Dick McTaggart produces
a superb display to beat hard-hitting
Ghanian Eddie Blay in their Light
Weight duel at the Rome 1960 Games.
McTaggart went on to take the bronze
medal.

West Ham in East London, was a former apprentice jockey who turned with great success to Boxing. He won the Flyweight division (51kg) in fine style, defeating Mircea Dobrescu of Romania on points in the final. He later turned professional and briefly became the British featherweight champion.

Scotland's Dick McTaggart, in contrast, was never tempted away from the amateur ranks. He won the Lightweight title at the 1956 Olympic Games, outpointing Harry Kurschat from Germany in the final and going on to be voted the Boxer of the Tournament. McTaggart went on to take the bronze medal in the Olympic Games in Rome four years later.

The 1956 Stoke Mandeville Games

In retrospect the 1956 Stoke Mandeville Games was possibly the breakthrough moment in gaining sufficient recognition to transform the event into something very much bigger. Ludwig Guttmann had always taken great care to invite politicians and movers and shakers in the sports world to the Stoke Mandeville Games, and in 1956 the guest of honour was none other than Sir Arthur Porrit, the New Zealand sprinter who settled in Britain and became surgeon to the Royal Family. Sir Arthur, later Lord, Porrit was by now an IOC member for Britain and, like others before him, was greatly impressed and moved by what he saw at Stoke Mandeville. He immediately wrote to Otto Mayer, Chancellor of the IOC, firstly to report on all the good work he had witnessed and then to nominate the Stoke Mandeville Hospital generally for their highly prestigious Fearnley Cup. This was duly awarded to Guttmann and his staff for their outstanding contribution to the Olympic ideal.

The Stoke Mandeville Games was beginning to win important friends in high places and

Guttmann was much encouraged by their support. In his opening speech at the 1957 Games he expressed the hope, long held privately, that the award of the Fearnley Cup might be the beginning of a much closer connection between the Stoke Mandeville Games and the Olympic Games. If Olympic sport, ultimately, is about human sporting endeavour and achievement, there was no logical argument for denying disabled individuals the chance to compete within their sphere.

The Stoke Mandeville Games continued to grow apace, and competition was now fierce. From 1958 a separate British championships had to be held a month prior to the Games themselves just to select a British team for the international competition itself. The momentum was with the Games, and the next Olympic Games would see its profile raised still further.

Rome 1960

Four years later, in the stifling heat of a Rome summer, it was back to pretty slim pickings for Britain at the Olympic Games. The USA continued their superpower rivalry with the Soviet Union, accounting for 174 of the available medals between them. The Soviets took an amazing 15 out of 16 possible medals in the women's Gymnastics, while the 'fastest woman on earth', Wilma Rudolph, became the first American woman to win three gold medals in Athletics (100m, 200m and 4 x 100m Relay) at a single Games. It was a remarkable achievement by the woman who became known as 'The Tornado' and had suffered from polio as a child. Another outstanding performance came from Australian Herb Elliott, who took the 1500m gold and set a new world record (3:35.60); 40 years later he was one of the last Torchbearers at the Opening Ceremony of the Sydney 2000 Olympic Games.

> 'Winning is great, sure, but if you are really going to do something in life, the secret is learning how to lose ... If you can pick up after a crushing defeat, and go on to win again, you are going to be a champion someday.'
>
> Wilma Rudolph, three times gold medallist for the USA in Rome 1960

Medal table from the 1956 Olympic Games				
Country	Gold	Silver	Bronze	Total
USSR	36	29	32	97
USA	32	25	17	74
Australia	13	8	14	35
Hungary	9	10	7	26
Italy	8	8	9	25
Sweden	7	5	6	18
United Team of Germany	6	12	7	25
Great Britain (8th position)	6	7	11	24

A sickly child, Wilma Rudolph (1940–94) overcame infantile paralysis to become the fastest woman on earth. Born in Tennessee during the years of racial segregation, Rudolph was the 20th of 22 children. Although her early years were spent wearing a brace to straighten her twisted left foot and leg, she went on to run for her country at the Melbourne 1956 Games. Aged only 16, she helped the USA win bronze in the 4 x 100m Relay. Four years later, at the Rome 1960 Games, she was at the height of her powers, winning gold in the 100m, 200m and 4 x 100m Relay – the first American woman to do so. She insisted that her homecoming parade in Clarksville, Tennessee be open to everyone, black or white – the first racially integrated event held in the town.

American champion Wilma Rudolph (centre), having just won the 200m event at the Rome 1960 Games, poses between German Jutta Heine (right), who was second and Britain's Dorothy Hyman (left), who finished third.

And the amateur boxer Cassius Clay, later to become world famous as Mohammed Ali, announced his arrival on the scene with a gold medal in the Light Heavy Weight division.

If there was a sense that 'the times, they are a-changing' at Rome 1960, many of the venues chosen for the Games harked back to the city's ancient past. In Cycling the Individual Road Race used the Via Cassia and the Via Flaminia, both ancient Roman roads, and the Marathon took place on the Appian Way itself, famously ending at the early fourth-century Arch of Constantine. Gymnastics took place in the Baths of Caracalla, Roman public baths built between AD 212 and 216, while

Wrestling was held in the Baths of Maxentius in the ancient Roman Forum. More recent times were also celebrated, with the Equestrian events (Dressage, Eventing and Jumping) taking place in the Piazza di Siena of the Villa Borghese gardens – one of the city's most beautiful landscape gardens, given a naturalistic 'English' flavour in the nineteenth century.

There were just two golden moments for Britain to savour, however: Don Thompson in the 50km Race Walk and Anita Lonsbrough in the 200m Breaststroke. The popular Thompson, who had switched from running to race walking following an injury to his Achilles tendon, had had enjoyed much success in the 52.5mile London to Brighton race

British athlete Don Thompson leads in the 50km Race Walk at the Rome 1960 Games, where he won the gold medal. Having collapsed in the heat at the previous Games in Melbourne, Thompson had trained for Rome by creating a steamroom effect in his bathroom and walking up and down on the bathmat.

It is a time of celebration for Britain's Anita Lonsbrough after winning gold in the 200m Breaststroke at the Rome 1960 Games in a world record time of 2:49.5.

between 1954–56 with two wins and had also taken line honours in the 100km Milan race.

He had participated in the 50km Race Walk at the Melbourne 1956 Olympic Games, but became dehydrated and had to withdraw after 45km, at which point he had been in fifth place.

Thompson was determined this would not happen again. He famously prepared for the Roman heat by training in a steam-filled bathroom at home, where he installed a paraffin heater to help crank up the temperatures after running a hot bath. After exercising for half an hour or more he found he used to faint, which he at first attributed it to the humidity, only later discovering that the leaky heater was giving off carbon monoxide fumes. He survived, however, and, armed with a bespoke Kepi hat made by his mother to ward off the sun, went on to prosper in a gruelling race (although his appearance

prompted the Italian press to nickname him *topolino* or 'little mouse'). The early leaders were disqualified for losing contact with the ground and he eventually defeated John Ljunggren of Sweden by 17 seconds, setting a new Olympic record of 4:25.30.

Lonsbrough, who had won two gold medals at the 1958 Commonwealth Games in Cardiff, was one of the favourites going into the pool at Rome, despite losing her world record to great German rival Wiltrud Urselmann just before the Olympic Games started. Come the final, however, and everything seemed to go to plan. The German went out hard over the first two laps; Lonsbrough pulled most of that advantage back in the third, and then overtook her great rival going down the final lap.

'When we had met in the past Urselmann had always given up once I had overtaken her, so I felt I had the race won,' recalls Lonsbrough. 'But with

'It is the Africans who possess this vitality, this muscular youth, this thirst for physical action which we are lacking. We have a magnificent motor at our disposal, but we no longer know how to use it'

Emil Zátopek reflects on East African dominance of long distance running

this being an Olympic Games she found something extra and started coming back at me unexpectedly. It made for an exciting finish, but I just got home. It was another fast race, with a world record of 2mins 49.5secs.'

Another British swimmer, the talented all-rounder Natalie Steward, won silver in the 100m Backstroke and bronze in the 100m Freestyle. Yet, unsurprisingly, it was Lonsbrough's achievements that caught the British public's imagination. She continued to make an impact after the Games, taking gold medals in 1962 at the European and Commonwealth Championships and becoming the first woman to win the BBC Sports Personality of the Year. Four years later, at the Tokyo 1964 Olympic Games, she became the first woman to carry the flag for Britain at the Opening Ceremony. She also met her future husband, cyclist Hugh Porter, was the only other British competitor to stay awake on the then interminable flight to Japan. He and Anita started talking and within a year they were married.

Lonsbrough had worked in local government during her swimming career, but after retiring from the sport in 1965 she turned to the media. For many years she worked as the *Daily Telegraph*'s swimming correspondent, and was indeed poolside filing copy at the Beijing 2008 Olympic Games. Forty-eight years after her great moment, Lonsbrough was reporting on the next British woman to win an Olympic gold swimming medal, Rebecca Adlington.

In Athletics Dorothy Hyman, like Lonsbrough a

'Even when I stood on the podium I was thinking, "I hope this isn't a dream and I am going to wake up". But later I was able to enjoy the moment'

Anita Lonsbrough remembers her 200m Breaststroke victory at the Rome 1960 Games

determined Yorkshire lass, raised Britain's spirits with a silver medal in the 100m and a bronze medal in the 200m. The real drama in the Athletics event came in the Marathon, however, run for the first time at night. To the astonishment of watching crowds, the first to reach the floodlit Arch of Constantine was an unknown Ethiopian in bare feet. Abebe Bikila, aged 28, achieved an extraordinary time of 2:15:16.2 over Rome's cobbled streets, shaving almost eight minutes off the great Emil Zátopek's Olympic record of 1952. Bikila had symbolically made his decisive move 40km into the race, just by the Ethiopian obelisk of Axum (looted on Mussolini's orders by Italian soldiers following their invasion of Ethiopia some 25 years before). Calm and efficient, Bikila simply eliminated the field to become the first black African to win an Olympic title. Four years later in Tokyo he became the first man to retain the Marathon title, winning gold in another world record time less than six weeks after having an appendectomy. Bikila's victories were to signal an East African dominance in distance running that has lasted to the present day.

Television was also a significant presence at the Rome 1960 Olympic Games. They were the first Games to be beamed across the world by television, the Italian National Olympic Committee having signed agreements with Eurovision for the rest of Europe and CBS for the USA who paid $394,000. The Olympic Games could now be viewed in 21 countries; a global phenomenon, it was now part of a technology-driven, rapidly changing sporting world.

Opposite page

He changed the world with his barefoot Marathon glory at the Rome 1960 Games, and here Ethiopian Marathon runner Abebe Bikila enters the Stadium at Tokyo 1964 for the finish of the race where he retained his title.

'I wanted the world to know that my country, Ethiopia, has always won with determination and heroism'

Ethiopian Abebe Bikila wins the Rome 1960 Marathon in a world record of 2:15.16.2 – running in the dark and barefoot

The barefooted Ethiopian, Abebe Bikila, leads the Rome 1960 Marathon through the streets of the Eternal City. A 28-year-old international novice, his victory on the Appian Way was to herald an era of African dominance in distance running.

*Medal table from the
1960 Olympic Games*

Country	Gold	Silver	Bronze	Total
USSR	43	29	30	102
USA	34	21	16	71
Italy	13	10	13	36
United Team of Germany	12	19	11	42
Australia	8	8	6	22
Hungary	6	8	7	23
Turkey	6	2	0	8
Great Britain (12th position)	2	6	12	20

Rome 1960 Paralympic Games

If the 1960 Olympic Games were generally
a disappointment for British competitors, the
remarkable flourishing of the Rome 1960 Paralympic
Games brought plenty of compensation. These were
held in Rome straight after the Olympic Games, for
the first time using the same venues, and drew on
the support of many other organisations. The World
Veterans Foundation, the Italian Olympic Committee
(CONI) and a giant Italian Insurance company INAIL
all rallied to help Guttmann and his staff and boost
the prestige of the Games.

With approximately 400 wheelchair-bound

athletes from 23 nations, the first Paralympic Games
was on a steep learning curve. Firstly, the Athletes'
Village was not completely wheelchair-accessible;
athletes had to be carried up and down stairs,
although Italian military personnel were on hand to
assist. Margaret Maughan, who went on to become
Britain's first Paralympic gold medal winner at the
Games, recalls, 'Nothing was on the ground floor.
The buildings were all on stilts. The Italians called in
the army, who were on duty day and night.' While
most of the competitions were held in the Village
area, Athletics and Wheelchair Basketball took place
at the Tre Fontane sports ground, some 40 minutes'

drive from the accommodation blocks. Innovative transport arrangements had to be made.

The Paralympic Games were held from 18 to 25 September, seven days after the Closing Ceremony of the XVII Olympiad. The Opening Ceremony of the Paralympic Games on 18 September saw a crowd of 5,000 spectators greet the colourful entry of the wheelchair athletes at the Acqua Acetosa Stadium. Camillo Giardina, the Italian Minister for Public Health, declared the Games open. The competitive programme included eight sport events considered beneficial and suitable for athletes with spinal cord injuries: Snooker, Wheelchair Fencing (Foil or Sabre), Javelin and Precision Javelin, Shot Put, Indian Club Throw (throwing a baton), men's Wheelchair Basketball and Swimming (Freestyle, Breaststroke and Backstroke). Other events included Table Tennis (singles and doubles), Archery, Dartchery (dart-style archery) and the Pentathlon (Archery, Swimming, Javelin, Shot Put and Club Throw).

Among the many outstanding individual performers was Britain's Dick Thompson, who won four gold medals in throwing events. Ron Stein of the USA, a polio sufferer, was also outstanding, taking gold medals in all three of his athletic events (the Club Throw, Open Pentathlon and Shot Put). The Americans unsurprisingly shone in men's Wheelchair Basketball, where they took both golds. Wheelchair Fencing was dominated by the Italian team, which won all nine medals in the Foil and Sabre events. As noted, Britain's first ever Paralympic gold medal went to Margaret Maughan in the Archery, barely a year after she was involved in a car accident in Nyasaland, now Malawi, which left her unable to walk. She was treated at Stoke Mandeville Hospital, where she met Guttmann, who told her, 'I had to start getting on with things and not feeling sorry for myself.' On leaving hospital she joined an archery club and was subsequently selected for the Games in Rome. She went on to win the women's Columbia round in the Archery competition, with a score of 484 points, although as she recollects it was a confusing process. 'The way they kept track of the scores was very complicated … We finished our competition and the scorers just went away, so we didn't have any idea how we'd done.' Only in mid-evening, when she was taken off the coach to return to the Village, did Maughan learn that she had won gold. Although the presentation was a low-key affair, it was still an emotional moment for her, as she acknowledges, 'I had a frog in my throat listening to the national anthem'. She also took part in Swimming, in the Women's 50m Backstroke Complete Class 5, winning in 1:49.02.

A big highlight for all those athletes and officials was an audience with Pope John XXIII at the Vatican, an occasion that brought the Paralympic Games further welcome publicity. 'You are the living demonstration of the marvels of the virtue of energy,' the Pope told the Paralympic athletes. 'You have given a great example, which we would like to emphasise, because it can be extended to all. You have shown what an energetic soul can achieve in spite of apparently

> ## 'Actually, we used the word 'Paralympic' right from the beginning … We were "the paras". We were very daring, you know'
>
> Margaret Maughan, winner of Britain's first ever Paralympic gold medal in 1960

Best of British

Margaret Maughan

Britain's first Paralympic gold medalist, Margaret Maughan was paralysed in a car accident in Nyasaland, now Malawi, in 1959. The following year she went to what was originally known as the 9th International Stoke Mandeville Games, now recognised as the first Paralympic Games, which were held in Rome straight after the Olympic Games. Maughan took the Columbia Round Archery contest with a score of 484 points, and it was the start of an illustrious 20-year career as a Paralympian. At those same Games Maughan also won the 50m Backstroke, when she was the only competitor. Some 12 years later in Heidelberg, she had switched to the Dartchery competition – a combination of darts and archery – winning a gold medal in the Pairs open. At Tel Aviv in 1976 she won a silver medal in the Pairs Open – and a silver in the Pairs lawn bowls – and she finished her Parlympian career by taking gold in the Lawn Bowls Pairs at Arnhem in 1980.

Medal table from the 1960 Paralympic Games

Country	Gold	Silver	Bronze	Total
Italy	29	28	23	80
Great Britain	20	15	20	55
Germany	15	6	9	30
Austria	11	8	11	30
USA	11	7	7	25
Norway	9	3	4	16
Australia	3	6	1	10

Right The Opening Ceremony of the Tokyo 1964 Games. It proved to be a superb Games for Britain in Athletics with Lynn Davies winning the men's Long Jump, Mary Rand winning the women's Long Jump, Ann Packer taking the 800m and Ken Matthews victorious in the men's 20km Race Walk.

insurmountable obstacles imposed by the body.'

Guttmann also attended and presented the Pope with the Stoke Mandeville pennant. He offered his summing up at the Closing Ceremony a few days later:

'The vast majority of competitors and escorts have fully understood the meaning of the Rome Games as a new pattern of re-integration of the paralysed into society, as well as the world of sport. It can now be concluded that the first experiment to hold the Stoke Mandeville Games as an entity in another country as an international sports festival comparable with the Olympic Games and other international sports events for the able-bodied has been highly successful.'

Toyko 1964

The going was still extremely tough for Britain at the Tokyo 1964 Olympic Games, but a golden generation of athletes, claiming four gold and 18 medals in total, captured the nation's imagination. Evolving technology continued to impress. Tokyo 1964 had intercontinental colour television coverage, provided courtesy of America's Syncom 3 satellite (launched just a couple of weeks before the Games started). For audiences at home the novelty of live action from the other side of the world only added to the drama of everything that unfolded.

In fact, even delivering this compelling television coverage was to prove a drama in itself. The pictures arrived in Britain via Syncom with impressive regularity and clarity, but the sound came a different route. It was transmitted via a cable from Japan to Honolulu, then on to the American mainland and finally on to Britain. Unfortunately a rogue fishing vessel managed to slice through the cable off Hawaii and for five days the BBC had pictures but no sound from their expert commentators in situ. A band of substitute commentators was hastily rounded up, including Norris McWhirter, a fount of all athletic knowledge who helped found the Guinness Book of Records, and Doran Williams who commentated

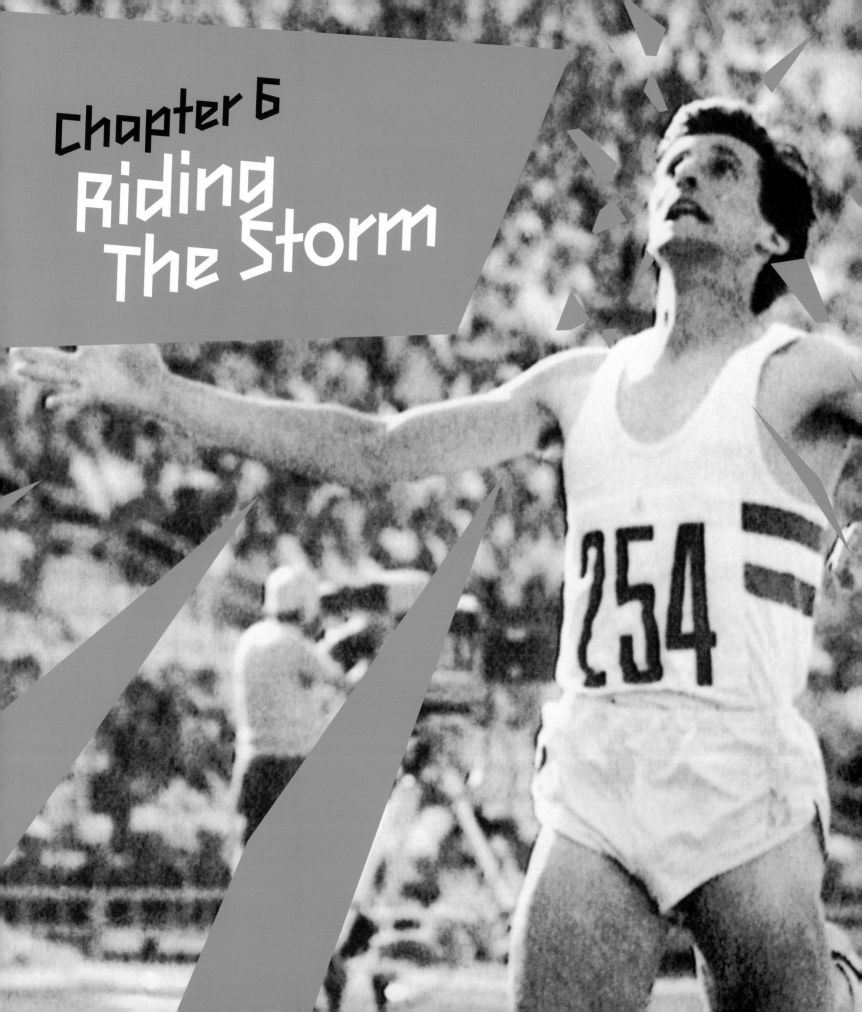

Chapter 6
Riding The Storm

Riding The Storm

THE YEARS AFTER THE TOKYO 1964 OLYMPIC GAMES WERE TO PROVE A CHALLENGING TIME FOR THE OLYMPIC MOVEMENT. MOST TRAUMATIC WAS THE KILLING OF 11 ATHLETES AND OFFICIALS OF THE ISRAELI OLYMPIC TEAM AT THE MUNICH 1972 OLYMPIC GAMES, BUT FINANCIAL PROBLEMS AND THE ISSUE OF PERFORMANCE-ENHANCING DRUGS ALSO EMERGED IN THESE YEARS. THE OLYMPIC GAMES HAD BECOME A HUGE GLOBAL STAGE ATTRACTING POLITICAL PROTESTS AS WELL AS CELEBRATIONS, AND THE AMATEUR ETHOS ON WHICH IT WAS FOUNDED HAD BEGUN TO BE A CHALLENGE IN AN INCREASINGLY PROFESSIONAL SPORTING WORLD.

Previous page

One of the greatest moments in Britain's Olympic history. It is Moscow 1980 and Sebastian Coe's face says it all as he bursts through to win the 1500m gold having lost the 800m to his rival Steve Ovett (centre) who finished third in this race.

Opposite page

An official poster for the Mexico City 1968 Games, now on display at the IOC Olympic Museum in Lausanne, Switzerland. Altogether, there were 2,120,000 copies of 159 posters printed for the Games.

Some countries were now directing large amounts of state money towards the Olympic Games in order to win gold medals and dominate the prestigious Games' medal tables. Britain, by contrast, operated in a much broader sporting environment than many countries, with interests focused on an array of sports, many of which were not featured at the Olympic Games. This gave British officials and the sporting public a valuable perspective and objectivity: its reputation as a sporting nation did not stand or fall by performances at the Olympic Games. Despite this Britain's support for the Olympic Movement and its ideals remained solid and consistent: not once did it succumb to the calls to boycott individual Games, leaving its reputation largely enhanced. Despite the diverse outlets for its sporting passions, the British public's fascination with the Games never diminished. Competition for gold medals had become intense, and although they were as hard as ever to come by, there were a number of stunning successes to savour in these difficult times.

The 1968 Olympic Games were hosted by Mexico City, part of the first developing (and Spanish-speaking) country to do so. It was also held at higher altitude than any previous games – 2,240m – which produced some curious results especially in jumping, throwing and shorter track events in Athletics. Many endurance athletes struggled in the thinner air, although East African runners from countries such as Kenya and Ethiopia prospered. The Paralympic Games, still known to contemporaries as the 17th International Stoke Mandeville Games, were also originally intended to be held in Mexico City, following the precedents of the Rome 1960 Games and Tokyo 1964 Games. However the altitude factor, among other concerns, saw them take place in Tel Aviv, Israel instead.

Political forces were starting to make their presence felt at the Mexico City 1968 Games. East and West German athletes competed in separate teams after having been instructed to send a combined team to the three previous Games. Czech gymnast Vera Cáslavská, winner of four gold and two silver medals and the Mexico City 1968 Games' single most successful athlete, looked down and away during the playing of the Soviet national anthem in the Victory Ceremonies for the Balance Beam and Floor Exercise competitions. Her action, witnessed around the world, was to see Caslavska forced into retirement by the authoritarian regime installed in Czechoslovakia after the Soviet Union's invasion of that country only two months earlier.

The most controversial protest of the Mexico City 1968 Games, the so-called Black Power Salute, occurred during the Victory Ceremony for the men's 200m. Tommie Smith and John Carlos, African-

de la XIX Olimpiada – Jeux de la XIXème Olympiade – Games of the XIXth Olympi...

1968

MEXICO

American members of the USA Team and 200m gold and bronze medallists respectively, each raised a black-gloved fist as a gesture of support for the Black Power movement, while the silver medallist, Australian Peter Norman, wore a Civil Rights movement badge of support. Smith and Carlos also wore black socks but no shoes, an apparent symbol of the poverty and poor conditions in which many black Americans lived. At a time of political protest in the USA, the salute made headlines around the world. To some officials it was seen as inflammatory and contrary to the spirit of the Olympic Games. Smith and Carlos were banned from future Olympic

'Black America will understand what we did tonight'

Tommie Smith after the Black Power salute with teammate John Carlos

Games for life, and Norman was omitted from the 1972 Australian Olympic team. Although booed on the podium by many of the crowd they remained defiant, with Tommie Smith declaring to a press conference that 'Black America will understand what we did tonight.'

A remarkable number of world records were set at the Mexico City 1968 Olympic Games, with the altitude undoubtedly playing some part. American sprinter Jim Hines officially broke the 10-second barrier in the 100m for the first time, with a time recognised after some debate as 9.95 seconds, in the first all-black final in the history of the Games. The men's Triple Jump world record was broken five times by three different athletes, but it was to be the Long Jump that saw the most extraordinary result. American Bob Beamon's incredible leap of 8.9m broke the 1965 world record by 55cm, setting a record that endured until 1991. The final, held on an unpromising cold, wet afternoon, actually started in lethargic and low-key mode. The first three competitors all performed 'no-jumps', but then Beamon took to the runway and transformed the event. He jumped so far that he landed beyond the new expensive optical measuring equipment, so an old-fashioned steel tape had to be used.

Beamon's feat is still often considered one of the single greatest performance in the history of the Games, a fact appreciated by other competitors. 'We all knew he could jump out of the pit one day if he got it right, but nobody expected him to get it all together. He proved us all wrong,' observes Welshman Lynn Davies, who had seen hopes of defending the Long Jump title he had won four years earlier in Tokyo dashed. Davies added: 'We expected something special to happen in the competition because we were at altitude. Everyone thought we could see the first 28ft jump – but what

The Victory Ceremony for the 200m at Mexico City 1968. Tommie Smith (centre) and John Carlos (right), both of the USA, stand up for their rights, making a gesture that showed the Olympic Games had become more than just sport.

Bob Beamon

At 3.46pm on 18 October 1968 in the Olympic Stadium, Mexico City, Bob Beamon took off down the runway and into the sporting history books. Jesse Owens, legend of the Berlin 1936 Games who was following Beamon through binoculars from the stands opposite, declared, 'His body went up five and a half to six feet in the air, and with his speed, that will do it.' Beamon had to wait what seemed like a lifetime to find out the result. The jump was beyond the range of the optical measuring device so had to be measured manually. When the result flashed up on the scoreboard, 8.90m, Beamon, who thought in feet and inches, still didn't know that he'd smashed the world record. It was up to Ralph Boston, gold medallist at Rome 1960 to tell him the incredible truth, 'You went about 29 feet 2 inches.' Beamon's world record stood for 23 years; he still holds the Olympic record.

'If someone had given me £1 million on the warm-up track to bet on someone jumping 29ft I would never have bothered. It seemed impossible'

Britain's defending champion Lynn Davies reflects on Bob Beamon's amazing Long Jump world record

Opposite page

This seminal photograph shows Bob Beamon leaping his way into Athletics history at the Mexico City 1968 Games with his extraordinary leap of 8.90m in the Long Jump, setting a record that was to stand for 23 years.

'Fred Housdon taught me to hurdle, Billy Smith to work and I added the third component, which is what's going on in the mind'

David Hemery

we got was the first 29ft jump. If someone had given me £1 million on the warm-up track to bet on someone jumping 29ft, I would never have bothered. It seemed impossible. Igor Ter-Ovanesyan, the great Russian athlete, came up to me and said, "compared to that we are all children". And even to this day I get asked more about Bob Beamon and *that* jump than I do about how I won my gold medal.'

The United States dominated the jumping events in Mexico. This was the Games in which Dick Fosbury introduced his now-famous 'Fosbury Flop' (a back-first style of high jumping), taking the gold medal with a new Olympic record of 2.24m. Britain had its own golden moments, however, with the most dramatic being David Hemery's unexpected victory in the 400m Hurdles. Like Beamon, the young Briton experienced one of those rare days in which everything is effortless; body and mind seeming to work in perfect harmony. As he later explained: 'My limbs reacted as my mind was thinking; total control which resulted in total freedom. Instead of forcing and working my legs, they responded with the speed and in the motion that was being asked of them.'

Such a state of grace was not achieved by chance: the rigour of Hemery's training regime was second to none. Almost 10 months previously, in December 1967, it had been snowing all day in Boston, Massachusetts, USA although had mercifully stopped by the time Hemery finished his lecture. He wrapped up as if embarking on a polar exploration and made his way down to the changing rooms at the Boston University athletics track. He expected to go through the formality of cancelling

"My limbs reacted as my mind was thinking, total control which resulted in total freedom."

David Hemery on how his body worked perfectly as he won the 400m Hurdles gold

his session that deep-winter afternoon, perhaps arranging a gym session by way of compensation. Waiting for him was coach Bud Smith, similarly wrapped up like a polar bear. As Hemery started to run through a checklist of gym exercises and things they could do to counter the cold blast, his breath freezing in front of him as he spoke, Smith led him through the changing room and out on to the track. There in the deep snow lay a virgin lane which Smith and his groundsmen had just cleared with their shovels. 'Out there', the coach explained, 'lies the road to Mexico.' Hemery nodded his head, turned sharply and started to get changed. It seemed like he would be doing his 400m training after all.

Hemery and his family had lived for a long while in America where his father's job took him and he came up through the American college system. This, contrary to common misconception, is not all about gilded wealth and world-class facilities. It is centred mainly on a very tough work ethic, weekly competition and constant assessment, both academically and on the sports field. There may have been a Corinthian whiff to Hemery in looks and demeanour but he was way ahead of his time compared with many British athletes in terms of hours devoted to training and the science behind that training. At Boston he earned his keep and paid for his education by representing the college throughout the year – a full indoors season in the winter, followed by an even busier summer season.

Yes the facilities were good, definitely better than in Britain, but it wasn't better facilities that set Hemery apart; it was old-fashioned dedication. Sand dune running on a deserted beach an hour from Boston was his favourite drill. Freezing winter afternoons would be spent

slogging his way up his chosen 30-metre dune 35 times – or 25 times up a longer, even crueller, 40-metre dune. Night had often fallen when the torture finished.

'I adored sand dune running,' Hemery recalls. 'It was totally exhausting and you can only make progress up a sand dune by running flat out, so there can be no short cuts. The less you put in the harder it is and the longer it all takes... Yet 10 minutes after you stop you feel fantastic and energised. Because there is no jarring on the muscles and bones it is actually very kind on the body while working it to the maximum.' He notes that Steve Ovett had been another great fan of sand dunes in training a decade later, 'and it didn't do him any harm.'

And so Hemery came to stand on top of the medal podium at Mexico City. He had not been on his rivals' radar at the start of the 1968 season and he seemed in many ways an unlikely gold-medal prospect. He had never run faster than 51.8, he was short-sighted and he was unable to hurdle off his left foot. When his stride got shorter with fatigue, he could thus not simply add a single stride – it had to be two. Yet he was to improve consistently through that season, beating Geoffrey Vanderstock (who went on to break the world record in the US Olympic trials) in the US national collegiate tournament. Above all, Hemery believed in himself: he had visualised himself winning, walking each of the eight lanes in Mexico City's Estadio Olimpico, and even though he and British teammate John Sherwood were the slowest among the eight finalists, they were to emerge with gold and bronze medals.

Above left David Hemery, with one of the finest Olympic Games performances by a Briton, leaps over the barrier on his way to gold and a world record in the 400m Hurdles final at the Mexico City 1968 Games.

Above right On the podium David Hemery (centre) with silver medallist Gerhard Hennige (left) and British teammate John Sherwood (right) who came third. David Coleman, commentating for the BBC, who was so excited by Hemery's win that he said 'Who cares who's third' later apologised to Sherwood.

Hemery didn't just beat his opponents in the final; he destroyed them. He didn't just break the world record; he decimated it – reducing the mark from 48.90 to 48.10. Hemery produced sporting perfection on the biggest stage, completing what many still consider the finest individual athletic performance by a British athlete at an Olympic Games. It was positively 'Beamon-esque', except that it was only three days later that the American's feat in the long jump pit brought this new word into the English language.

Those watching Hemery live on television back in Britain (with a memorable commentary by the BBC's great David Coleman adding immeasurably to the occasion) were thrilled. 'It's Hemery of Great Britain, Hemery of Great Britain,' screeched Coleman as the magnitude of the triumph became apparent – even to those who knew precious little about the blonde hero rippling over the hurdles. Indeed it was – but although Hemery was undoubtedly British to the core, this victory also came with a 'Made in the USA' stamp.

Elsewhere the now customary sporadic smattering of British success (a tally of five golds, five silvers and three bronzes) left the team 10th in the medal table. The Equestrian events were a particular success, with Marion Coakes taking the Individual silver medal, only four faults behind American champion Bill Steinkraus, and her teammate David Broome taking the bronze. Major Derek Allhusen and his horse Lochinvar won not only silver in the Individual Three-Day Eventing competition, but also gold (with Richard Meade, Jane Bullen and Ben Jones) in the Team event. The circumstances were challenging, to say the least. A sudden storm dramatically changed conditions to the cross country test; one team's horse drowned in a flooded ditch and the non-swimming rider of another had to be rescued. The final phase of Jumping in the arena was also extremely hazardous, with the British team being one of only two nations who managed to get four horses to complete the course.

Four years later, in the Munich 1972 Olympic Games Meade was to go one better. Riding Laurieston, a horse loaned to him by Allhusen, he took two golds in the Eventing, winning both the Individual and Team events: a magnificent result.

In Yachting, Rodney Pattisson began his distinguished Olympic career at Mexico City 1968. Together with London solicitor Iain MacDonald-Smith he first won the Olympic trials and then took gold medal in the Flying Dutchman class. In their elaborately named boat *Supercallifragilisticexpidalidocious* (shortened, unsurprisingly, to *Superdocious*), they won five out of six races held in Acapulco, Mexico, with one disqualification, and claimed gold with a huge win over the highly successful West Germans Ullrich Libor and Peter Naumann. Pattisson, the first Scot to win Olympic gold in any sport for 12 years, also went on to repeat his success in 1972, this time crewed by Chris Davies, to beat the French pair of Yves and Marc Pajot. He took silver in the 1976 Olympic Games in Montreal, where he was a flag bearer for the British team, and became a huge inspiration for a later generation of British sailors such as Ben Ainslie, Michael McIntyre and Shirley Robertson.

Chris Finnegan, a bricklayer from Buckinghamshire, became a typical British rags-to-riches hero by winning a Middle Weight gold in Boxing; it was to be Britain's last gold in the sport until Audley Harrison triumphed at Sydney 2000. Finnegan had a hard path to the gold medal, having to survive two standing counts in a semi-final against the American Alfred Jones (and only narrowly coming through with a 3-2 verdict) before taking on the Soviet Union's Aleksei Kiselyov in the final. Even getting to Mexico City was a minor miracle for Finnegan; a sympathetic Slough magistrate agreed that he could defer payment of money owed on unpaid National Insurance stamps for five weeks until his return from the Olympic Games. The unnamed magistrate expressed the

Medal table from the 1968 Olympic Games

Country	Gold	Silver	Bronze	Total
USA	45	28	34	107
USSR	28	31	30	89
Japan	11	7	7	25
Hungary	10	10	12	32
German Democratic Republic	9	9	7	25
France	7	2	5	14
Czechoslovakia	7	2	4	13
Great Britain (10th position)	5	4	3	12

'I knew I'd won before the announcement because the ref squeezed my hand as we waited for the decision. Mind you, I thought, if he's winding me up I'm going to knock his head off.'

The late Chris Finnegan reflecting on his Boxing glory

The boxer Chris Finnegan, who won Middle Weight gold for Britain at the Mexico City 1968 Games, in training during his professional career. He became a British and Commonwealth Light Heavy Weight champion.

hope that Finnegan would bring the gold medal with him when he next attended to pay the debt – whether he did we sadly do not know.

Finnegan became a national sporting celebrity on the back of his Olympic gold and turned professional with a contract from promoter Harry Levene. Another gold medallist at Mexico City, however, was to remain resolutely amateur in approach. Bob Braithwaite took Shooting gold in the Mixed Trap event, which was held 50 miles away from the main Games. All the competitors faced having to hit 200 clay targets in eight stages over two days, and Braithwaite's performance was extraordinary. He missed two targets (the 5th and 13th) on the first day, and so entered the second day in second place. Gold seemed out of the question, requiring a world record score, but by the end of the day every one of Braithwaite's 175 targets had been struck. It was

a fantastic result for the busy vet who practised on a simple trap near the family's Cumbrian farm – a triumph for the gifted amateur in a Games where highly funded professionals were making their mark.

The saddest story of the Mexico City 1968 Games must be that of Lillian Board, a hugely

'When it was found out, most surprisingly, that I had won they had no national anthem out there ... we had to wait ages for it to come.'

Bob Braithwaite, winner of the Shooting Mixed Trap at the Mexico City 1968 Games, an event held 80km away from the rest of the Olympiad

Lillian Board

Lillian Board may not have won gold at Mexico City 1968, the one Olympiad that the Fates allowed her to compete in, but for a few short years she was undoubtedly the 'Golden Girl' of British athletics. Highly photogenic but also very natural she immediately captured the hearts of British fans and from the off was clearly an exceptional athletic talent. She put aside her dramatic defeat in the 400m at Mexico City, winning the 800m at the European Championships in Athens in 1969 with a blistering run. She then exacted a small measure of revenge over Colette Besson by overhauling the French girl on the last leg of the 4 x 400m Relay to finish with another gold medal. The world was at her feet, but after running a fast mile race in Rome in May next year she started to complain of stomach pain. Diagnosed at first as a virus, then Crohn's disease, it was in fact colorectal cancer and an exploratory operation in September suggested she might have only two months to live. As a last resort she sought treatment at the Ringberg Clinic of Dr Josef Issels in Bavaria but to no avail and after being moved to Munich University Hospital she died there on Boxing Day 1970.

talented athlete who won silver in the 400m and set a UK record of 52.12 seconds in the process. She had been favourite for gold, coming a comfortable second in her heat and winning the semi-final in a personal-best time of 52.56. In the final itself she took the lead about 100 metres from the finish, apparently certain to win, but she was caught by Colette Besson of France just before the line, and beaten into second place by 0.09 seconds. Despite her potential, Board never got the opportunity to compete in another Olympic Games. In September 1969 she won the 800m with a superb race at the European Championships in Athens, winning by a clear eight metres over her rivals and setting a new championship record. She is still the only British woman to have won the title. She then tragically

developed colorectal cancer in 1970 and died in December of that year, aged just 22.

Every medal at Mexico City 1968 was incredibly hard earned and savoured accordingly. A couple of months after the Games, a story with interesting resonance for Britain's sporting future emerged. At the Mexico City 1968 Games, John Sherwood just sneaked in behind Hemery and Gerhard Hennige for a bronze medal – famously unnoticed by commentator David Coleman ('Hemery takes the gold, Hennige, of West Germany the silver and who cares who's third. It doesn't matter') – while his wife Sheila claimed a silver medal in the Long Jump. A promising couple by any criteria – yet on their return, as the winter set in and they set their sights on the 1969 European championships, there were simply

French athlete Colette Besson breaks the tape to win the women's 400m at the Mexico City Games on 20 October 1968. Lillian Board, of Britain, was second, and Natalya Pechonkina, of the Soviet Union, was third. Just over two years later, Board died aged 22.

no indoor facilities of any sort in Yorkshire where they lived. Eventually they resorted to transforming a long corridor at Myers Grove Comprehensive School in Sheffield, where Sheila worked, into an ad hoc running lane – here they could sprint and put down a few hurdles. Yet such resourceful, inventive stuff from the Sherwoods pinpointed the problems that British athletes faced. With limited funding and resources, it was becoming increasingly difficult to compete against the superpower nations – those devoting almost unlimited effort towards winning events at the Olympic Games.

But that is not quite the end of the story – for among the 12-year-olds watching grainy pictures of the Mexico City 1968 Games in a large school hall was a boy named Sebastian Coe. Nearly four decades later, in a speech to the IOC delegates, the defining moment of Britain's bid for the London 2012 Games, he recalled the impression it made on him. 'Two athletes from our home town were competing. John Sherwood won a bronze medal in the 400m Hurdles. His wife Sheila just narrowly missed gold in the Long Jump. By the time I was back in my classroom, I knew what I wanted to do – and what I wanted to be. Thirty-five years on, I stand before you with those memories still fresh. Still inspired by this great movement.' There are many unexpected links in Britain's long history of involvement with the Olympic and Paralympic Movements, but this was to prove one of the most significant.

Meanwhile the Paralympic Games also had problems to overcome during this period. The Mexican authorities felt they lacked the experience or expertise to stage the event in Mexico City, and the additional health issues posed by the extreme altitude were a major concern. After discussing the matter with the Paralympic Games organisers, Israel stepped into the breach. The 1968 Paralympic Games were promoted as both a celebration of the 20th anniversary of the first Stoke Mandeville Games, held on the day of the opening of the 1948 Olympic Games, and the 20th anniversary of the founding of the State of Israel.

Although the Opening Ceremony was staged at Tel Aviv, the Games themselves were held at nearby Ramat Gan, headquarters of Israel's Foundation for Handicapped Children. The scale of the event was tribute to the Games' success. In 1948 just 16 competitors from a single country had contested one sport at a hospital lawn in Buckinghamshire. In 1968 there were approximately 750 wheelchair athletes from 29 nations. Sir Ludwig Guttmann's dream of a truly international Paralympic Games, considered ridiculously grandiose by some, was beginning to be realised. And Britain was again to the fore, ranking second behind the USA with a total of 69 medals, 29 of which were gold.

One of Britain's medal winners was Davina Ingrams, 18th Baroness Darcy de Knayth and a direct descendent of Clive of India. She had married publisher Rupert Ingrams in 1960 and had three children, when she was involved in a car accident in 1964 that killed her husband and left her paralysed from the neck down. Stoke Mandeville played a huge part in Ingrams' rehabilitation; she won a place in Britain's Swimming team for the 1968 Games and proceeded to win a gold medal in the 25m Backstroke, followed by a bronze medal in Table Tennis at the 1972 Games, held in Heidelberg. After taking up her seat in the House of Lords in 1969, Ingrams became a powerful supporter of Britain's Paralympians, and of the Games in general. She was made a Dame for her services to people with disabilities in 1996.

After the Paralympic Games in Israel, Stoke Mandeville continued to develop its reputation as the world centre of Paralympic sport. The following year the Queen opened both the 21st anniversary Games and the newly constructed Stoke Mandeville Stadium, built at a cost of just over £350,000.

Medal table from the 1968 Paralympic Games

Country	Gold	Silver	Bronze	Total
USA	33	27	29	99
Great Britain	29	20	20	69
Israel	18	21	23	62
Australia	15	16	7	38
France	13	10	9	32
Federal Republic of Germany	12	12	11	35
Italy	12	10	17	39

Right An official poster from the Munich 1972 Games on display at the IOC Olympic Museum in Lausanne, Switzerland.

Far Right The incredible swimming star Mark Spitz, who won seven gold medals with seven world records at the Munich 1972 Games.

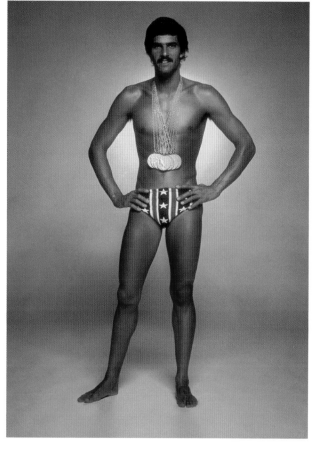

Olga Korbut

Her amazing acrobatics may have won her four gold medals at the Olympic Games, but it was her radiant smile and personality that won Olga Korbut millions of fans the world over and encouraged thousands of little girls to take up the sport. Born in Belarus, then part of the USSR, in 1955, Korbut started training as a gymnast when she was eight. At the Soviet national championships in 1969, she demonstrated a difficult backwards aerial somersault on the balance beam and a backflip-to-catch on the uneven bars. The latter was the first backward release move performed by a woman on the bars and became known as the Korbut Flip. At the Munich 1972 Games, Korbut won Individual gold in the Balance Beam and the Floor competition, and overall Team gold. However she made a mistake in her strongest event, the Uneven Bars, and had to be satisfied with silver. Korbut returned to the Olympic Games at Montreal 1976, but although she was part of the winning USSR team she failed to win an individual gold.

Munich 1972 Games

The Munich 1972 Olympic Games have left indelible memories for all the wrong reasons. Yet Germany, still recovering from the devastation of the Second World War, had tried hard to create a peaceful and welcoming atmosphere, with student security guards in floppy caps and quiet young Army conscripts serving as drivers and attendants. Jesse Owens, now working as a commentator with United Press International, was an honoured guest in the Media Centre, and an imaginatively designed stadium overlooked the new Olympic Park. As an event the Games were still growing healthily, attracting over 7,000 athletes from more than 120 nations. Men's Handball, Canoe Slalom and Kayaking made their debut as Olympic sports.

The 1972 Paralympic Games could not be held in Munich, but the German authorities, keen to maintain the momentum built up by the Stoke Mandeville International Games, offered the university town of Heidelberg as a more suitable venue. This time the Paralympic Games took place before the Olympic Games. Heidelberg rolled out the red carpet, erected a massive beer tent in which everybody congregated at the end of each day and promoted the Games locally under the banner '1000 competitors, 1000 winners' – although in reality there were 984 competitors, from 43 nations. Non-medal visually impaired events, such as Goalball and 100m Sprint, were introduced on an experimental basis and proved a great success. Britain again enjoyed a successful Games, winning 16 gold medals, 15 silver and 21 bronze to take third place in the medal table behind West Germany (first) and the USA (second).

Back in Munich the Olympic Games, prior to the terrorist attack with which they are always associated, proved a fascinating competition. American swimmer Mark Spitz dominated the Games with an astonishing seven gold medals, while 15-year-old Australian Shane Gould turned

Far Left A leaping Mary Peters on her way to gold in the Pentathlon at the Munich 1972 Games.

Left Mary Peters celebrates her Pentathlon win, flanked by silver medallist Heide Rosendahl of West Germany (left) and Burglinde Pollak of East Germany (right), who was third.

in an inspired performance to take three Swimming golds, a silver and a bronze. Another teenager, Olga Korbut, captivated millions as she helped the Soviet gymnastic team to its sixth straight Olympic title; she was aged only 17 and looked even younger. A last-minute replacement for an injured teammate, Korbut also won two individual gold medals and one silver, while the Soviet Union went on to head the medal table with an impressive tally of 99.

Intense rivalry between the East and West German Teams underlay many events, with Renate Stecher winning gold in the 100m and 200m and yet another teenager, 16-year-old Ulrike Meyfarth, delighting the Munich spectators with her High Jump gold. Home favourite Heide Rosendahl took gold medals in the Long Jump and 4 x 100m Relay, but was beaten into second place in the women's Pentathlon by Britain's Mary Peters. It was a wonderful win by Peters who did it the hard way from start to finish; she achieved personal bests in four of the five events and broke the world record en route.

Such gritty determination had been a feature of Peters' career. Born in Lancashire but living in Belfast, Northern Ireland from the age of 11, she suffered from a chronic lack of facilities in her adopted city; political tensions were rising and 'the Troubles' in the Province biting hard. She had represented Northern Ireland since 1958, and Munich was her third Olympic Games for Britain, with fourth place at Tokyo

> **'I wasn't daunted by the crowd, I rose to them. It was like being on stage at the theatre'**
>
> Mary Peters, Pentathlon gold medallist at the Munich 1972 Games

Best of British

Mary Peters

For some, glory comes early in their sporting careers; for a very few, it comes at the end. Mary Peters falls into the second category. Munich 1972 was Peters' third and last Games. She had been fourth in the Pentathlon at Toyko 1964, and ninth at Mexico City 1968, but in Munich everything came together. On day one, the 33-year-old, set personal bests in the hurdles, shot put and high jump, ending up in the lead with an impressive 301 points. The next day, however, a poor performance in the long jump cut her lead, meaning that everything rested on the 200m. This was Heide Rosendahl's event and the West Germany was running in front of her home crowd, so Peters knew she would have to run a personal best to keep her dreams of a gold medal alive. She did just that, clocking 24.08, to finish second behind Rosendahl who won in 22.96. There was an agonising wait until the results were announced. Peters had won by 10 points and her total of 4801 was a new world record! Finally, Mary Peters was able to take her place on the podium and receive Britain's only Athletics gold of the Games.

New events

The Munich 1972 Games saw the appearance of some new events and the return of some old friends.

Archery, which featured four times between 1900 and 1920, made a reappearance after 52 years.

Handball debuted in 1936 but was then excluded until 1972.

Canoe Slalom was first held in 1972.

Badminton and Water Skiing made their first appearances at an Olympic Games as demonstration sports.

1964 being her best performance to date. It was now or never for 33-year-old Peters, who had viewed herself primarily as a team support to Mary Rand in previous Games. In Munich she responded with the competition of her life to defeat her great friend Rosendahl by 10 points – the equivalent of just a 10th of a second in that final 200m race. It was Rosendahl's specialist discipline, but this was Mary Peters' day. Peters set a world record of 4,801 points and became the third British woman to take an Olympic Athletics gold medal (following in the footsteps of Mary Rand and Ann Packer). Afterwards she still wasn't sure whether she had taken gold. 'I couldn't work it out, I couldn't do the maths,' she recalled. 'Not even a simple subtraction. Then someone came and put an arm around me. I turned and saw that it was Heide Rosendahl, and she had the answer written in her face. The gold medal was on its way to Belfast.'

Britain also played a significant part in the outcome of the men's Basketball final, even though this was between the USA and the Soviet Union. The intervention of the International Basketball Federation (FIBA) Secretary General Renato William Jones made a crucial contribution to the USA's dramatic defeat by the Soviet Union. The Italian-born son of a Scottish father, William Jones was a British national who had been brought up in Germany and the USA. He was a huge figure in the world of basketball, serving for decades as Secretary General of FIBA, the world-governing authority. FIBA was often seen as being European-orientated and involved in a power battle with the American NBA. William Jones was also Patron of the Amateur Basketball Association of England.

Later christened the 'War on the Floor', the final started just before midnight local time (at the request of American television companies which were transmitting the match live). The dramatic finish had the USA trailing 49-48 when their player Doug Collins was fouled with three seconds left. Two free

Dwight Jones of the USA tips off against Alexander Belov of Russia during the controversial men's Basketball final on 9 September at the Munich 1972 Games. There were astonishing scenes in the final seconds of the game, when the USA thought they had won before a timing device was re-set and the Soviet Union took the title.

throws were awarded and Collins, still shaken from the tough challenge, which saw him almost knocked out on the basketball stanchion, scored two points from them. This gave the USA the lead, and the Soviet Union quickly restarted the game, attacking without threat down the right-hand side of the court. With just one second left, however, the referee, Brazil's Renato Righetto, noticed an argument at the timekeepers' table and called an administrative time-out. Soviet officials claimed they had requested a time-out during the free throws, although according to the law they had called it too late. Missed time-outs are not unknown in basketball, but this was a critical match and tempers flared. Righetto ordered play to continue with one second on the clock. The Soviet Union were unable to win and the Americans started celebrating victory. They had never lost a Basketball game in the history of the Games, and had previously secured 62 consecutive wins.

At this point William Jones, a man who ruled the global game outside of the NBA with a rod of iron, came down from the stands (where he may have had a better view of events). He was also an accomplished linguist – not insignificant as the Soviet officials were complaining that the language barrier (they spoke poor English, the referee Portuguese and the timekeepers German) had been a factor in the time-out being missed. Despite having no official role in the match William Jones insisted that play should have been restarted with three seconds on the clock. After a long delay the two teams lined up yet again, the Soviets having had time to concoct a last-ditch plan between long-pass specialist Ivan Edeshko and centre Alexander Belov. Edeshko threw a full-court pass direct to Belov who, according to some, pushed one of the American defenders before completing a simple lay-up to win the match.

Uproar ensued. Referee Righetto refused to sign the official score sheet saying the finish had been 'irregular'; he was extremely unhappy that the time-out decision had been taken out of his hands. Eventually William Jones decreed that a five-man committee chaired by Hungary's Ferenc Hepp should rule on the matter. Poland and Cuba unsurprisingly supported the Soviet Union while Italy and Puerto

"I don't want to lose this game later tonight sitting on my butt'

Hank Ibia, head coach for the USA Basketball team, in the confused Olympic final later known as the 'War on the Floor'

'I devise and bequeath at my death that my wife Rita and children Jill and Bryan and their descendants never accept a silver medal from the 1972 Olympic Games in Munich, West Germany'

Kenneth Davis, captain of the defeated Basketball team in the 1972 Olympic final

Rico voted firmly for the USA, leaving Hepp to cast the deciding vote in favour of the Soviet Union. None of the Americans collected their medals and some, such as captain Kenny Davis, later made wills insisting that no family member be allowed to accept silver medals on their behalf after their deaths. Britain may not have much of an Olympic Basketball history, but William Jones' intervention is still discussed whenever fans of the sport gather.

Yet such Cold War skirmishes were put into perspective by the horrific attack that took place on the Israeli team in the Olympic Village. Eight members of Black September, a wing of the Palestine Liberation Organisation, climbed the Village fence at around 3am on 5 September and forced their way into the Israeli accommodation block. Two of the team, weightlifter Yossef Romano and a wrestling coach, Moshe Weinberg, held up the terrorists for precious seconds, in which many of the team and officials escaped, before they were shot dead. Nine hostages were taken and tense negotiations began.

Everybody of a certain age in Britain remembers something of the Munich Massacre, as it was later called. News started filtering out early on the morning of 5 September, with the severity of the situation seeming to develop hour by hour. All day, television cameras tracked events, featuring chilling images of hooded terrorists on the accommodation block balcony. The BBC's office overlooked Connolly Strasse, the street housing the Israeli

A pin from the Munich 1972 Olympic Games, with the Olympic Rings above the Munich 1972 Emblem. Otl Aicher's timeless symbol represents a crown of rays of light.

Medal table from the 1972 Olympic Games

Country	Gold	Silver	Bronze	Total
USSR	49	27	22	98
USA	32	30	30	92
German Democratic Republic	20	23	23	66
Federal Republic of Germany	13	11	16	40
Japan	13	8	8	29
Australia	8	7	2	17
Poland	7	5	9	21
Great Britain (12th position)	4	5	9	18

'We were extremely isolated from it all ... You are in a cocoon and you do not know the significance of anything'

Brendan Foster, member of the British team at the 1972 Games, describes competitors' confusion as the Munich disaster unfolded

Medal table from the 1972 Paralympic Games

Country	Gold	Silver	Bronze	Total
Federal Republic of Germany	28	17	22	67
USA	17	27	30	74
Great Britain	16	15	21	52
South Africa	16	12	13	41
Netherlands	14	13	11	38
Poland	14	12	7	33
France	10	8	15	33

Opposite page

On 6 September 1972, the Olympic Flag flying at half-mast in the Olympic Stadium in Munich during the memorial service for the 11 members of the Israeli team who were killed by terrorists the previous day.

accommodation block, and commentator David Coleman drew a vast audience. He later recalled putting in a 16-hour shift in front of BBC cameras as the story developed, played out live in the rolling news coverage that we take for granted today. At least two British reporters, Doug Ibbotson and Gerald Seymour, managed to get into the Village and provided a stream of dramatic eyewitness updates.

For competitors, such as 24-year-old Brendan Foster, information was initially scant. There were no televisions in the athletes' rooms, so Foster only discovered that something was going on when officials tried to stop him re-entering the Village after a morning run. He climbed over a fence instead and went on to breakfast, where the situation became apparent. Like the rest of the world, athletes relied on television for information; Foster has described it as being, 'in a cocoon... you do not know the significance of anything'. All the competitors could do was speculate and try to make plans. Foster, together with fellow athletes American Jim Ryun and Kenyan Kipchoge 'Kip' Keino, determined that if the Games were cancelled they would run a 1500m race on the warm-up track.

The press at the Games knew little more as Murray Hedgcock, a member of the Games reporting team for Australia's News Limited, remembers, '...inside the compound there was little news. Here again was the hazard of the news reporter, able only to be in one place at one time. People back in Britain watching television knew far more than we did'. British newspapers were also struggling to cover a fiendishly difficult developing story. Soon after midnight they heard

apparent confirmation that the hostages were safe and the terrorists killed or captured – welcome news that quickly went round the world. Then, after all the late editions had gone, as Murray Hedgcock remembers, the terrible truth emerged. 'At 3am those of us inside the still-closed Village were called to a press conference, in a big bare room. We stood in a circle around a group of politicians, police officers and Games officials, to be told in stunned silence by the Bavarian Interior Minister, Bruno Merk, that all nine remaining hostages, five terrorists and a policeman had been killed.' The rescue attempt at Fürstenfeldbruck, a military airport just outside Munich, had gone disastrously wrong.

When the bloody denouement to events was eventually revealed many felt that the Games should be cancelled there and then. Among them was Willi Daume, president of the Munich Olympic Games Organising Committee. Athletes were divided: some felt overwhelmed by the tragedy while others were more determined than ever to continue. Avery Brundage, the president of the IOC, and other IOC members decided that the Games should go on – a decision fully supported by the Israeli authorities. A memorial service was held at the Athletics stadium on the following day. Then, just 34 hours after the terrorists first climbed over the fence of the Olympic Village, the Games recommenced.

Yet, as Brendan Foster, who came fifth in the 1500m observed, nothing would be the same again. 'Before 1972 the Olympics was a celebration of sport, like a party. But after 1972 it became extremely serious... a world phenomenon.'

'Come and look at all these tanks around the fencing, I wonder what they're for?'
Janet Simpson, British Olympic team member, voicing general bewilderment in the early hours of the Munich disaster

Montreal 1976 Olympic Games

Security at the Montreal Olympic Games four years later was inevitably tight, but events ran like clockwork

Lasse Virén

The 'Flying Finns', middle- and long-distance runners, had dominated their events during the first decades of the twentieth century. Names such as Hannes Kolehmainen, Paavo Nurmi and Ville Ritola had won Athletics gold medals at multiple Games. But Finnish supremacy of the sport had been in abeyance for some years before Lasse Virén came on the scene. A policeman from Myrskylä in the south of Finland, Virén started running as a hobby. He chose his competitions carefully, working hard to be in peak condition for the Olympic Games: 'Times were different then. It was not a full time profession and you were not running for money'. After winning the 5000m and 10,000m at Munich 1972 he repeated his success at Montreal 1976 – the first and only man to win the double twice.

and it was in many ways a success. The financial burden imposed on the city was severe, however, with Montreal citizens making up the shortfall for decades afterwards. Only in 2006 was the main stadium finally fully paid for, 30 years after its construction.

Politics again impacted on competing nations, with 28 African countries and Guyana from South America boycotting the Games. They were protesting at the IOC's refusal to ban New Zealand, following the All Blacks rugby team's tour of South Africa, then governed by an oppressive apartheid regime, in 1976. Britain, who maintained close links to South Africa through rugby and cricket, kept its head down – the British and Irish Lions rugby team had toured South Africa in 1974 and would do so again in 1980. The decision of rugby authorities to keep sporting links open played a large part in encouraging British athletes to attend both the 1976

and 1980 Games, although political pressure was significantly greater in the latter following the Soviet Union's invasion of Afghanistan in 1979.

It was to be a Games of surprises, with outstanding performances in several fields. Romanian gymnast Nadia Comaneci, aged only 14, became an icon for a generation of schoolgirls too young to remember Olga Korbut; she took three gold medals, including one for the prestigious All Around event, and received seven 'perfect 10' scores – baffling the electronic scoreboard in the process. (This unfortunate piece of technology, not programmed to show a perfect score, resorted to displaying 1.00.) The American Boxing team, one of the strongest in the history of the Games, carried all before it, with five great competitors – Sugar Ray Leonard, Leon Spinks, Michael Spinks, Leo Randolph and Howard Davis Jr – taking golds. Swimming was dominated

by two countries: East Germany winning all but two of the women's gold medals and America all but one of the men's. Meanwhile the great Finnish runner Lasse Virén repeated his Munich 1972 success with consecutive gold medals in the 5000m and 10,000m. A police officer, he had fallen in the 10,000m final in Munich, but still recovered to win the race and break a seven-year-old world record. There was to be no such drama in 1976, however, where Virén won both events with ease. He became the first man ever to win the 5000m in consecutive Games, but a disappointing (for him) fifth in the Marathon – run only 18 hours after the 5000m final – left Czech runner Emil Zátopek's record of three golds in 1952 intact.

Canada, the host, suffered mixed fortunes; it won five silver and six bronze medals but became the first host of a Summer Games to take no golds at all. (Australia also failed to win a single gold, leading to the foundation of the Australian Institute of Sport, a world-class training facility responsible for much of the country's more recent international success.) For Britain the Montreal 1976 Games was to prove particularly disappointing in Athletics. Only a single medal was gained from track and field events, in those days still an amateur sport. Brendan Foster, in his second Olympic Games, took bronze in the 10,000m, which was won by the legendary Lasse Virén. Bronze was not what Foster wanted, and he swiftly stuffed the medal into a drawer in the room he shared with teammate Steve Ovett (then a European 800m silver medallist who went on to finish fifth in the Olympic final). At the end of the Games Foster was still the only British athlete to have made the podium – and it was hard to believe that a golden age of British athletics lay just around the corner.

The overwhelming 'good news' story for Britain in 1976 was served up in the swimming pool by David Wilkie. Sri Lankan-born, American-trained but Scottish to the core, he destroyed a world-

'... the most beautiful fluid technique, powered by the strongest legs in swimming. It was like watching a periscope cut through the water'

'... a man of steel in the pool. Once he started taking the sport and his event seriously, it was always a matter of who would finish second'

both David Haller, coach to Olympic gold medallist David Wilkie

Top left Magnificent. A perfect 10 score, although the scoreboard was unable to show it, as Romanian Gymnastics champion Nadia Comaneci celebrates after the acrobatic compulsory at Uneven Bars at Montreal 1976.

Top right A glorious day for Britain as Scotland's David Wilkie wins gold in the 200m Breaststroke at Montreal 1976 after taking silver four years earlier at Munich 1972. He finished second in the 100m Breaststroke at Montreal 1976 as well.

Opposite page

Double Olympic Sailing gold medallist Rodney Pattisson carries the flag for Great Britain at the Opening Ceremony of the Montreal 1976 Olympic Games on 17 July 1976.

class field to win the 200m Breaststroke gold medal, breaking the world record by more than three seconds as he did so. No British Olympic Swimming gold medal has come close, either in quality or impact. The only non-American to win gold in the men's Swimming in Canada, Wilkie's swim was unanimously voted the performance of the Games; it is still spoken of with awe in swimming circles. He retired a month later at the age of 22, a youngster by today's standards, but his timing was impeccable.

Wilkie was very much of his time and something of a cult figure: his distinctive long hair, moustache, trademark goggles and swimming cap made him instantly recognisable. He was in fact the first male swimmer to wear either goggles or a cap in competition – the former to combat a lifelong allergy to chlorinated water and the second to tuck away his locks and to help his streamlining. Wilkie's victory in Montreal was far from unexpected as he had won the previous two World Championships and remained undefeated at 200m breaststroke for four years. Yet the majesty of his triumph still took everybody by surprise. In one day everything came together. Wilkie finally married technique and strength in such perfect union that the existing world-record holder, America's John Hencken, was left treading water.

David Haller was Wilkie's coach in Britain, while Charlie Hodgson supervised his training in America. Haller seems to have been one of the few who sniffed something special in the air. He was astounded by Wilkie's performances in training during the months leading up to the Olympic Games. The Scot, both

> ## 'The emotion of winning an Olympic gold medal is like getting all your Christmas presents wrapped up in one'
>
> David Wilkie reflects on Olympic Swimming gold

arms holding a float, would reel off a 'legs only' 200m breaststroke in 2:40, and repeat the exercise in sets of 10. Even today you would struggle to find anybody to match that.

'He was absolutely phenomenal. His swim in 1976 is still probably the greatest individual performance I have witnessed,' insists Haller. 'Of course these days you are allowed to duck your head under the surface and can go even quicker, but David is still comfortably the best the event has ever seen. And such a gentleman, possibly the nicest bloke I have met. Never a cross word at training, just working together quietly – but a man of steel in the pool. Once he started taking the sport and his event seriously, it was always a matter of who would finish second.'

Down the final length Wilkie's swim turned into a commanding performance, as he later acknowledged. It was a race against the clock and he deliberately took his time in checking the result, revelling in anticipation of a good score. 'I wanted to capture the whole glory of the moment and finding out my time was going to be the icing on the cake... And when I did look around and saw 2:15.11 on the scoreboard I couldn't believe it. When you have broken the world record and your own best by more than three seconds, it's a great feeling.' He later confessed to waving only at those in the crowd sporting British flags, despite his debt to the intensive training in Miami. 'A lot of people looked on me as being very American and perhaps I was scared to take their acclaim, even though I shall be eternally grateful for what Miami did to me. But I wanted to show the British supporters that I was swimming for Britain and that I was proud to be British.'

Elsewhere all the drama centred on the Modern

Best of British

David Wilkie

Born in Sri Lanka to Scottish parents, David Wilkie returned to Scotland to go to boarding school. It was then that he joined the Warrender Baths Club, a Victorian pool that Wilkie described as 'like swimming in the Forth. It was choppy; it was cold.' His first medal in an international competition was at the 1970 Commonwealth Games, held in Edinburgh, when he won a bronze in the 200m Breaststroke. Many were surprised at the 16-year-old's success, including Wilkie himself who said, 'I was a total amateur in those days. I hardly trained. I didn't know what to expect – I really didn't know what swimming was all about, competing at that level.' At the Munich 1972 Games, he came from nowhere to win silver in the 200m Breaststroke, in the process coming to the attention of the University of Miami who offered him a sports scholarship. There followed years of intensive training and study in Florida. The effort paid off. At Montreal 1976, Wilkie was untouchable in the 200m Breaststroke, knocking more than three seconds off the world record. Of the 13 men's gold medallists in the Swimming events, Wilkie was the only non-American.

Pentathlon competition, firstly with the exposé by the British Press of one of the greatest scandals in the history of the Games, and then with the unexpected gold medal by the British team on the final afternoon. On the first day the British captain, Jim Fox, was mystified that his opponent in the fencing section of the event, Boris Onishchenko, seemed to be registering scores on the automatic electronic device without actually hitting him. Fox knew Onishchenko very well; they had become firm friends after a decade of fierce opposition, during which time he had no cause to doubt the Russian, but on this occasion Onishchenko's 'scoring' when he had not landed a hit was so flagrant that Fox and the British delegation felt compelled to make an official complaint. An extraordinary deception was revealed. Onishchenko had wired his sword so that it could trigger the electronic scoring system with his hand and register a hit at will.

Boris was immediately dubbed 'Disonischenko' or 'Boris the Cheat' by the British media. He was disqualified from the event and thrown out of the Games. Meanwhile Britain kept ticking over quietly, going into the final day and last event, a 4km cross country run, in fifth place and with an outside chance of a bronze medal. Or so they thought. Adrian Parker, a music company director from Croydon, then ran the race of his life to finish first, Danny Nightingale pushed hard to come fourth and the 34-year-old Fox responded with an incredible effort to finish sixth. From nowhere Britain had advanced to not only win a medal, but to take gold – the most dramatic final-day turnaround in Modern Pentathlon history.

Yet Fox had mixed feelings about exposing his former friend, for whose situation he felt some responsibility. In a typical moment of generosity he told Doug Ibbotson of the *Evening News* that he wished a simpler solution had been possible. 'I wish I had just taken him outside and punched him on the nose. Then it would have been over and forgotten… and we would have been friends again.' In the

Medal table from the 1976 Olympic Games				
Country	Gold	Silver	Bronze	Total
USSR	45	40	35	130
German Democratic Republic	40	25	25	90
USA	33	35	25	93
Federal Republic of Germany	10	11	16	37
Japan	9	6	10	25
Poland	7	6	13	26
Bulgaria	6	9	7	22
Great Britain (13th position)	3	5	5	13

Left Boris Onishchenko of the Soviet Union takes a breather during practice as he prepares for the fencing event of the Modern Pentathlon competition at the Munich 1972 Games. Four years later, he was disqualified for cheating during a clash in the fencing with Britain's Jim Fox. Onishchenko's Epee had an illegal device that registered a score without a strike being made.

Medal table from the 1976 Paralympic Games

Country	Gold	Silver	Bronze	Total
USA	66	44	45	155
Netherlands	45	25	14	84
Israel	40	13	16	69
Federal Republic of Germany	37	34	26	97
Great Britain	29	29	36	94
Canada	25	26	26	77
Poland	24	17	12	53

Medal table from the 1980 Olympic Games

Country	Gold	Silver	Bronze	Total
USSR	75	66	45	186
German Democratic Republic	46	37	42	125
Bulgaria	8	16	16	40
Cuba	8	7	5	20
Italy	8	3	4	15
Hungary	7	10	15	32
Romania	6	6	13	25
Great Britain 9th position	5	7	9	21

complex world of the modern Olympic Games, this was sadly no longer an option.

The authorities in Montreal, already under huge financial pressure in trying to deliver the main Olympic Games, were not in a position to stage a Paralympic Games. However, Toronto City Council and the State Government of Ontario stepped in and provided $1 million funding to ensure the Paralympic Games at least took place in Canada. They too came under considerable pressure not to support an event featuring a team from South Africa, a country banned from the Olympic Games because of the policies of its apartheid regime. For a time it appeared the Canadians would withdraw their financial support from the Games, but Dr Guttmann spent long hours gently persuading them to stay on board.

He succeeded, but the South Africans were not thereafter allowed to compete at the Paralympic Games until 1992.

These were the last Paralympic Games that Guttmann was to attend. He suffered a heart attack in November 1979 and died in March 1980, some months before the Arnhem 1980 Games. His pipedream had expanded dramatically, and was growing all the time. The 1976 Games featured more than 1,600 athletes from 40 countries, including , for the first time, amputees and visually impaired athletes. York and Toronto Universities were used to accommodate the athletes, while fleets of specially adapted buses provided the transport. The Paralympic Games were becoming a very slick operation – and were attracting large audiences. In 1976 over 25,000 fans attended the opening ceremony at the Woodbine Race Track.

Britain garnered a remarkable 94 medals in 1976 (29 gold, 29 silver and 36 bronze). Such was the growth of the Paralympic Games, however, that this haul was only good enough for fifth place in the medal table behind USA, Netherlands, Israel and West Germany. In British terms the Games were

notable mainly for the first appearance, at the age of 31, of Mike Kenny, a highly talented athlete who went on to win a total of 16 gold medals before retiring in 1988. In Toronto Kenny helped himself to three gold medals – the 25m Freestyle, Backstroke and Breaststroke in the 1A category – a hat-trick he would go on to repeat four years later at the 1980 Paralympic Games, held at Papendal close to Arnhem in Holland.

In total, Britain would win 5 gold medals at the 1980 Games, but a total of 21 (7 silver and 9 bronze) brought only ninth place in the medal table. In the Paralympic competition over 3,000 medals would be on offer, and 1973 athletes from 42 nations would compete for them. South Africa would not attend, following the Dutch government's decision that the country's apartheid policies made its presence 'undesirable' – the first time that it did not participate in the Paralympic Games since 1964.

There were to be several new developments at the 1980 Paralympic Games as the event continued to evolve. For the first time cerebral palsy athletes would compete (125 in total) and the four major disability groups would be clarified as amputee athletes, visually impaired athletes, cerebral palsy athletes and wheelchair athletes. Sitting Volleyball was to be admitted to the Paralympic programme, with the host nation, the Netherlands, winning gold by a 3-0 victory over Sweden. Thirteen sports were to feature in the 1980 programme (Archery, Athletics, Dartchery, Goalball, Lawn Bowls, Shooting, Swimming, Table Tennis, Volleyball, Weightlifting, Wheelchair Basketball, Wheelchair Fencing and Wrestling), each represented by its international sports federation and united in one venue for the first time.

Moscow 1980

To go to the Moscow 1980 Olympic Games or not? That was the stark question confronting British

Left The Opening Ceremony of the Moscow 1980 Games with performers making a human tower. It was a controversial Games that was overshadowed by the USA's boycott because of the Soviet Unions's invasion of Afghanistan.

political pressure to withdraw. Jimmy Carter, by then the outgoing American President, had called for a mass boycott of the Moscow 1980 Games in late 1979, and Britain's Prime Minister, Margaret Thatcher, agreed. She wrote in the strongest terms to Fellows, stressing that, 'the Games will serve the propaganda needs of the Soviet government', making participation by British athletes 'against British interests and wrong'. Another concern, not widely discussed at the time, surrounded the plight of many Jews in the Soviet Union whom, it was claimed, were not being allowed to leave to start new lives elsewhere. The BOA received many letters from British Jews asking them to consider a boycott on those grounds also. The boycott issue was debated for six hours in Parliament and the Foreign Secretary, Lord Carrington, held numerous meetings with the BOA, even travelling to Lausanne in an attempt to persuade the IOC to change the venue of the Games. He did not succeed.

It was a complex situation with no easy resolution. Taking everything into account, Fellows and Palmer opted for a democratic mandate. The BOA invited its constituent organisations – the separate governing bodies of Britain's Olympic sports – to vote on the matter. The result was that 15 sports voted for definitely attending the Games with just one, Hockey, voting in favour of a boycott. Four sports, Fencing, Equestrian, Swimming and Yachting, abstained, but were happy to accept the consensus.

Fellows announced the decision by saying, 'We believe sport should be a bridge not a destroyer'. Britain's athletes had themselves decided to attend

'I have a 90 per cent chance of winning the 1500m'

Steve Ovett, shortly before the start of the 1980 Moscow Games

The cuddly bear Misha, mascot of the 1980 Olympic Games, delighted audiences around the world.

competitors in 1980, after the Soviet Union's invasion of Afghanistan the previous year. In the end 65 nations within the Olympic Family decided to boycott the event by way of protest, but Britain was not among them. The debate raged fiercely at the time and it is possible to argue that both sides emerged with honour. In hindsight the 1980 Games provided an opportunity for Britain to show democratic support for the Olympic Movement, and to surmount international tensions with some quite extraordinary sporting achievements.

Dennis Fellows, chairman of the British Olympic Association (BOA), and his chief executive Dick Palmer were well aware that there was a genuine matter that needed to be addressed, but they resisted

Right A sporting legend in Britain, Duncan Goodhew showing off his gold medal after winning the 100m Breaststroke at the Moscow 1980 Games.

Best of British

Sharron Davies

Born in Plymouth, Devon, Sharron Davies learnt to swim by the age of five, and was training seriously before she was eight. A child prodigy, she swam for Britain aged only 11 and competed in the Montreal 1976 Games at just 13 – the youngest member of the team. In 1978, at the Commonwealth Games in Canada, she won two gold medals and set a new Commonwealth record in the 200m Individual Medley. Two years later at Moscow 1980, Davies (now, aged 17, a veteran of the Games) took the silver medal in the 400m Individual Medley behind Petra Schneider. The East German has since admitted being part of a state-run systematic doping programme, but Davies's calls for a reallocation of medals and titles from this period have so far fallen on deaf ears. For the following nine years Davies retired from Swimming and worked on her career in the media. She returned to the pool in 1989 and competed at the Barcelona 1992 Games. Things had gone full circle as time, aged 29, she was the oldest swimmer on the team!

although, of course, any individual was free to withdraw and make their own protest that way. Some significant changes were also made. British competitors did not attend the Opening Ceremony, Olympic Flags replaced the Union Jack on the podium and the national anthem was not played for the nation's five gold medal winners.

It was to prove a strange Games. Revealing tensions emerged within the Soviet bloc, with East German and Polish competitors being relentlessly booed by Russian fans. The Cold War attitudes continued until the Closing Ceremony, with Soviet officials declining to raise the Stars and Stripes of the USA. Instead they hoisted the flag of Los Angeles, the next Host City – an action perceived as an insult at the time, although it has now become the norm.

One area in which Margaret Thatcher appears in retrospect over-strident lay in her inference that Moscow 1980 would be an 'inferior' and vastly devalued Games. In a letter to Fellows she wrote that 'As a sporting event, the Games cannot now satisfy the aspirations of our sportsmen and women... Medals won at Moscow will be of inferior worth and the ceremonies a charade... the Games will not be worthy of the name Olympics'. Although only 80 nations competed, those countries between them had accounted for 71 per cent of the gold medals awarded at the Montreal 1976 Olympic Games. The Moscow 1980 Games may have been controversial, but the quality of the action and the medals won cannot be seriously called into question. New Olympic records were set 241 times over the Games, and world records were beaten 97 times. Certainly Britain's modest total of five golds was to come from some of the country's greatest ever Olympians.

Boycott or no boycott, Britain was always going to be a force to be reckoned with at Athletics in Moscow. As it turned out athletes took four of the five British golds, with swimmer Duncan Goodhew taking the fifth. Daley Thompson was imperious in

the Decathlon, although his finest moment was to come four years later in Los Angeles. Irresistibly talented, he probably approximated more closely to the ancient Greek ideal of the all-round athlete than any modern Olympian. Scottish runner Allan Wells landed an unlikely gold in the 100m – the last time white runners have appeared in the final, let alone won the event. His achievements in Moscow are often qualified with the observation that top American sprinters were not present because of the boycott, but this is unfair to the powerful Scot. 1980 was by no means a golden era for American sprinting, and both before Moscow and in the season following the Games Wells regularly defeated the best Americans – Mel Lattany, Stanley Floyd, Harvey Glance and a young Carl Lewis before his glory years. Wells actually ran his best 100m race in the semi-final, with a then British record of 10.11, but the final was, as often happens, a much tenser affair. By 60 metres it was a two-horse race between Wells and the Cuban Silvio Leonard, and it became the closest 100m for 28 years. An extreme 'dip' from Wells clinched gold by the narrowest of margins, and

Left Backed by the screams of his wife and coach Margot, Allan Wells produces the performance of his life to win the 100m at Moscow 1980 – running from the outside lane.

both athletes were credited with the same winning time, 10.25. After the race an emotional Wells, the first British 100m winner since Harold Abrahams, said he was actually thinking of Eric Liddell, the great Scottish runner of 60 years before.

Duncan Goodhew, famous for his bald head (a medical condition rather than cosmetic streamlining), won two Swimming medals at the Moscow 1980 Games – bronze for the 4 x 100m Medley Relay and gold for the 100m Breaststroke, in which he beat the strong Soviet favourite, Arsens Miskarovs, into second place by half a second. The women's events were dominated by East Germany who won 11 out of 13 gold medals, but Britain's Sharron Davies won silver in the 400m Individual Medley, as did the women's team in the 4 x 100m Medley Relay.

However, the Swimming star of the Games was the Soviet Union's Vladimir Salnikov, who took three golds and became the first swimmer in history to break the 15-minute barrier in the 1500m Freestyle. He missed the Los Angeles 1984 Games because of a reciprocal boycott, but regained the 1500m Freestyle title at Seoul in 1988.

East Germany also dominated the Rowing competition, taking an astonishing 11 gold medals out of 14 events. The East German men almost achieved a clean sweep by winning seven out of eight events, while the women won four out of six – including surprise victories over the Soviet Union who had triumphed in the last two Olympic Games. Britain's great Rowing achievement was a silver medal in the Rowing Eights, a remarkable feat from a team that had never before rowed together before the Olympic trials and had only 10 weeks to prepare for the Games. The stroke, Richard Stanhope, had never stroked an eight-man shell before, and the team were disadvantaged in the final when their steering broke, but they still finished a very creditable 0.74 seconds behind a strong East German crew.

Yet for many – not only British fans – the 1980 Games is best remembered for the epic, head-to-head Athletics battles between Britons Steve Ovett and Sebastian Coe. The media presented the two men as a clash of opposites, although neither public image was entirely correct and both possessed one or two qualities attributed to the other. However, they were

Best of British

Allan Wells

Allan Wells was a former triple and long jumper who switched events mid-career. An idiosyncratic figure who went about Athletics his own way, Wells attributed much of his impressive upper body strength to the extensive use of a boxer's speed ball and punch bag in training. He was also the first top athlete to start wearing the lycra style cycling shorts that have now become commonplace, but at the time caused quite a stir. His wife, Margot, herself a former Scottish 100m and 100m hurdle champion, organised his training with military precision and they very much took on the world as a team. Following his win in the 100m at the Moscow 1980 Games, Wells prepared for the 200m. This was a high quality race featuring the legendary Jamaican Don Quarrie and the then world record holder Pietro Mennea of Italy. The latter eventually by only 0.02 seconds with Wells clinging on to take silver and claim another British record with a time of 20.21. After retiring from athletics Wells continued to work as a systems engineer and also coached the GB Bobsleigh squad.

Coe and Ovett: Rivals and Records

The rivalry between Sebastian Coe and Steve Ovett was legendary. The British pair dominated middle-distance running in the late 1970s and first half of the 1980s, trading records like football stickers. In a remarkable 41 days in 1979, Coe set new word records for the 800m, 1500m and mile. Going into the Moscow 1980 Games, however, Ovett had broken Coe's mile record, and it was Ovett who drew first blood at the Games, beating Coe to win gold in the latter's favoured 800. Six days later their positions were reversed, when Coe took gold in Ovett's preferred 1500m – a title he was to retain four years later at Los Angeles 1984. After the Moscow 1980 Games their rivalry continued. In a remarkable 10 days in 1981, between them they traded the world record for the mile three times, Coe being the eventual winner with a time of 3:47.33.

Medal table from the 1980 Paralympic Games

Country	Gold	Silver	Bronze	Total
USA	74	66	54	195
Poland	74	50	52	177
Federal Republic of Germany	68	48	46	162
Canada	47	32	21	100
Great Britain	47	32	21	100
Netherlands	33	31	36	100
Sweden	31	36	24	91

Opposite page

Sebastian Coe (centre) celebrates his 1500m gold medal at Moscow 1980 with British teammate Steve Ovett (right), bronze medal-winner here and 800m champion, and East German Jürgen Straub (left), who took silver.

undoubtedly the greatest middle distance runners of their era. Each had a beautiful, fluid, economical style of running – dissimilar, but both close to perfection in their different ways. You didn't need the stopwatch to know you were watching timeless genius when Coe or Ovett were racing.

When they met twice on the biggest stage, in Moscow, the nation stopped and held its breath. The 800m and 1500m events were pieces of great sporting theatre, following on from two years of apparent intense rivalry. In 1979 Coe set an amazing three world records in just 41 days, for the 800m, 1500m and one mile. Prior to the Games, Ovett broke the mile record and equalled Coe's 1500m time, becoming the favourite for the latter event in Moscow. Such predictions were famously turned on their head when both Coe and Ovett lost the Olympic finals they were 'meant' to win and triumphed in the race they were tipped to lose. These moments of human drama defined the Olympic Games for a whole generation. Thirty years on, people can still remember where they were as those races were run, so great was their impact at the time.

As the world record holder – with a phenomenal time of 1:41.73 that remained unbeaten until 1997 and would have won world and Olympic gold medals 30 years on – Coe was clearly the man to defeat in the 800m. Yet on the day, by his own admission, he ran the worst tactical race of his life. Ovett, second favourite and tactically adroit in any middle-distance race, could hardly believe his luck as

'I chose this day of all days to run the worst race of my life'

Sebastian Coe after finishing second to rival Steve Ovett in the 800m – his best event

'Perhaps somebody, somewhere, loves me after all'

Sebastian Coe on why he looked to the sky on the podium as he celebrated winning the 1500m at Moscow 1980 a few days after his 800m silver medal

he cruised home impressively, leaving Coe to take silver.

There followed the most testing three days of Coe's athletics career as he tried to recover from the shock of defeat and prepare himself for the heats, semi-final and eventually the final of the 1500m. At one stage, in despair, he started talking about withdrawing from the race but was talked out of that by Daley Thompson and others. Eventually he regained his composure and set about the task of defeating Ovett, who had reeled off 45 consecutive wins over three years in 1500m and mile races, using his tactical mastery and withering finishing speed to good effect.

Ovett was confident, not only of winning the 1500m but of taking as much as four seconds off the world record. Coe, on the other hand, had run only eight 1500m races in the last four years. Yet once again, expectation was overturned. Coe gloriously redeemed himself by running a tactically perfect race to win with some ease, covering the last 800m in just 1:49. He collapsed briefly to the ground after the finish with the emotion of it all and then, after a brief embrace with third-placed Steve Ovett, set off on his lap of honour.

For Britain, the rivalry of Coe and Ovett was a powerful symbol of how much Olympic medals still mattered. Despite the turmoil of the last decade, the Games had moved beyond politics to become a compelling showcase of sporting endeavour.

Chapter 7
An Evolving Games

An Evolving Games

AFTER A DIFFICULT DECADE FOR THE OLYMPIC GAMES IT WAS PERHAPS NOT SURPRISING THAT ONLY ONE CITY, LOS ANGELES, BID TO HOST THE 1984 GAMES. IT BECAME THE FIRST TO BE STAGED WITH NO FINANCIAL SUPPORT FROM GOVERNMENT WITH THE EXCEPTION OF A A VELODROME AND THE OLYMPIC 'SWIM STADIUM' AQUATICS CENTRE, BOTH OF WHICH WERE FUNDED BY CORPORATE SPONSORS. THE GAMES RETURNED A VERY RESPECTABLE PROFIT OF $223 MILLION AND ESTABLISHED A FINANCIAL TEMPLATE FOR SUBSEQUENT OLYMPIC GAMES.

Medal table from the 1984 Olympic Games

Country	Gold	Silver	Bronze	Total
USA	79	59	30	168
Romania	19	15	17	51
Federal Republic of Germany	18	19	22	59
China	15	8	10	33
Italy	14	6	12	32
Canada	10	17	16	43
Japan	10	7	14	31
Great Britain 11th place	5	10	21	36

The 1984 Olympic Games

Following the boycott of the 1980 Games by the USA and other nations, a reciprocal boycott from the Soviet Union and its allies – 15 nations in all – was probably no surprise to the organisers. Britain, mercifully, had no agonising to go through as there was no moral issue at stake on this occasion, only Cold War retaliation. The absentees impacted on the Games sporadically, with just a few individual sports being significantly reduced in quality. The Weightlifting competition, for example, missed 29 of the 30 medallists from their last World Championships before the Games, while Freestyle Wrestling lacked 23 of its most recent World Championship medallists.

Those who did attend found a colourful, well-marketed Games. Sam the Olympic Eagle was the official mascot and based on the USA's national bird the Bald Eagle while John Williams composed the rather regal 'Olympic Fanfare and Theme' which proved such an instant hit it has been used ever since. Graphic design also came to prominence with an inspiring logo called 'Stars in Motion' – a horizontal arrangement of five blue, red and white stars plus vivid alternating streaks to give an impression of power and speed.

The emerging American talent, Carl Lewis, making the first of his four appearances at the Olympic Games, began with a comfortable win over fellow American Sam Graddy in the 100m, beating him by 0.2 seconds with a time of 9.99. Lewis went on to take gold in the Long Jump, 200m and 4 x 100m Relay; in the last two races he set new Olympic and world records respectively. His tally of four golds in these events equalled Jesse Owens' achievement in 1936. This has always been a major ambition for Lewis who went on to win three further Long Jump gold medals at the Seoul, Barcelona and Atlanta games. He also went on to win the 100m in Seoul, after originally finishing second behind Ben Johnson, and was a member of the successful USA 4 x 100m Relay team in Barcelona.

For Britain, Los Angeles can be seen as another middling Games, with a total of five gold medals – a tally the same as in Moscow four years earlier and repeated in the Olympic Games of 1988 and 1992. Such consistency began to beg a rather disturbing question. Had Britain reached its natural level – apparently that of a useful second tier sporting nation, occasionally able to produce stars of world renown yet lacking depth across the board in Olympic sports.

It was a reasonable concern, and yet the 1984 Olympic Games felt much better than that. Part of the reason, of course, was because two of the nation's greatest ever Olympians, Sebastian Coe and Daley Thompson, were at career peaks and taking centre

'There was only one man in that race and that man was Seb Coe'

Steve Cram, who took silver, in the 1500m final at Los Angeles 1984

stage with magnificent performances. Also on the Athletics track, the incident between Zola Budd and Mary Decker became the talking point of the entire Games. So one way or another Britain seemed to be always at the heart of the action.

Coe's achievement of becoming the first man to win consecutive gold medals in the 1500m is even more remarkable in the context of a miserable 1983 season. He fell ill with toxoplasmosis – a type of blood poisoning – and was forced to spend several months going in and out of hospital and taking strong medication. He was unable to run from July 1983 to Christmas of that year, until the infection had finally cleared his system. No lasting damage had been done, however, and he set about preparing for the 1984 Olympic Games.

Coe once again missed out in the 800m final, taking silver behind the outstanding Joaquim Cruz from Brazil. His time of 1:43.64 in second place was exceptional for an athlete concentrating on the longer 1500m, however, and it augured well. Coe was to dominate the 1500m final, simply running away from the world-class field to smash the Olympic record and post a time of 3:32.53 that was scarcely half a second outside his personal best. He had delivered like very few 1500m runners in history, despite the fact that he was competing in his seventh race in eight days amid the heat and smog of Los Angeles which many found so debilitating – including Steve Ovett who struggled to breathe properly from the moment he arrived. 'There was only one man in that race and that man was Seb Coe,' observed Britain's silver medallist Steve Cram afterwards. Coe's record of four individual Olympic medals on the athletics track is still the best ever for a British competitor, while his 800m time of 1:41.73 set on 10 June 1981 in Florence, remains an unbeaten British record. He may have concluded his own Olympic career with style in 1984 – but his association with the Olympic and Paralympic movement was very far from over.

Britain's Daley Thompson in action during the javelin element of the Decathlon. Thompson is on his way to winning gold at the inaugural World Championships in Athletics in Helsinki, Finland in 1983.

Daley Thompson celebrates after having thrown a personal best of 46.56m in the discus on his way to winning the Decathlon with a world record points total of 8847 at the Los Angeles 1984 Games.

Previous page

It is the 1500m final at the Los Angeles 1984 Games and (left-to-right) Steve Ovett and Steve Cram trail Sebastian Coe who is heading to a dramatic and glorious defence of his title.

Yet despite his heroics in Los Angeles, Coe had to share the limelight. He was happy to do so, as his big mate Daley Thompson was in the middle of an incredible run in which he didn't lose a Decathlon competition for nine years. Thompson was without any doubt the greatest all-round athlete of his era, and in the opinion of many, possibly the most gifted decathlete of all time. Highly talented but also driven, Thompson was known for extremely rigorous training. He famously put in three sessions a day all the year round, even training on Christmas Day in the sure knowledge that his most dangerous opponents would have given themselves the day off and

> **'Training was a complete joy, even in the rain and cold … I wasn't making a huge sacrifice. It was why I lived'**
>
> Daley Thompson, the greatest all-round athlete of his time

he would be fractionally ahead of the game. Yet he denied any sense of martyrdom. 'I was lucky because very early in life, I discovered exactly what made me happy,' he explains. 'I can think of perhaps five days maximum in 15 years when I had to force myself to train because I felt ill or lacked motivation. Training was a complete joy, even in the rain and cold. People go on about my dedication but they get it wrong… I wasn't making a huge sacrifice. It was why I lived. It would have killed me not to have trained.'

By 1980, still only 21, he seemed unstoppable, setting a world record in May and then crushing the opposition at the

'I was lucky because very early in life, I discovered exactly what made me happy … running, throwing and jumping. In other words, the Decathlon'

Double Olympic champion Daley Thompson reflects on the Decathlon's impact on his life

Moscow Olympic Games. Of course one can always speculate on who would have won medals if there had been no boycott of the Moscow Games. Yet Thompson would arguably still have won gold medals, whatever generation he had been part of. His ability to rise above everybody else was exceptional. Four years later he was still unbeaten, and seemingly unbeatable, with his two great German rivals Jürgen Hingsen and Guido Kratschmer – both brilliant athletes in their own right – despairing at ever defeating Britain's finest. Los Angeles was a commanding performance. Thompson again broke the world record with 8,847 points to become, among many things, the first athlete in history to be the reigning world-record holder, Olympic champion, European champion and Commonwealth champion.

Thompson was an incredible and uninhibited raw talent who cared little about convention, tradition and athletics etiquette. He has no recollection of watching the Olympic Games on television or reading about them in the newspapers. One day he just found himself competing in them. He was intensely patriotic and emotional, but sometimes affected not to care because actually he grew to care so much. 'Losing was never a problem,' he once told me. 'But training to finish second is totally and completely unacceptable and is a very big problem indeed. You always train to be first, but if you get beaten by a better man you shake his hand and smile. I was training to beat, not just match, an incredible athlete like Jürgen Hingsen. That was the making of me. Training to beat Jürgen took me to the very top.'

The flip-side to the undiluted majesty and glory of Coe and Thompson was the curious, headline-grabbing tale of Zola Budd. She was an amazingly talented long-distance running prodigy from South Africa, a country barred from the Olympic Games because of its government's oppressive apartheid policies. Budd thus seemed destined to miss out on the opportunity to compete at the very highest level, until the *Daily Mail* newspaper took up her story.

The *Mail*'s interest and support of the British Olympic cause dates back to 1908, so it is not surprising that it came up with the idea of getting her to run for Britain. Budd had a British grandparent and was perfectly entitled to apply for a British passport – many cricketers and rugby players have done the same over the years – but at the time it caused a considerable fuss. The speed with which Budd's passport application was approved, in particular, attracted a good deal of comment. Changing countries was definitely not then the norm in athletics' circles, although the practice now is rife, and some critics saw the *Mail*'s interest and considerable financial investment as part of an ongoing circulation war. However the British public, no less than any in the world, craved success at the Games and were well disposed to the teenage athlete. Budd was legitimately qualified and clearly had potential.

And so the *Mail*'s reporters headed off to South Africa to bring her back to Britain. Her first race, in Dartford, attracted live television interest

Opposite Page

Daley Thompson clears the bar in the pole vault at the Seoul 1988 Games, where he finished fourth in the Decathlon. It proved to be his final Games.

Who could have imagined the drama this 3000m final would bring at Los Angeles 1984 when American star Mary Decker fell over after her accidental clash with Britain's Zola Budd?

Mascots

Above London 2012 mascots Wenlock (left) and Mandeville (right) during the opening of the London 2012 shop in Paddington Station on 1 November 2010. They are going to be among the 'stars' of the Games.

Above right Sam the Eagle, the mascot of the Los Angeles 1984 Games, marches around the Olympic Stadium during the Opening Ceremony.

Right Izzy, the mascot for the Atlanta 1996 Olympic Games, makes a visit to New York. Izzy was the first computer-generated mascot.

Far right Hodori, a tiger cub and the mascot of the Seoul 1988 Games, holds aloft the Torch on top of a mountain of flowers.

Above It is Beijing 2008 and three of the official Games mascots (left to right) Jingjing, Nini and Huanhuan are on court during the China–Lithuania men's quarter final at the Olympic Basketball Gymnasium in Wukesong Culture and Sports Center.

Below Misha the bear made an appearance at the Opening Ceremony of the Moscow 1980 Games to wish everyone luck. She is better known, however, for her tear at the Closing Ceremony.

Right Mary Decker is helped away by her future husband, the British Discus thrower Richard Slaney, after she crashed to the ground in the dramatic 3000m final and was unable to carry on.

'I knew Mary had fallen but I did not pay much attention. All I thought was that I had to go for it; I just focused on my own race'

Wendy Sly, who beat Zola Budd and American Mary Decker to win the silver medal in the 3000m

on the BBC's then flagship sporting programme, *Grandstand*. It turned into a media frenzy, a remarkable occasion for the small track in Kent where she won the 3,000m in 9:2.60. Such was the foundation for an amazing few months that ended in a controversial clash in the 3,000m final at the Los Angeles 1984 Games.

Budd started as one of the fancied runners although the favourite was undoubtedly American athlete Mary Decker. The press build-up had been all about the impending Decker/Budd showdown and many in Britain were captivated, even though the live race took place at about 4am. Decker set the initial pace, but in the fifth lap the barefoot Budd went to the front, with Decker right behind. Decker, unused to running in the pack, was running too close. She nearly tripped once when her right thigh made contact with Budd's left foot. Decker maintained her close position and made contact a second time. This time she hit Budd's calf before tangling with her for a third, final time when she fell painfully. Her future husband, Richard Slaney, competing in the Discus for Britain, carried her away from the track, and Decker's contorted face, streaming with tears, became an iconic image of the Los Angeles 1984 Olympic Games. Meanwhile the 100,000-strong crowd booed Budd continuously for the remainder of the race – with echoes of the Anglo-American controversies back in 1908 – but with no good cause. Her teammate Wendy Sly kept her focus and composure to take silver for Britain, leaving Budd to finish an undistinguished seventh.

The incident had been Decker's fault and the IAAF jury lost no time in absolving Budd of any blame, although the American media proved less forgiving. Decker pointedly refused to accept Budd's attempt to shake hands after the race, although she has indicated in subsequent years that perhaps it was her fault after all. For a long time Budd, unfairly, seemed to be public enemy number one in the USA, although ironically she now lives in the country. She continued

to represent Britain for a number of years, winning the world cross-country championship in 1985 and 1986 before returning to South Africa. In the Barcelona 1992 Olympic Games she competed for the land of her birth in the 3,000m, but did not come through the heats.

The 1984 Games saw a number of significant firsts, not least Steve Redgrave's gold for the Coxed Four in Rowing which set him on the road to becoming one of Britain's greatest ever Olympians. New events at the Games included Synchronised Swimming, Rhythmic Gymnastics and Windsurfing, as well as the women's Marathon, in which Joan Benoit took gold in the latter event to become its first ever female Olympic champion. The archer Neroli Fairhall from New Zealand was to become the first paraplegic to compete in the Olympic Games, finishing a very respectable 35th out of 56 competitors. Fairhall had previously taken gold in the wheelchair women's Doubles Archery competition at the 1980 Paralympic Games, followed by a victory in the Commonwealth Games when archery was first included there in 1982.

The 1984 Paralympic Games

For organisational reasons it was not possible to hold the Paralympic Games in Los Angeles in 1984. Instead the original intention was to divide the Games into two parts, both held within the USA. All wheelchair competitions were to take place in Champaign, Illinois and all other Paralympic categories – amputee, cerebral palsy, visually impaired and les autres (a new category which mainly included blind competitors) – were to be hosted by Hofstra University in New York.

The latter went ahead as planned, with 1800 athletes from 45 countries competing for 900 mdeals. President Reagan officially opened the Games on 17 June, and events encompassed Archery, Athletics, Boccia, Cycling, Equestrian (Dressage), Football, Shooting, Swimming and Table Tennis, with Powerlifting appearing as a demonstration sport. There were exceptional performances in several fields, including the 100m wheelchair race, where American amputee Jim Martinson set a new world record of 17.13 seconds. Another American, visually impaired Winford Haynes, won the gold medal in the 100m dash in 11.78 seconds, and a third, Charles Reid, won the Powerlifting competition to establish himself as a world class cerebral palsy athlete. Media coverage was more extensive than ever, with the major US television networks and press featuring the Paralympic Games, as well as the BBC and Dutch, West German and Swedish radio and television channels.

Monica Saker of Sweden celebrates after winning gold in the 800m – 4 at the Los Angeles 1984 Paralympic Games, although the wheelchair events were held at short notice at Stoke Mandeville.

Champaign, Illinois, was an outstanding venue with 'absolutely world class' facilities, according to a British official who later became involved in hosting the Games. He noted that the Champaign basketball stadium seated 35,000 people and the athletics stadium held twice that, while the track itself had ten lanes rather than Stoke Mandeville's six. Unfortunately, however, Champaign had to withdraw at very short notice when their organising committee failed to secure the funds needed to stage the Games. This presented a huge problem for the authorities as the wheelchair events were by far the

'We will build a Sports Stadium and an Olympic Village so that the disabled athletes of the world will always have their own Olympic facilities here at Stoke Mandeville'

Dr Ludwig Guttmann, speaking at the opening of the Stoke Mandeville Stadium in 1969

Chris Hallam

One of the people credited with raising awareness of disability sports, Chris Hallam was paralysed below the chest in a motorcycle accident two days before he was due to be selected for the Welsh swimming team. Twice winner of the London marathon, setting course records in his victories in both 1985 and 1987, Hallam held world records on the track at 100m and 200m in his class and held world short and long course records in the pool for 50m Breaststroke. He won medals in Swimming and Athletics in three successive Paralympic Games: New York/ Stoke Mandeville 1984, Seoul 1988 and Barcelona 1992. Hallam's success has encouraged others to give disability sports a go. Indeed, Dame Grey-Thompson saw him in the 1985 marathon. 'I remember saying to my mum that I was going to do the London marathon one day.' Hallam is now one of the UK's leading disability sports coaches, encouraging young athletes such as Daniel Lucker and Josie Pearson. In 1986 he was named Disabled Sports Personality of the Year and two years later he was awarded an MBE.

Medal table from the 1984 Paralympic Games

Country	Gold	Silver	Bronze	Total
USA	136	131	129	396
Great Britain	107	112	112	331
Canada	87	82	69	238
Sweden	83	43	34	160
Federal Republic of Germany	79	77	74	230
France	71	69	45	185
Netherlands	55	52	28	135

biggest category and arguably – the core sport of the Paralympic Games. Britain reacted quickly, not for the first time, and agreed, with less than four months notice, to host the wheelchair section of the Paralympic Games at the Stoke Mandeville Stadium between July 22 and August 1.

There was more than a whiff of 'backs to the wall' at the London 1948 Olympic Games known as the 'Austerity Games' but the British spirit of improvisation responded to the occasion. The British Paraplegic Sport Society organised the Stoke Mandeville Games, led by its long-serving Secretary General Joan Scruton and supported by the local community in Aylesbury. Along with a number of loyal sponsors and donors, they all set about somehow making the Games a reality. A total of £420,000 was raised in no time at all, essential in an era well before lottery funding. Money came from various sources – German television rights, individual companies and the normal loyal support network Stoke Mandeville had built up through the decades. Donations came via many small Rotary and Round Table clubs around the land and Aylesbury Vale District Council, with the National Federation of Self-Employed and Small Businesses also lending a timely hand.

The accommodation at Stoke Mandeville was not big enough to hold 1,500 competitors and officials. Hampden Hall, part of the nearby agricultural college was hurriedly pressed into service, as was the RAF Halton Camp at Wendover. Here Kermode Hall was converted in just 48 hours after the apprentices had left for their summer break, with specially adapted portable lavatories and showers being installed. Old buses were loaned from London Transport's 'graveyard' in Grays, Essex where they had been placed in store for rather obscure reasons so as to be available in the case of a national emergency. Stoke Mandeville's need was pretty pressing, so somewhere in Whitehall a 'national emergency' was quietly declared and the vehicles released to help with the

Paralympic Games' transport needs. A fleet of 12 buses was the result, and London Transport sportingly made one of their mechanics available for a fortnight to service all the vehicles.

British Telecom installed a telephone exchange and also ran the Stadium switchboard. A daily newspaper, *Pursuit*, produced to entertain all involved with the Paralympic Games, included reports on the previous day's action. The Stadium Supporters' Committee erected and ran a huge beer tent and the Prince of Wales rearranged his diary so he could officiate at the Opening Ceremony.

Wheelchair racing saw some spectacular individual achievements at the 1984 Games, especially from the Swiss. Heinz Frei won three golds in the 1500m, 5,000m and Marathon, while Franz Nietlispach took a further four golds and a silver. This was also the first time that the Games had been able to stage a Paralympic Marathon over the classic distance – a real breakthrough moment. Thames Valley Police assisted hugely with the event, which was performed on public roads between Chalfont St Peters and the Stoke Mandeville Stadium, built in 1969. The race was won by Canada's Rick Hansen, nearly nine minutes ahead of Frenchman Jean-François Poitevin, in a time of 1:49:52.06. Wheelchair Marathon racing was becoming immensely popular and provided a spectacle that the wider sporting public could appreciate and support.

Among those embarking on their Paralympic career in 1984 was Chris Hallam. He won a gold medal in the 50m Breaststroke and went on to win medals in the next two Games, held in Seoul and Barcelona respectively. Hallam became even better known as the winner of the wheelchair section of the London Marathon in 1985 and 1987, setting course records on both occasions. A larger-than-life character, he was the competitor whom Dame Tanni-Grey Thompson always credits with motivating her to become a Paralympian. Overall, across both sides of the Atlantic, Britain performed exceptionally well, claiming a total of 107 gold medals – second only to the USA. Yet undoubtedly their greatest success was getting the wheelchair section of the Games staged at all.

The 1988 Olympic and Paralympic Games

The 1988 Games, hosted by Seoul in South Korea, was the second Summer Games to be held in Asia after Tokyo 1964. The tit-for-tat boycotts were thankfully over but North Korea and its allies Cuba, Nicaragua, Ethiopia and Madagascar refused to attend while Albania and the Seychelles also stayed away. Otherwise it was business as usual, with 159 nations and 8,391 competitors making these the largest Games to date. A dramatic Opening Ceremony featured a skydiving team descending in a pattern of the five Olympic Rings, and a record 33 broadcasters showed the event across the world.

The 1988 Games were in retrospect the end of an era. They became the swansong of two powerhouse Olympic nations, the Soviet Union and East Germany, both of which had ceased to exist by 1992. They departed in some style, however, with Kristin Otto of East Germany taking six Swimming golds and the Soviet Union's Vladimir Artemov winning four golds in Gymnastics. Meanwhile the slow, inexorable death of amateurism continued, with the reintroduction of Tennis to the Games and the appearance of millionaire superstars such as Steffi Graf and Gabriela Sabatini, who took gold and silver medals respectively.

In many ways Seoul 1988 was Britain's 'nearly' Olympic Games, especially at the athletics track where there were six high-profile but frustrating silver medals, not least with Peter Elliott in the 1500m, Colin Jackson in the 110m Hurdles and Linford Christie in the 100m and the 4 x 100m Relay. Such near misses made the Games feel rather more successful than they were, but the gold medal tally remained just five – this time from five different

Left The Opening Ceremony of the Seoul 1988 Games, which took place on 17 September 1988 at the Jamsil Olympic Stadium.

217

Adrian Moorhouse

One of the best breaststroke swimmers Britain has ever produced, Adrian Moorhouse achieved his first major international success at the 1983 European Championships when he won the 200m Breaststroke. He made his Olympic debut at the Los Angeles 1984 Games, finishing fourth in the 100m Breaststroke. Wins in the 100m breaststroke at the 1985 and 1987 European Championships followed, as well as at the Seoul 1988 Games, repeating the successes of Duncan Goodhew. Despite being ranked number one in the world at this time, Moorhouse had failed to break the world record. This all changed in the heats of the 1989 European Championships in Bonn, when he clocked 1:01.49 and shaved 0.16 seconds off the world 100m Breaststroke record set by the American Steve Lundquist at the Los Angeles 1984 Games. Moorhouse went on to equal his own world record another two times during his swimming career.

'Shooters are made, not born. You have to work on every little bit of your technique until it improves. And that, from the age of 14, is exactly what I did'
Malcolm Cooper, Shooting gold medallist at the 1984 and 1988 Games

Gold! Britain's Adrian Moorhouse celebrates winning the 100m Breaststroke at the Jamsil Indoor Swimming Pool at the Seoul 1988 Games after finishing one-hundredth of a second faster than Károly Güttler.

sports. Britain eventually finished 12th in the medal table, with a total of 24, but this included some truly remarkable performances.

A long tradition of Breaststroke excellence was maintained in the pool by Adrian Moorhouse. After finishing a disappointing fourth in Los Angeles, where he had been tipped for gold, Moorhouse was initially devastated, but he recovered to become the established world number one early in 1988 after a victory in the 100m breaststroke at the US Indoor Championships. He took gold at the Seoul 1988 Games, winning a tense race with an extremely close finish. Moorhouse's time of 1:02.04 was only one-hundredth of a second ahead of Károly Güttler of Hungary, while long-standing rival Victor Davis of Canada was beaten into fourth place and the Soviet swimmer Dmitri Volkov, who had looked certain to win at the 75m mark, took the bronze.

Further British success came from Michael McIntyre and Bryn Vaile in the men's Star class at the

Sailing regatta – yet another close contest. McIntyre and Vaile went into the last race knowing they could only take the gold medal if they won and the American team of Mark Reynolds and Hal Haenel finished in worse than sixth place. In the event the British pair did win, and the unfortunate Americans had to retire with a broken mast – a sweet reward for McIntyre, who had placed seventh in the Finn class at the Los Angeles 1984 Games .

Seoul proved another happy hunting ground for the relentless Steve Redgrave. Partnered by Andy Holmes, he took gold comfortably in the Coxless Pairs as well as bronze in the Coxed Pairs. Redgrave was to become a fixture on the podium over successive Olympic Games, although Holmes retired from Olympic competition after Seoul 1988. Both were key figures during the 1980s, a period when British rowing got its act together again. It was a welcome upturn after three decades with no Rowing gold medal success at the Olympic Games.

Best of British

Andy Holmes

Outside of the Rowing world not many will remember the name of Andy Holmes, but this is a 'warrior' who collected two gold medals and a bronze in the two Games in which he competed. Initially a rugby player at Latymer Upper School in Hammersmith, where he played in the same team as actor Hugh Grant, his physicality and aggression were noted by the school's rowing coach Jim Clark – a silver medal winner for Great Britain in the Eights at Montreal 1976. Working on building sites as a 'hoddie' to further develop his strength, Holmes also gradually developed a refined touch with his stroke and by Los Angeles 1984 had become a powerhouse in the GB Coxed Four that won gold. At Seoul 1988, four years later, he teamed up with Steve Redgrave and won a gold medal in the Coxless Pairs and a bronze medal in the Coxed Pairs. Nearly two decades later he was to make a comeback as a coach and recreational sculler, but tragically was to die in a matter of days from leptospirosis or Weil's disease.

Above left Life on the ocean waves is golden for Britain's Michael McIntyre (rear) and Bryn Vaile on their way to victory in the Star class at Seoul 1988.

Left Steve Redgrave signals being No. 1 with teammate the late Andy Holmes after their triumph in the Coxless Pairs at Seoul 1988. Tragically, Holmes died in 2010.

Elsewhere, Malcolm Cooper – known as 'Cooperman' to the press – claimed a second consecutive gold medal in the 50m Rifle 3 Positions, to be precise. Cooper had been virtually unchallenged as the world's greatest marksman for a decade or more, with his wife Sarah Robinson also competing internationally at the sport. The pair were so dedicated that they refused to have a television in the house lest it should prove a distraction from training.

The most remarkable team victory of the Games – certainly for British fans – came in the men's Hockey competition, which saw Britain defeat the favourites West Germany in the final 3-1. The semi-final against Australia was a punishing match in itself. A 2-0 lead for the British team, courtesy of Sean Kerly, was immediately reduced to one within 20 seconds, and with 13 minutes to play Australia equalised. An extraordinary lunge by Kerly, which he has described as 'half a dive and half a belly flop', eventually resulted in the winning goal for Britain, although the hat-trick hero thought it had bounced back off the post rather than the backboard of the goal. Thus reprieved to fight another day, the team had to confront Germany in the final – a team to whom they had already lost in the group stages. This time their performance was magnificent, with an attack brimming with pace and guile. Imran Sherwani scored the first and third goals and Kerly the second from a penalty corner, confusing the Germans who were expecting the powerful Barber to strike. In a Coleman-esque moment the commentator Barry Davies, delighted at the third goal that had secured the gold for Britain, uttered his famous remark, 'Where were the Germans?' answering his question

with a brutal honesty shared by hundreds of British fans, 'But frankly, who cares?'

The eventual 3-1 score was a huge disappointment to the silver medallists who had lost consecutive Olympic finals. For the British team it was a moment to relish and their victory party swiftly expanded into an unofficial team celebration. This was a squad that partied as they played, famously draining the Seoul Hilton of champagne as they toasted the achievement of an impossible dream.

For the Hockey team's story was a wonderfully British tale of extraordinarily talented amateurs taking on an increasingly professional sporting world and emerging victorious. It was a ripping yarn – amateurism's last hurrah if you like – that gladdened the heart and gave hockey a massive, albeit short-lived, boost in Britain. And back home the viewing and reading public became very curious as to exactly who these amateurs were. These were ordinary people, not sporting superstars, who moved among them in everyday life doing normal jobs.

That was the great appeal of the team, together with the fact that this was clearly the best British Hockey team in generations. The squad had been together for a long time, winning a bronze medal in Los Angeles in 1984 and then taking silver in the 1986 World Championships. The 1988 Games represented their last chance to land the big title they craved before they were forced to concentrate full-time on life, family and careers – as amateurs must do.

So who were these guys, and what gave them the edge? The team was a very individual, highly motivated group – to succeed at that level they had to be.

'If nothing else happens in our lives we'll know that we stepped up to the plate and made it happen'

Sean Kerly reflects on winning the Hockey gold medal at the Seoul Olympic Games

'I can't recall a moment in the final when I doubted that Britain would win'

BBC commentator Barry Davies looks back on the men's Hockey final of the 1988 Games

Medal table from the 1988 Olympic Games

Country	Gold	Silver	Bronze	Total
USSR	49	30	45	124
German Democratic Republic	36	35	30	101
USA	36	31	26	93
Republic of Korea	11	8	11	30
Bulgaria	10	12	13	35
Hungary	10	6	6	22
Federal Republic of Germany	9	14	15	38
Great Britain (11th position)	5	10	9	24

Opposite page

What a day. Stephen Batchelor leads the celebrations as Britain beat West Germany 3-1 in the Hockey final at the Seoul 1988 Games to win gold in the event for only the second time – the last occasion being 68 years earlier in Antwerp.

'... a moment encapsulated in my life, which will never disappear'

David Whitaker, coach of Britain's gold medal winning Hockey team, describes the 1988 Games

> 'I looked into the back seat to see Johnson staring out. He looked lost, somehow out of place and diminished by the vastness of the car interior, and I remember thinking that he didn't look like a man who had just won the greatest prize in sport.'
>
> Tom Knight, journalist, describes his encounter with Ben Johnson after the 100m final in Seoul, 1988

Goalkeeper Ian Taylor was a teacher who later went into PR before becoming chief executive of the British Ice Hockey Super League; he then went on to work with the London Irish rugby club. Reserve goalkeeper Veryan Pappin, a parachute instructor in the RAF, was last heard of running a diving school in the UAE, while ice-cool defender Jon Potter worked for Nestlé in Eastern Europe before becoming a global brand director for Guinness, based in Connecticut.

Imran Sherwani was developing a career in the police when he gave the job up to become a newsagent, a job which guaranteed he could train five afternoons a week and play every weekend as he chased his Olympic dream. Martin Grimley was a high-flying teacher before he was threatened with the sack if he went on another England hockey tour. He chose to leave, and switched to the financial sector after the Games. Paul Barber was a quantity surveyor who now runs his own construction company, while Richard Dodds was already an orthopaedic surgeon by the time of the Seoul 1988 Olympic Games, a career he was to continue.

Richard Leman was a young businessman who was soon to set up his own personnel recruitment agency; he is now the president of the GB Hockey Board and a director of the British Olympic Association (BOA). Steve Batchelor, a highly regarded tennis coach at the time of the Olympic Games, became a teacher and housemaster at Cranleigh School, while Robert Clift was soon to become a leading banker in Hong Kong. Ace goal scorer Sean Kerly was a free spirit who basically lived for hockey, although he could also be found working as a marketing manager at a leading Kent public school.

Russell Garcia was an 18-year-old student hairdresser. Ulsterman Jimmy Kirkwood returned to Belfast as a senior bank manager with HSBC. Kulbir Bhaura is the CEO of a sports retailer in London and Stephen Martin became deputy chief executive of the BOA. David Faulkner is now the performance director of British Hockey, helping two more highly regarded teams, male and female, prepare for the London 2012 Games. Almost a quarter of a century later the drama of the 1988 Games remains; a moment, as coach David Whitaker observed, 'encapsulated in my life, which will never disappear'.

Yet for many the overriding memory of Seoul is a sober one – the spectacle of an extraordinary runner being stripped of his gold medal and 'world record' for taking a banned steroid, Stanozolol. The shock in Britain, when Ben Johnson's fall from grace was announced on the BBC's Olympic Grandstand, was as great as anywhere, although athletes and competitors themselves were aware of the problem of drugs in elite sport. A number of high profile athletes did complain to the authorities about the inefficiency of drug testing at major athletics events. It was clear that not everyone was adhering to the same rules but this was a difficult situation to change. The lingering Cold War attitudes did not help as they created a climate of suspicion and uncertainty.

Ben Johnson arguably changed the face of sport forever, with his very public disgrace proving a turning point in the battle against illicit drugs. The Olympic Movement responded to the challenge, with the controversial 100m of the 1988 Games leading in due course to the formation of the World Anti-Doping Agency. Professor Arne Ljungqvist, the distinguished member of the IOC and renowned anti-doping campaigner, acknowledges the beneficial long-term consequences of a very regrettable affair. In his biography *Doping Nemesis*, Ljungqvist pinpointed the controversy surrounding Johnson as a 'wake-up call' to which the international sporting community had to respond. 'After the Johnson scandal the whole world's opinion changed about drugs in sport; he observed. It was to make Ljungqvist's own path rather easier to pursue.

The Seoul 1988 Games was to prove a milestone for Paralympic sport as it was the first event for 24 years to take place in the same

From left, Richard Leman, Imran Sherwani and Martyn Grimley celebrate Great Britain's gold medal winning 3-1 victory over Germany in the men's Hockey at Seoul 1988.

city as the Olympic Games. After the logistical challenges of the 1984 Games everything went much more smoothly, with the entire Paralympic Family being brought under the one administrative roof – the International Coordinating Committee (ICC). The ICC worked closely with the progressive Seoul organisers, to the extent that the Paralympic Games became fully integrated and received a $12,857,143 grant from the Seoul Olympic Organizing Committee. All the main facilities used during the Olympic Games, were also used by the Paralympic Games, while on this occasion a separate Paralympic Village was provided, just 4km from the Olympic Stadium. For the first time ever Britain's Paralympic athletes and 70 coaches were given permission to wear the same uniform and the same competition kit as their Olympic colleagues.

Sir Ludwig Guttman's dream was now clearly a reality, and from this point onwards the organisation of the Paralympics has gone hand in hand with the Summer Olympic Games.

The 1988 Paralympic Games featured 17 sports, including Wheelchair Tennis as a demonstration sport. It attracted 3,059 athletes from 60 countries and saw the first, and last, appearance of the Soviet Union. Participating only in Athletics and Swimming, the USSR won 56 medals including 21 gold. Britain's impressive haul of 180 medals, 65 gold, 65 silver and 53 bronze, put them third in the table behind the USA and second-placed West Germany. The undoubted star was Rob Matthews, an athlete blind since the age of 20. He repeated his extraordinary hat-trick first achieved at the 1984 Games, winning the Athletics BI 800m, 1500m and

Medal table from the 1988 Paralympic Games

Country	Gold	Silver	Bronze	Total
USA	92	90	91	273
Federal Republic of Germany	76	66	51	193
Great Britain	65	65	53	183
Canada	54	42	55	151
France	47	44	50	141
Sweden	42	38	23	103
Korea	40	35	19	94

'I knew I could do it and when I came down the final straight there was no way I was going to lose'

Sally Gunnell, gold medallist in the 400m Hurdles at the 1992 Games

5,000m. Matthews subsequently emigrated to New Zealand, a country he now represents at triathlon. Also in Athletics, his teammate Peter Carruthers took gold in the B1 100m, Nigel Coultas won the A6/A8 100m and 200m and Colin Keay the C6 200m and 400m, with fellow Briton Gordon Robertson taking silver in the 400m event.

The 1992 Olympic and Paralympic Games

Barcelona, which hosted the 1992 Olympic and Paralympic Games, realised the events' potential for urban regeneration with extraordinary success. The Games became the catalyst for a vast economic and cultural transformation, from which Barcelona emerged as one of Europe's most popular tourist destinations and business capitals. A new port and stylish Olympic Village were built in the run-down neighbourhood of Poblenou and modern sports facilities were constructed in the Olympic zones of Montjuïc, Diagonal and Vall'd'Hebron. Sightlines helped to showcase Barcelona's dramatic architecture with Diving, for example, taking place within view of the famous Sagrada Familia structure. The investment has left an enviable infrastructure of world-beating facilities and top class coaching, as well as an enduring culture of sport that has brought Spain outstanding international success. Barcelona remains the inspiration for modern Olympic and Paralympic Host Cities, would-be and actual, in using the Games to enhance its reputation across the world.

The glamour and drama of the 1992 Games were captured in Britain by the specially commissioned song *Barcelona*, which was performed by Queen's Freddie Mercury ,who co-wrote the song with Mike Moran, and the acclaimed operatic soprano Montserrat Caballe, a native of the city. The BBC fronted their coverage of the Games with this stunning aria, set against footage of the dancing fountains at the foot of Montjuïc – a memorable celebration of an event which, being on virtually the same time zone as Britain, attracted a huge television audience.

The first Games of the 1990s also reflected the political earthquake that had taken place since Seoul with the dissolving of the old Soviet empire. Twelve states from the former USSR competed as a unified team and eventually topped the medal table with a haul of 111 that consisted of 44 gold, 38 silver and 29 bronze. The USA came second, with a total of 107, of which 37 were gold, followed by the first unified German team since 1964, which took 32 gold medals and 80 overall. Israel won its first ever Olympic medal when Yael Arad took silver in Judo, on the 20th anniversary of the Munich massacre. Barcelona 1992 was also the first Games to feature a South African team since 1960, leading to a heart-warming moment in the women's 10,000m. South African Elana Meyer lost a very tight race to Derartu Tulu of Ethiopia, after which the white and black athletes joined in a victory lap, which they ran hand in hand.

Britain was to end a disappointing 13th in the medal table, with a total of 20 medals including five gold (again) and three silver. In Athletics, Linford Christie, the men's team captain, won the 100m, becoming the third Briton to do so after Harold Abrahams and Allan Wells. The Commonwealth and European champion powered through the race with

> ## 'It is all about putting the pieces together and it was all about the mind games, and mentally preparing'
>
> Sally Gunnell celebrates her gold medal in the 400m Hurdles in Barcelona

Barcelona transformed

Once a scene of urban decay, Barcelona used the 1992 Olympic Games as a vehicle for reform, revitalising the city and giving it a reputation as a world leader in innovative planning. Olympic facilities were spread over four neglected urban areas, with the Olympic Village developed on abandoned industrial land close to the coast. The construction of six artificial beaches either side of the Olympic Port had the most impact: for the first time in its history, Barcelona was able to benefit from the recreational advantages of its position on the Mediterranean. The Games were used as a springboard to build more than 200 parks, plazas, schools and other public facilities. Of the 43 venues used at Barcelona 1992, 15 were new while 10 were refurbished. Taken together, the positive impact of the Games on the city is impossible to overestimate.

Previous page

Brought up on a farm in Essex, Sally Gunnell went from jumping over barrels of hay to leaping her way to 400m Hurdles gold for Britain at Barcelona 1992.

Best of British

Sally Gunnell

These things are all subjective, but possibly the greatest athletics performance from a British competitor during this period was Sally Gunnell winning the 400m Hurdles gold medal at the Barcelona 1992 Games. Nearly 20 years on that time comfortably remains a British record. Gunnell also produced an extraordinary final leg to help the GB team to a bronze medal in the 4 x 400m Relay. Born and raised on an Essex farm less than 10km from the London 2012 site, Gunnell was an outstanding long jumper and heptathlete before she turned to hurdling. Like Hemery, she started with the shorter sprint hurdles event 100m in the case of women – refining her technique and winning the Commonwealth title in 1986 before moving onto the longer event that she was to make her own. In addition to the 1992 Olympic title she won the 1993 World Championship and in 1994 completed the clean sweep by adding the European and Commonwealth titles, the only woman in history to achieve such a Grand Slam.

Daddy's golden girl. Steve Redgrave and Matthew Pinsent show off their medals to Redgrave's daughter, Natalie, after their success in the Coxless Pairs at Barcelona 1992.

typical strength, pulling away in the second 50m to take gold in 9.96. The women's team captain, Sally Gunnell, set an equally inspiring example with a spectacular victory in the 400m Hurdles, swapping her leading leg from her favoured left to right and back again. Despite the pressure Gunnell timed her run perfectly, taking command in the home straight and beating her great American rival Sandra Farmer-Patrick into second placewith a time of 53.23. She became only the fifth British woman to win an Athletics gold medal at the Olympic Games, which she agreed had been a hard-won victory: 'It has taken weeks, months and years of work to achieve my dream of becoming Olympic champion.' Gunnell still holds the British record of 52:74 secs which was a world record time when she recorded it at the 1993 World Championships in Stuttgart and she remains the only woman to have held 400m Hurdles titles from the Olympic Games, Commonwealth

Games, European and World Championships at the same time – a remarkable feat.

Rowing was another success story for Britain at the 1992 Games. Steve Redgrave continued his inexorable progression to five consecutive golds, this time taking number three in the men's Coxless Pairs, partnered by Matthew Pinsent. Brothers Greg and Jonny Searle also triumphed in the men's Coxed Pairs, with Garry Herbert as cox. Britain and Australia came joint fourth in the Rowing medal table, while the powerful unified German team dominated overall with ten medals, four of them gold.

For Britons watching at home, Chris Boardman's Cycling gold medal in the 4km Individual Pursuit captured the imagination. Rather like Harry Llewellyn sharing the limelight with his horse Foxhunter in Equestrian, Boardman has learned to share equal billing with his beautiful Olympic mount – the carbon-fibre composite, monocoque Lotus 108 bike on which

Britain's Chris Boardman heading for victory on his Lotus superbike during the 4000m Individual Pursuit Final in the Velodrome at the Barcelona 1992 Games. His bicycle, a masterpiece of engineering, is now in the Science Museum, London.

he won his gold medal. Nearly 20 years on it is still the most perfect looking bike, which became an unsurprising template for the majority of pursuit bikes that followed. None has ever looked quite so good, however. Norfolk-based bike designer Mike Burrows is the man who deserves most credit. In 1987 he was at an advanced state of design for the bike, which he initially called the 'Windcheetah', when the Union Cycliste Internationale (UCI), always suspicious of such radical changes, declared monocoque frames illegal.

In 1990 the UCI lifted the ban and Burrows' plans were taken to Lotus Engineering, well used to such high-tech projects from their time working in Formula 1 motor racing. Titanium inserts were incorporated at the load-bearing points and the flush composite rear wheel was also very distinctive. Lotus engineer Richard Hill ran a range of wind-tunnel tests to fine-tune its racing set-up. The fast emerging Boardman was already forging a reputation in the sport and

early in 1992 a formidable combination of rider and machine was born. In the new professional era it was a textbook operation, with designers, engineers and athletes sharing a single dream. Only 15 such bikes were made, and the whereabouts of just three are known. One is now in the Science Museum in South Kensington – the one Boardman rode in Barcelona, it's claimed. Another is held at the Lotus factory at Hethel in Norfolk, and the third was donated by Boardman himself to the Liverpool Museum in 2010.

Yet one of the most dramatic moments in Barcelona did not involve a victory at all. It was a timely reminder of one of the modern Olympic Games' founding principles – that being a 'winner' does not necessarily mean taking gold. The British crowds, quick to sympathise with a heroic underdog, recognised this is in their response to Dorando Pietri in 1908. It is thus not difficult to understand why many of those watching Derek Redmond in the

Opposite page

His face says it all as Derek Redmond is aided by his father Jim, determined to finish the 400m semi-final of the Barcelona 1992 Games after the trauma of a hamstring injury stopping him on the back straight. He received one of the biggest cheers of the Games as he hobbled home – and his spirit sums up what the Games is all about.

Medal table from the 1992 Olympic Games

Country	Gold	Silver	Bronze	Total
Unified Team (ex USSR)	44	38	29	111
USA	37	34	36	107
Germany	32	20	28	80
China	15	22	15	52
Cuba	14	6	10	30
Spain	13	7	2	22
Republic of Korea	12	4	10	26
Great Britain (13th place)	5	3	12	20

Athletics 400m saw in his brave battle to complete the course the biggest story of the 1992 Games.

Redmond was a very fine 400m runner indeed. A former British record holder, he had been bedevilled by injuries and had undergone eight operations in the years leading up to Barcelona. At the Seoul 1988 Games he had withdrawn from the 400m just 10 minutes before the start, when a suspect achilles again let him down. In the lead up to the Barcelona 1992 Games, Redmond had enjoyed an injury-free run and suddenly appeared to be in the form of his life. Certainly in his heat and quarter-final – won comfortably in 45.03 and 45.02 respectively – Redmond's speed and easy, economical running style indicated that a race time in the low 44 seconds might be just around the corner. That was definitely medal territory, so the omens were good.

On semi-final day at the Montjuïc Stadium all seemed to be set fair as Redmond settled into his blocks in lane five – although he later admitted that he was fretting slightly over a poor night's sleep in an uncomfortable bed. Nonetheless he powered out of the blocks and was moving smoothly down the back straight when he tore his hamstring high up on his right thigh. Not a gentle strain or pull – an agonising rip that virtually stopped him in his tracks. Or rather it didn't. Redmond, like other athletes before him when confronted by pain and disappointment, went into denial; his brain would not take on board the reality and awfulness of the situation. His Olympic Games, and indeed his season, were all over, but mentally he was still a competitor with a race to finish.

After kneeling for a few seconds Redmond stood up straight and started to hop around the top bend on his left leg. It was desperately sad and uplifting at the same time. Suddenly the 65,000 capacity crowd, having seen American Steve Lewis (the eventual silver medallist) win the race, turned their attention to the bravely battling Brit, trying to finish what he had started with as much dignity as he could muster. The astonished murmur was replaced with a growing roar of approval and heartfelt encouragement as he entered the home straight, supported by that point, by his father Jim who had jumped out of the crowd to be with his son.

The applause grew louder as somehow his struggle morphed into a metaphor for sport and life in general. Many in the crowd, and the millions more watching on television, will have suffered a crushing disappointment and setback at some stage of their lives, yet tried to battle on. Redmond was a symbol that seemed to validate their often unheralded, unremarked struggles. It was a hugely powerful emotional image that went around the world. At one stage a Spanish official tried to motion father and son off the track – the race was over, it was time for the next heat – but he had missed the point entirely and eventually the duo crossed the line. David Coleman, as he often did, found the perfect words: 'In the greatest arena in sport, he gets the biggest cheer'. Rather cruelly, the official records list Redmond as DNF. If anybody in the history of the Olympic Games demonstrably 'finished' a race, it was Derek Redmond.

'It seemed to touch a lot of hearts,' says Redmond, remembering his struggle. 'I suppose the biggest thing about it was the fact that it was a dad who came to protect his son. Every parent can relate to that, to being there for their child... I've had people telling me how it has helped them overcome illness, and helped them in their studies. I've had kids in Canada writing to say their athletics teams have not been doing well recently, but how they have all been determined to go out and improve after watching me. It seems to have touched a lot of people's lives, and given them a sense of hope.'

That moment seemingly resonates louder and louder; a timeless Corinthian moment at the first officially professional Games. It became a focal point of the official Barcelona 1992 Olympics Games film, 16 Days of Glory by Bud Greenspan, and featured in the International Olympic Committee's Celebrate

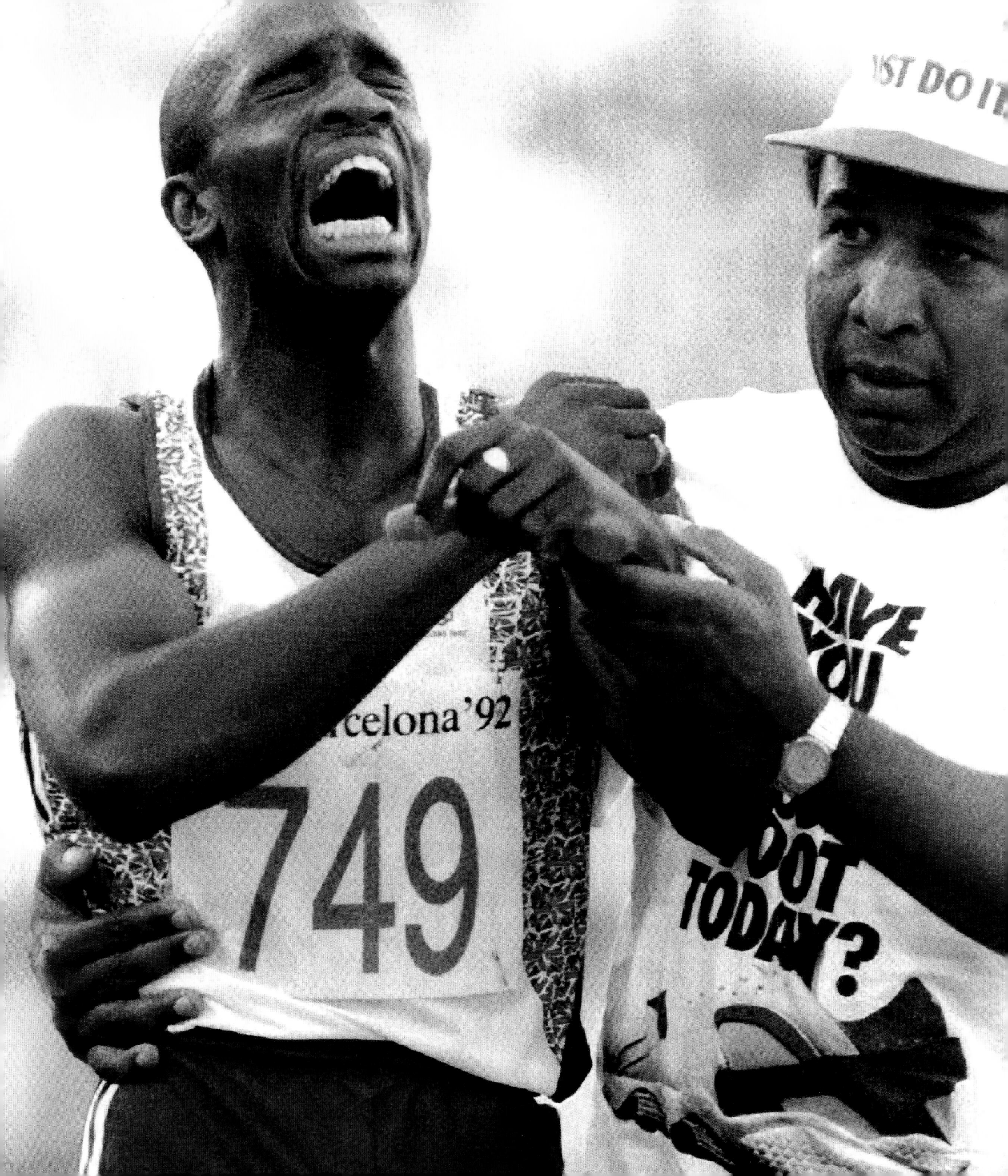
749
TODAY?

Best of British

Tanni Grey-Thompson

The world of the Paralympic Games is full of heroes and heroines, but none more so than Carys Davina 'Tanni' Grey-Thompson – now Baroness Grey-Thompson, DBE. Grey-Thompson was born with spina bifida, but has made light of that lifelong disability to win 11 Paralympic gold medals in the track events between Barcelona 1992 and Athens 2004 at distances varying from 100m to 800m. She was christened Carys Davina Grey, but her sister referred to her as 'tiny' when she first saw her, pronouncing it 'Tanni', and the name stuck. At Seoul 1988 she sampled the Paralympic Games atmosphere for the first time and won a bronze medal in the 400m – 3; by Barcelona 1992 she was at the height of her powers, taking a grand slam of gold medals in all four events from 100m to 800m. In Atlanta four years later she found the going much tougher, with just one gold medal in the 800m – T52 to her name, but she was back to her dominating best at Sydney 2000 with another four gold medals in her favourite events. Even at Athens 2004 she remained a steely competitor, taking gold in the 100m – T53 and 400m – T53. Tanni was made a life peer in March 2010 and sits as a cross-bencher in the House of Lords.

Tanni Grey-Thompson of Britain is all smiles after winning the gold medal in the 400m in the TW3 Wheelchair event at the Barcelona 1992 Paralympic Games. It was one of four gold medals that she would win at that competition.

Humanity campaign in 2008, as well as one of VISA's Olympic commercials. Redmond was amazed, but gratified, to even find himself being mentioned in person by US President Barack Obama in a speech to support Chicago's bid for the 2016 Olympic and Paralympic Games.

The Paralympic Games, held without question in Barcelona, took place straight after the Olympic Games. The Paralympic Movement had become entirely streamlined following the creation of the International Paralympic Committee (IPC) which formalised the integration that had already become a reality in Seoul.

Britain enjoyed a wonderfully successful Games,

taking 40 gold medals and 128 in total to finish in third position behind the USA and Germany. The undoubted British stars of the Games were wheelchair athlete Tanni Grey-Thompson and blind swimmer Chris Holmes. Grey-Thompson, who was born with spina bifida, had won her first medal, a bronze, in the Paralympic Games at Seoul 1988. Four years later she was resplendent, winning a grand slam of medals in the 100m, 200m, 400m and 800m in the TW3 Wheelchair Events. Chris Holmes took an incredible six gold medals in the B2 50m Freestyle, 100m Backstroke, 100m Freestyle, 200m Backstroke, 200m Individual Medley and 400m Freestyle.

Both champions have become fantastic

supporters of the Paralympic cause and inspired later generations of Paralympic athletes. Holmes, awarded the MBE for his services to sport, has served on the Disability Rights Commission and is currently working as the Director of Paralympic Integration for the London 2012 Olympic and Paralympic Games. Grey-Thompson continued to compete at the top level until 2007, finishing her career with a remarkable tally of 11 Paralympic gold medals. She became Baroness Grey-Thompson in 2005 and is a high-profile supporter of the Paralympic Movement and the disabled cause in general.

Another success story of the 1992 Paralympic Games was swimmer Peter Hull. He was born with no legs and shortened arms but became a powerhouse in his sport, taking three golds at the Disabled European Swimming Championships in 1991. A year later he won three Paralympic gold medals in the 50m Backstroke, 50m Freestyle and 100m Freestyle at Barcelona, all three in world-record times. Such victories must have been all the sweeter after the disappointment of the Seoul 1988 Paralympic Games, when Hull suffered the frustration of finishing fourth in each of his three races. He himself acknowledges the important role that mental toughness and resilience have played in his success, noting that, 'It's not just physical fitness, it's mental as well. If you achieve in sport as in life or business, it gives you confidence and makes you feel good about yourself.'

The Games of the 1980s and early 1990s spanned a period of considerable change, both political and in attitudes to sport. By 1992 the Olympic Games was officially accepting professional athletes, a once-unthinkable position; tennis legends and basketball stars such as Michael Jordan and 'Magic' Johnson could now compete for Olympic gold medals. The Paralympic Games had finally fulfilled the great dream of its founder, Sir Ludwig Guttman, receiving the status and recognition of an integral event and being backed by its own

It is the Barcelona 1992 Paralympic Games and Britain's Peter Cordice balances the baton during the 4 x 100m Relay TS2,4. The event was won by Australia in a world record time of 45.95.

organising committee. So much seemed to be new: even the once dominating powerblocks of East Germany and the USSR were evolving into new forms as the political landscape shifted. And yet in one of the Games's most inspirational moments, Derek Redmond's battle to complete his race, the essential values of Olympic and Paralympic competition were shown to be as strong – and as profoundly moving to witness – as they had ever been.

Best of British

Peter Hull

Despite being born with no legs and shortened arms, Peter Hull won three gold medals at the Barcelona 1992 Games – all in world record times. He has competed in long-distance events, mainly to raise money for charity, and successfully finished six London marathons. 'Sport got me where I am today. I've got a quality of life – I work and live independently. It's not just physical fitness, it's mental as well. If you achieve in sport as in life or business, it gives you confidence and makes you feel good about yourself.' In 1996, Hull featured in a Nike poster campaign with the slogan 'Peter is not like ordinary people. He's done the marathon.'

Medal table from the 1992 Paralympic Games

Country	Gold	Silver	Bronze	Total
USA	75	52	48	175
Germany	61	51	59	171
Great Britain	40	47	41	128
France	36	36	34	106
Spain	34	31	42	107
Canada	28	21	26	75
Australia	24	27	25	76

Chapter 8
From There To Here

From There To Here

ONE OF THE MOST DYNAMIC AND EXCITING EPISODES IN BRITAIN'S LONG OLYMPIC AND PARALYMPIC GAMES HISTORY IRONICALLY BEGAN WITH PROFOUND DISAPPOINTMENT. THE ATLANTA 1996 OLYMPIC GAMES BROUGHT JUST ONE GOLD MEDAL FOR GREAT BRITAIN, WON BY THE EVER-RELIABLE STEVE REDGRAVE AND FELLOW OLYMPIC LEGEND MATTHEW PINSENT IN THE MEN'S PAIRS IN ROWING. TOGETHER WITH EIGHT SILVER AND SIX BRONZE MEDALS, BRITAIN ACHIEVED A TOTAL OF 15 AND AN UNDISTINGUISHED 36TH PLACE IN THE MEDAL TABLE. A SINGLE GOLD EQUALLED BRITAIN'S PREVIOUS WORST-EVER GAMES AT HELSINKI 1952, LEAVING A SENSE OF SHAME AT HOME THAT A RELATIVELY WEALTHY, SPORTS-MAD COUNTRY OF NEARLY 60 MILLION PEOPLE COULD, FRANKLY, NOT DO BETTER.

A snow globe featuring the Olympic mascot, Izzy, commemorates the Atlanta 1996 Games. This was the fourth time the USA had hosted the summer Games.

Up until 1992 a small band of exceptional competitors had brought the consolation of quality if not quantity. There was also the fact that Britain, unlike many participating nations, adhered to the essential amateur ethos that underpinned the resurrection of the modern Games in 1896. With the official recognition by the IOC in 1992 that the Games must now be considered 'open', however, the landscape radically changed. Private funds and money that did not come from the taypayer could now be freely directed towards sport in general, and the Olympic and Paralympic Games in particular. A new era had dawned for competitors, coaches, sponsors and all involved with the Games.

Certainly there was a new, more commercial feel to the Atlanta 1996 Games. The organisers closely followed the financial model of the Los Angeles 1984 Games, funding both the Olympic and Paralympic Games through commercial sponsorship and ticket sales. The 'open' Games had a vibrant, colourful atmosphere; an Opening Ceremony featuring cheerleaders and pick-up trucks combined with an innovative fantasy mascot named Izzy to reflect Atlanta's individual 'take' on the event. Some overcrowding on transport and in the venues showed the popularity of the Games with local people, keen to see the sights. The Centennial Olympic Stadium, built specifically for the Games,

showing the Opening and Closing Ceremonies and the Athletics events. After the Games it was successfully adapted into the Turner Field, a new home for the local baseball team, the Atlanta Braves. The Stadium, along with the Georgia Dome, the Georgia Tech Aquatic Center and the Georgia World Congress Center, was part of Atlanta's three-mile 'Olympic Ring', with other events being held at Stone Mountain, about 20 miles from the city. The Wassaw Sound at Savannah hosted the Sailing competition, while the soccer tournament was spread across many Southern cities, including Birmingham, Athens, Washington DC and Miami, to maximise accessibility.

Yet there were also positive notes in this new-look Games. All the current IOC member nations attended, including several former Soviet republics, and a record 79 of the 197 nations attending (in itself a record) won at least one medal. 10,000 competitors took part and new sports or disciplines such as Softball, Beach Volleyball and Mountain Biking were introduced, along with women's Football and Lightweight Rowing. A poignant moment occurred when Muhammad Ali, winner of a Boxing gold medal in the Light Heavy Weight class at the Rome 1960 Games, and now suffering from Parkinson's Disease, lit the Olympic Flame during the Opening Ceremony.

Right Michael Johnson's performance in the 200m final in Atlanta caused disbelief. How could a man run so fast? The American's record-breaking time of 19.32 remains one of the greatest feats in the history of track and field, the gap between second place Frankie Fredericks of Namibia, left, showing the different class that Johnson was in that night.

Michael Johnson

The only male sprinter in history to have won both the 200m and 400m at the same Olympic Games, Michael Johnson set the world on fire in 1996 when he achieved his historic double. Wearing his custom-made golden spikes, Johnson began his Atlanta campaign by running the 400m final in 43.49, a new Olympic record. Three days later he smashed the 200m world record, leaving the rest of the field standing. Johnson was 32 years old by the time of the Sydney 2000 Games. Despite this, he successfully retained his 400m title – the only man to have won two consecutive 400m titles.

'19.32 isn't a 200m time, it's my grandfather's birthday'
Bronze medallist Ato Boldon (Trinidad and Tobago) expresses awe at Michael Johnson's performance

Unsurprisingly the USA dominated the medals, coming top of the table with 101 (including 44 golds), with Russia in second place with 63 medals, 26 of which were gold. Amy Van Dyken won four Swimming gold medals, becoming the first American woman to win four titles in a single Games; Shannon Miller led the women's Gymnastics team, described by the media as the 'Magnificent Seven', to its first team gold medal by defeating the Russians for the first time ever; and the USA also took gold in the inaugural women's Football competition. In the men's events, Andre Agassi took the Tennis gold medal, becoming the first male player to achieve the unofficial Career Golden Slam, winning all four Grand Slam tournaments and the Olympic gold, while Carl Lewis, now aged 35, claimed a fourth Long Jump gold, bringing his personal tally of gold medals to nine.

Yet another American, Michael Johnson, dominated other Athletics events, becoming the first man ever to win golds in the 200m and 400m at the same Games. Johnson set a new world record of 19.32 seconds in the 200m – breaking the one he had set just a month earlier at the US Olympic Trials, by more than 0.3 seconds. Johnson executed his magnificent Olympic display in a curious but highly effective running style, unusually upright and with short steps. His idiosyncratic style was further evidence that you don't need to be "textbook" to be a world beater as shown by the successes of both Eric Liddell and Emil Zátopek, whose running styles were criticised by some before they started defeating all-comers. Johnson's 400m gold was achieved in an Olympic record time of 43.49 seconds, almost a full second ahead of his nearest rival.

In Swimming, a strong discipline for the former Soviet Union, Alexander Popov, a 'giant' at just over two metres tall, took two golds for the Russian Federation. He won the 50m Freestyle and 100m Freestyle, followed by silvers in the 4 x 100m Freestyle Relay and 4 x 100m Medley Relay – a compelling mirror image of his achievement in the Barcelona 1992 Games. Popov was the first man to repeat two Swimming victories in consecutive Games since Johnny Weissmuller, who later became a screen legend as Tarzan. Weissmuller won gold in the 100m Freestyle, 400m Freestyle and 4x200m Freestyle Relay at Paris 1924, followed by the 100m Freestyle and 4x200m Freestyle Relay at Amsterdam 1928, before turning to Hollywood and a movie career.

Gold medals eluded Britain, however, with the exception of Steve Redgrave and Matt Pinsent in the Coxless Pairs. Both were Olympic veterans, good friends as well as rowing partners, and by the Atlanta 1996 Games they had become equals in the boat, a subtle change since their last Olympic gold four years before. The Olympic final, their 100th race together, saw the pair establish a big lead of 3.04 seconds by the halfway point of the race and go on to defeat Australians David Weightman and Robert Scott in a comfortable victory. Redgrave's fourth gold in as many Games placed him alongside legends such as the Danish sailor Paul Elvstrøm, American discus thrower Al Oerter and chasing veteran Hungarian fencer

'I've had enough. This is it for me. If anyone sees me near a boat they can shoot me'

Steve Redgrave after taking his fourth gold medal in as many Olympic Games

Aladár Gerevich's seven gold medals. Redgrave had found the battle to win Great Britain's solitary gold medal in 1996 particularly gruelling and his elation on winning with Pinsent was immediately followed by an almost despairing aside to the cameras: 'This is it for me … If anyone sees me anywhere near a boat you can shoot me.' Happily nobody took Redgrave up on his offer and after a well-deserved rest he started to think more positively about competing in Sydney in 2000.

Other medals, albeit in silver and bronze, reflected solid performances in a range of events. Roger Black, an outstanding 400m specialist who had set the British 400m record in July that year, took the silver medal in the 1996 Games, behind Michael Johnson. He also contributed to Britain's silver in

Best of British

Roger Black

One of the most talented athletes of his generation, Black's career was plagued by injury. Two years after a brilliant start to his international career – when he won gold in the 400m and 4 x 400m Relay at the European Championships and Commonwealth Games – Black had to miss the Seoul 1988 Games. Barcelona 1992 was also a no-show as he recovered from the combined effects of a serious foot injury and a virus. Fit at last for Atlanta 1996, Black knew that if Michael Johnson was on form he was unbeatable. Deciding to run his own race, he kept his nerve and got the result he wanted: as Johnson stormed away to win gold in 43.49, Black was second in 44.41.

Matthew Pinsent salutes his second gold medal after winning the Coxless Pairs with Steve Redgrave, who had just achieved his fourth Olympic gold. The duo had just produced Britain's only winning performance at Atlanta 1996.

Medal table from the 1996 Olympic Games

Country	Gold	Silver	Bronze	Total
USA	44	31	25	100
Russian Federation	26	21	16	63
Germany	20	18	27	65
China	16	22	12	50
France	15	7	15	37
Italy	13	10	12	35
Australia	9	9	23	41
Great Britain (36th position)	1	8	6	15

Jonathan Edwards

With its origins in the Ancient Olympics, the Triple Jump has appeared at each one of the modern Games. Since 7 August 1995 the world record for the discipline has been held by British athlete Jonathan Edwards, who jumped an incredible 18.29m at the 1995 World Championships in Gothenburg. Edwards was understandably hopeful of a gold medal at the Atlanta 1996 Games, but instead had to settle for silver when USA's Kenny Harrison jumped 18.09m – the longest jump ever with a negative wind reading. Four years later in Sydney, Edwards finally won his Olympic gold with a season's best of 17.71m. His success continued into the twenty-first century – at one point in 2002 he held gold medals for the Olympic Games, World Championships, Commonwealth Games and European Championships – until his retirement in 2003. In 1995 Edwards was named BBC Sports Personality of the Year.

Medal table from the 1996 Paralympic Games

Country	Gold	Silver	Bronze	Total
USA	47	46	65	158
Australia	42	37	27	106
Germany	40	58	51	149
Great Britain	39	42	41	122
Spain	39	31	36	106
France	35	29	31	95
Canada	24	22	24	70

the 4 x 400m Relay, assisted by teammates Iwan Thomas, Jamie Baulch and Mark Richardson. Ben Ainslie, arriving on the scene as a teenage sailing prodigy, immediately challenged the Brazilian Robert Scheidt, then considered the world's best dinghy sailor, all the way in the Laser class. Ainslie finally had to make do with the silver medal, but this would be the last time he was bettered in a race that really mattered. Steve Smith from Liverpool won bronze in the High Jump, the first British man since 1908 to win a medal in the event, and Steve Backley, a lynchpin of Britain's athletics team for over 15 years, took silver in the Javelin, sandwiched between a bronze in the Barcelona 1992 Games and another silver at Sydney in 2000. Backley thus became the only British track and field competitor to win medals in three different Olympic Games.

Perhaps the athlete most frustrated by his second place was Jonathan Edwards who went into the 1996 Games as Triple Jump favourite and world record holder. American jumper Kenny Harrison won the gold medal with an astonishing leap of 18.09m, leaving Edwards the consolation of knowing that his distance of 17.88m was the longest ever *not* to win the event.

The Atlanta 1996 Olympic Games may have yielded a largely disappointing outcome for Britain, but the Paralympic Games remained a tour de force. The nation finished fourth in the medal table with 39 gold medals, 42 silver and 41 bronze; only the USA (47), Australia (42) and Germany (40) secured more gold medals. Equestrian entered the full programme, with Sailing and Wheelchair Rugby (formerly known as Murderball) being introduced as demonstration events. The Games had the most participating nations ever, 104, and 269 new world records were set in a remarkable flowering of Paralympic talent. For the first time athletes with a learning disability were accorded full medal status, alongside those with spinal cord disabilities, cerebral palsy, amputations, les autres and visual impairments.

The 1996 Paralympic Games generated some impressive numbers. They were large in scale, attended by 3,259 athletes and 1,717 delegation staff, while a total of 388,373 spectators attended and 2,088 media reported on the Games. They were also the first to receive mass media sponsorship, and had a budget of $81m – the latter much needed as 8,000 rooms were set aside to accommodate competitors and back-up staff and 12,000 volunteers were recruited for general help. Nineteen sports – 7 full medal sports and two demonstration events, Sailing and Wheelchair Rugby – were spread across 508 events at the Games, held between 16–25 August 1996. Tanni Grey-Thompson then unmarried as Tanni Grey, won four medals, taking gold in the T52 800m and silver in the 100m, 200m and 400m. Britain's success in the Paralympic Games was in marked contrast to its limited medal haul in the Olympic Games.

The British public and media were swift to draw a veil over the disappointments of the Atlanta 1996 Olympic Games. Steve Redgrave remembers being warned by BOA officials in Atlanta that he and Matthew Pinsent were likely to be mobbed on their return and would be the focus of all the media attention. As Britain's only gold medallists they were to be prepared for the spotlight. In the event their return went virtually unannounced and unheralded. Yet the issue was already in hand. Behind the scenes sports administrators had already undertaken a major re-think about the best way of funding sport in Britain after 1992. Whether the creation of the National Lottery in November 1994 was a case of happy coincidence, synchronicity or divine intervention doesn't really matter. It arrived, changing the British sporting scene to a massive degree and probably in perpetuity.

It was the moment that many involved in sport in the country had been waiting for, providing a large, steady and reliable influx of non-state money that was ring-fenced for sport. The monies thus earmarked started to come on stream in February 1995. This was too late to have any significant effect on the 1996 Games, especially as in these very early days the financing was targeted unambiguously on medium to long term projects and the upgrading of facilities, ranging from the building of the Millennium Stadium in Cardiff to assisting with new showers at local football or cricket clubs and installing wheelchair ramps and other facilities for disabled competitors. Elite sport was not initially a priority, with the total funding for Britain's Olympic Track Cycling squad in 1996, for example, being just £22,700.

But change was on the way. Shortly after Atlanta, early in 1997, the World Class Performance Programmes (WCPP) were drawn up and gradually introduced. Money became available for elite level athletes judged by the governing bodies of their respective sports to be either medal prospects or potential medal prospects further down the line. This is the system that has brought about such a radical upturn in Great Britain's Olympic fortunes and is underpinning the nation's efforts heading towards London 2012. Since Lottery funding kicked in properly following the Atlanta 1996 Games, Great Britain has accumulated 39 gold medals in just three Olympic Games, only one less than in the nine Games between Rome in 1960 and Barcelona in 1992. The continuation of such funding is constantly reviewed, towards both the sport and the individual, and is performance related.

The financing helped in a number of ways. Firstly it paid the competitors' basic living bills, enabling them to concentrate full time on their sports. In effect they could become full-time athletes – something that may have been the *de facto* situation for a number of them before the watershed of 1992, when amateurism was abolished, but was far from being the case for the majority, especially in the less well funded sports. In addition to that extra financing was made available for specialised equipment, training camps and, probably most importantly of all, for the expert coaches and back-up staff such as

conditioners, physiotherapists and sport scientists. This area had been much neglected throughout Britain's Olympic and Paralympic history, with coaches rarely getting the support they required and the status they deserved.

Performance directors have gradually been employed in all the sports. The level of funding is constantly reviewed, both towards the sport and the individual, and is performance-related. Sport governing bodies have been empowered to employ some of the very best coaching talent in the world. Sometimes such coaches were already working closely with British competitors, for example Jürgen Grobler. He has coached medal-winning Rowing crews at every Olympic Games from 1972 to 2008, the first five Games of which were with the East German squad. Track Cycling employed a brilliant young sports scientist named Peter Keen, who had long felt that, given sufficient funding, he could make great strides very quickly in what was then a small niche sport. Keen drew up the WCPP for Cycling, appointing Dave Brailsford as the WCPP Programme Director and hiring German coach Heiko Salzwedel who was responsible for setting up the successful cycling programme at the Australian Institute of Sport. Other Olympic sports, finally granted the luxury of money to spend on top coaches, trawled the world. The Modern Pentathlon fraternity turned to Jan Bartu from the Czech Republic and Hungarian István Németh, while Swimming eventually persuaded the legendary Australian coach Bill Sweetenham to revamp their entire coaching structure.

This organised, scientific approach to winning and competing, with a couple of exceptions, was new territory for British sport. The general consensus was that it would not really impact until the Athens 2004 Olympic Games at the earliest, by which time a new generation of highly-motivated, brilliantly-coached and savvy competitors would begin to repair Britain's fortunes. The system was at last in place – and how it would have pleased the visionary

Bottom left Aborigine dancer Djakapurra Munyarryan brings atmosphere to the occasion at the amazing Opening Ceremony of Sydney 2000. It was a fabulous start to what proved to be a sensational Games for Britain, where the team won 11 golds.

Bottom right Only one person could light the Olympic Cauldron in Sydney – the darling of Australian sport herself, Cathy Freeman. The Aboriginal megastar lived up to all expectations by going on to win the 400m gold medal.

Sir Arthur Conan Doyle who had recognised the problems nearly 80 years earlier. However, the the national sporting federation governing bodies expected that Britain's sporting public would have to remain patient for a while longer before seeing the success of these changes.

That was not the case, though. The new generation lapped up the change in approach, appearing to gain fresh motivation and impetus overnight. It was now totally acceptable to be hungry and ambitious, absolutely professional and relentless in your pursuit of victory. No stigma was attached to that anymore; the days of the brilliant talented amateur were over, and Britain's competing elite rose to the challenge.

The Sydney 2000 Games in general were breathtaking and quite superb – only Barcelona 1992 can seriously claim to have matched them for enjoyment and atmosphere in modern times. A spectacular Opening Ceremony celebrated Australia's past with 120 stockhorses and their riders tracing the pattern of the Olympic Rings, a procession of Ned Kellys on stilts and explorers on bicycles and, finally, Aboriginal athlete Cathy Freeman's lighting of the Olympic Cauldron. Dressed in a protective white body suit, she appeared to walk on water over a glistening pond to ignite a ring of fire with the Olympic Torch.

It was an extraordinary beginning to an event that was to raise the bar for the Games in the twenty-first century. A heady mixture of confidence, informality and sporting passion gave the Games a true Australian flavour, and Cathy Freeman's performance symbolised a nation looking to the future. Yet

Cathy Freeman

Born in Mackay, Queensland in Australia in 1973, Cathy Freeman started running at school. In 1990, aged 16, she competed in the Commonwealth Games, where she won gold in the 4 x 100m Relay. Four years later in Victoria, she won two more Commonwealth Games gold medals, in the 200m and 400m. Although she had run in the 400m at the Barcelona 1992 Games, she had not made the finals. In 1996 things were different, and Freeman won silver in the 400m, coming second to the formidable Marie-José Pérec. Freeman's successes were not going unnoticed back home, and in 2000 she was given the honour of lighting the Olympic Cauldron at the Opening Ceremony of the Games in Sydney. At those Olympic Games, with the hopes of the nation running with her, she fulfilled her dream of winning gold in the 400m. After the race the crowd wildly cheered her on her victory lap as she proudly carried the Australian and Aboriginal flags.

Australia also acknowledged its proud sporting past. Herb Elliott, who took gold and set a new world record in the 1500m at the 1960 Games, carried the Torch into the Stadium. It was then passed between several great female medallists – Betty Cuthbert (suffering from multiple sclerosis and assisted in her wheelchair by Raelene Boyle), Dawn Fraser, Shirley Strickland de la Hunty, Shane Gould and Debbie Flintoff-King – to celebrate the anniversary of one hundred years of women's participation in the Olympic Games.

It was to be the talismanic Cathy Freeman who provided the iconic image of the Games, winning the 400m in a highly charged Olympic Stadium with impressive composure and ease. The pressure on her to win, as a symbol of reconciliation over an often divisive past, was immense, and she chose a sensible rather than flamboyant route to victory; as she herself acknowledged, 'I forced myself to be practical. I ran one of the most conservative races of my life.' Her psychological strength paid off, and a video of her run is now part of Team GB's preparation for the London 2012 Games. Freeman's lap of honour, holding both the Australian and Aboriginal flags, became a defining image of the Games all over the world, a spectacle of hope which was integrally linked with the Olympic Movement itself.

There were plenty of other memorable moments at the Sydney 2000 Games. Ian Thorpe, Australia's teenage swimming sensation, took gold in the 400m Freestyle, 4 x 100m Freestyle Relay and 4x200m Freestyle Relay, as well as silvers in the 4 x 100m Medley Relay and 200m Freestyle. The most successful athlete of the Games, Thorpe was chosen

Medal table from the 2000 Olympic Games

Country	Gold	Silver	Bronze	Total
USA	36	23	31	90
Russian Federation	32	27	29	88
China	27	16	14	57
Australia	16	25	17	58
Italy	14	8	13	35
France	13	12	11	36
Germany	12	15	24	51
Great Britain 8th position	11	10	7	28

'I can't quite understand what has happened to me of late. It's overawing, overwhelming. I feel like an outsider looking in at it all'

Cathy Freeman, national icon, after taking gold in the 400m at the 2000 Games.

Left Cathy Freeman, wearing her distinctive all-in-one costume, edges ahead in the 400m final. The evening of her victory was anticipated by the home crowd from the moment the Athletics schedule was announced and they were not disappointed thanks to her dramatic win.

Iain Percy

The achievements of Iain Percy sometimes get overlooked, with Ben Ainslie's three gold medals in three successive Games dominating the headlines. However, Percy is a formidable opponent having won the Finn gold medal at Sydney 2000 and then the Star Class, with Andrew Simpson, at Beijing 2008. He has also twice won the Star World Championships, in 2002 with Steve Mitchell and 2010 with Simpson. Percy, renowned as probably the fittest sailor on the water, took up sailing as a four-year-old and has scarcely been off the water since. The Star is the oldest and in many ways most prestigious Olympic class, and the high-quality competition at the Beijing 2008 Games featured no less than eight Olympic gold medallists and seven former world champions. It was always going to be a brutal event to win, and Percy and Simpson had to battle all the way before finally overcoming the leaders on the final day. After Beijing, Percy became a key member of Ainslie's Team Origin crew and in 2010 won the world Match Racing World Championship before again setting his sights on London 2012.

Right On the first night of competition at Sydney 2000, Jason Queally won gold for Britain in Cycling's 1km Time Trial. In that one moment the whole team was lifted as Britain had won as many golds in that opening day as they did during the whole of Atlanta 1996. Another 10 golds were to follow.

Far right It was the moment that Jonathan Edwards had spent a career planning for – and he delivered in style to win the Olympic Triple Jump title with a leap of 17.71m.

to carry his country's flag at the Closing Ceremony before going on to take two more golds (400m Freestyle and 200m Freestyle) and a silver in the 4 x 200m Freestyle Relay in Athens four years later. His performance in Sydney helped Australia to finish fourth in the final medal table, with a total of 58 medals, of which 16 were gold.

Ethiopian athletes also provided some of the Games' great moments, with Haile Gebrselassie taking his second consecutive 10,000m gold. He defeated Paul Tergat of Kenya in a superb final lap, becoming only the third man to defend his title after the great Emil Zátopek and Lasse Virén. The men's Marathon, the last event of the Games, saw Ethiopia take both gold and bronze. The 22-year-old Gezahegne Abera's victory was Ethiopia's first Marathon gold since Abebe Bikila won in Tokyo at the 1964 Games.

'It's incredible. I don't know where the time came from'

Jason Queally on his victory in the 1km Time Trial, sparking Britain's 'Gold Rush' at the 2000 Games

Britain's love affair with the Sydney 2000 Olympic and Paralympic Games was a genuine response to the feel-good factor of the 'athletes' Games', but it was surely magnified by the success that the nation enjoyed from the start. On the first full day of competition the previously unheralded Jason Queally dispelled the negativity of Atlanta, surprising the cycling world by winning the 1km Time-Trial (Kilo) in style. A fine victory in itself, it also created a great surge of confidence throughout the squad. The new system was working. Talented but previously underachieving individuals were emerging as top international competitors – and with some speed, as Queally had only taken up cycling competetively in 1995 having previously been a British Universities waterpolo representative. Great Britain was on a roll, and the medals starting coming with pleasing regularity.

Jonathan Edwards and Ben Ainslie made up for the disappointment of silver medals in Atlanta by striking gold in the Triple Jump and Sailing Laser class respectively. The latter was to prove a particularly nail-biting finish, with the final two races being held on 29 September. Ainslie needed to hold off the challenge of Brazilian Robert Scheidt who by winning the previous two races had closed the gap between the two men to only four points. In the final medal race Ainslie turned the tables on Schiedt, sailing him down the back of the fleet by staying in front and giving him 'dirty air', whilst later in the race ensuring that Scheidt incurred a penalty.

Commentators assumed that in the end the Briton would blink first and settle for another 'valiant' silver. But Ainslie's motto is to never give up. Ever. He may occasionally come second, but the other bloke has to excel to win. Ainslie's was a ruthless clinical approach that spoke volumes for the new kind of Olympian that Britain was spawning.

Sailing proved a rich source of medals overall for Great Britain with Iain Percy winning the Finn class and Shirley Robertson taking the Europe class.

In the 49er class Ian Barker and Simon Hiscocks won silver, and Ian Walker and Mark Covell did the same in the Star class. Walker had previously won a silver medal in the 470 class at Atlanta 1996 with John Merricks, but the latter was tragically killed in a road accident the following year. The total of five medals placed Britain at the top of the Sailing medal table, just ahead of Australia with two golds, a silver and a bronze.

And still the medals kept coming, as other sports joined the party as well. Audley Harrison became the first British boxer to win the Super Heavy Weight boxing gold medal. Dr Stephanie Cook marked the introduction of the women's Modern Pentathlon to the Olympic Games by promptly taking the gold medal, with her teammate Kate Allenby winning bronze. It was another close finish, with Cook lying fourteenth after three events and eighth after four. Her particular strength lay in running, however, with the 3,000m race the last event. In this Cook successfully made up 49 seconds on American athlete Emily deRiel to take the inaugural gold.

Richard Faulds won another gold for Britain in the

Top left Iain Percy on his way to gold in the Finn class Sailing at Rushcutters Bay on Day 15 of the Sydney 2000 Games. His victory was one of three Sailing golds for Team GB at the Games.

Top right No need to guess who has won – it is Britain's Audley Harrison after victory in Boxing's Super Heavy Weight division against Kazakhstan's Mukhtarkhan Dildabekov in Sydney in 2000.

Steve Redgrave

The club of Olympians who have scored gold medals at consecutive Games is an exclusive one and remaining at the top of one's sport for four years is such a challenge. To stay at the top for 16 years is almost unbelievable, and those Olympians who have won a gold medals at five consecutive Games are in the most exclusive club of all. At Los Angeles 1984, Steve Redgrave began his Olympic Rowing career, wining the Coxed Four with Martin Cross, Adrian Ellison, Andy Holmes and Richard Budgett. Four years later in Seoul he won the Coxless Pair with Andy Holmes. Barcelona 1992 saw him team up with Matthew Pinsent in the Coxless Pair, a winning partnership that would be repeated in Atlanta 1996. Redgrave's final Olympic outing, at Sydney 2000, was a much less predictable affair. He had battled ulcerative colitis and Type 1 diabetes over the last decade and was unsure whether he could or indeed should make the team. However, on 23 September 2000, in the Coxless Fours with Matthew Pinsent, Tim Foster and James Cracknell, experience paid off and Steve Redgrave and crew brought the gold home for Britain.

'I made a conscious decision that diabetes had to live with me, not me with diabetes. I couldn't let it change the mechanics and processes of what we were trying to do'

Steve Redgrave on training for his fifth consecutive gold medal at the Sydney 2000 Games

Shooting, Double Trap Shotgun, while back on the athletics track Denise Lewis proved a popular winner of the Heptathlon. She progressed steadily through the seven events, with only the high jump causing a blip when she achieved well below her personal best. She recovered to take first place, but had to run the final event, the 800m, with her leg bandaged because of a calf and Achilles tendon injury. Lewis's time, rather than her position, would prove vital. Her two close rivals, Yelena Prokhorova of Russia and Natallia Sazanovich of Belarus, both finished ahead of the Briton, and a tense wait ensued while the scores were calculated. At last it was declared that Lewis's time of 2:16.83 was sufficient to give her the gold medal, with Prokhorova taking silver and Sazanovich, just four points behind her, the bronze.

Once again Rowing was a success story for the British team, who finished third in the event table behind very strong Romanian and German competition. Britain's men won gold in the Eight, beating Australia into second place with times of 5:33.08 and 5:33.88 respectively, while Guin and Miriam Batten, Gillian Lindsay and Katherine Grainger won silver in the Quadruple Sculls – Britain's first Olympic medal in women's Rowing. The victory that undoubtedly transfixed the nation, however, was that of Steve Redgrave claiming an extraordinary fifth consecutive Rowing gold medal – the end of one of the great British Olympic crusades.

The path to a fifth consecutive gold was anything but straightforward for Redgrave. His initial decision to retire after Atlanta 1996, where he had won his fourth gold, was overturned by the prospect of making Olympic Games history, but it was undeniably a struggle. The decision was made to move Redgrave and Pinsent into the Four alongside Tim Foster and James Cracknell, but only one year into the Olympic cycle, with everything going relatively to plan, Redgrave started to feel weak and fatigued. He complained of raging unquenchable thirsts, and a BBC film crew, working on the

documentary *Gold Fever*, captured the moment when he collapsed virtually unconscious while undergoing fitness testing against other members of the squad on an indoor rowing machine. Something was clearly seriously wrong. After extensive medical tests diabetes was diagnosed and daily self-injections of insulin prescribed.

'When I was told I had it, the consultant also said to me "there is no reason it should affect your dreams",' recalled Redgrave. 'He admitted to me later that he had no idea how I was going to do it. No one had done it before … I made a conscious decision that diabetes had to live with me, not me with diabetes. I couldn't let it change the mechanics and process of what we were trying to do. I had to fit in to what the others were doing, however hard that may be. And it was hard, believe me.'

In contrast to the Atlanta 1996 final when Redgrave had felt 'controlled panic' beforehand, on this occasion he was calm. His experience and mental strength were talismanic to the crew, and they needed his conviction after the disappointing fourth place of Ed Coode and Greg Searle in the Pairs final, held just before the Four. Cracknell had not previously rowed at an Olympic Games, while Foster had done so only once, taking a bronze in the Four in Atlanta. But Pinsent and Redgrave had a partnership lasting 11 years and had enjoyed tremendous success together; this could not stop now.

And it did not, with the British team quickly moving ahead of their rivals. They were in front after only eight lengths, then the Italian crew made up ground, with Britain pulling ahead again in the third quarter. They eased off towards the end, resulting in a close finish: 5:56.24, as opposed to the Italians' 5:56.62, with the Australian crew taking bronze. Only after the race did Redgrave reveal the strain he had been under. 'As we crossed the line, the emotional release was overwhelming. God, my legs were killing me. But I do remember thinking: this pain isn't going to last long and I'm going to be five-time Olympic champion

Steve Redgrave celebrates in Sydney in 2000 after winning his fifth gold medal as a member of the men's Coxless Four. He was part of the team along with Matthew Pinsent, James Cracknell and Tim Foster.

Canada and the USA. This was a vintage Games for Britain. Leading Paralympic athletes were benefitting from the Lottery funding as much as their Olympic counterparts, and some of the biggest names in British Paralympic sport, Tanni Grey-Thompson, Lee Pearson, David Roberts and Sarah Bailey (now Sarah Storey), were all at their magnificent peak.

The Paralympic Games in Sydney featured 3,881 athletes from 123 countries and awarded 1,657 medals. It was the first time that the Paralympic and Olympic Games were organised by the International Paralympic Committee (IPC), the Sydney Paralympic Organising Committee (SPOC) and the Sydney Organising Committee for the Olympic Games (SOCOG) shared departments and a mission to deliver the best possible conditions for elite athletes with a disability. The organisers adopted a seamless approach to technology, ticketing and transport systems. Paralympic and Olympic athletes lived in the same Village, sharing access to catering, leisure facilities and medical care. A record 1.2 million tickets were sold for the Paralympic Games. It was a memorable Paralympic Games all-round, with the emphasis upon integration within the wider Olympic Movement. This was highlighted by some clever touches, such as Kylie Minogue, who sang 'Dancing Queen' in the Closing Ceremony before also opening the Paralympic Games with 'Waltzing Matilda' and 'Celebration'. In the Paralympic Games' own Closing Ceremony the Australian group *The Seekers* sang their song 'The Carnival is Over', with lead singer Judith Durham, who had recently broken a hip in a car accident, performing from a wheelchair.

'Sydney 2000 will always hold a special place in the hearts of everyone who was there,' says Grey-Thompson who, with four gold medals under her belt, understandably returned from Australia with happy memories. 'The Aussies love their sport and they treated us simply as sportsmen and women. We weren't regarded as role models or inspirations, we were competitors.' Her personal haul of four

Medal table from the 2000 Paralympic Games				
Country	Gold	Silver	Bronze	Total
Australia	63	39	47	149
Great Britain	41	43	47	131
Canada	38	33	25	96
Spain	38	30	38	106
USA	36	39	34	109
China	34	22	17	73
France	30	28	28	86

for the rest of my life. I can live with that pain.'

The appeal of Redgrave is not difficult to understand. Five consecutive Olympic gold medals is an 'athletic' achievement almost beyond compare, but it even transcended that. Here was a very British hero – the no-nonsense dyslexic son of a builder from Marlow triumphing in what had been perceived, rightly or wrongly, as an elitist sport. Now that rumour was dispelled – anyone, given will and dedication, could truly conquer the world.

While Britain's Olympic competitors were enjoying a phoenix-like resurgence after the 1996 Games, the Paralympians continued to be a force to be reckoned with. They had done well in Atlanta but they did even better in Australia four years later. The Paralympic team of 215 competitors took 41 gold, 43 silver and 47 bronze medals, coming second in the medals table to Australia ahead of

'Sydney was an athletic Disneyland, it was where magic happened'

Tanni Grey-Thompson, four times gold medal winner at the Sydney 2000 Paralympic Games

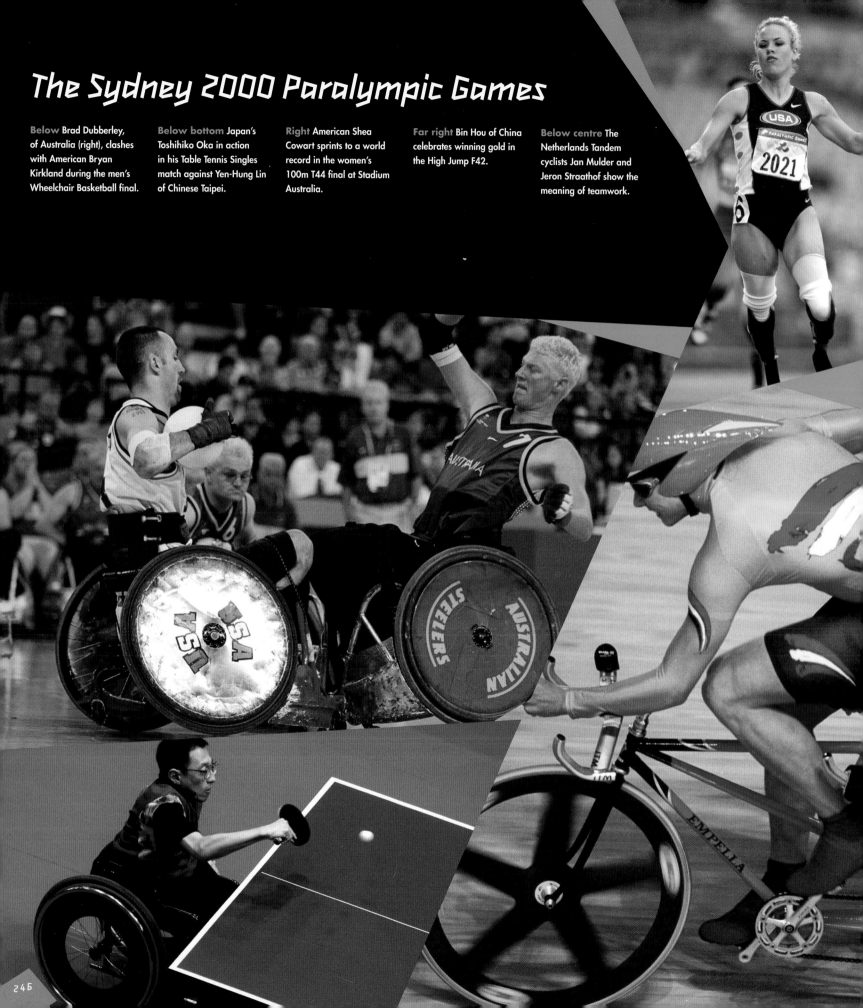

The Sydney 2000 Paralympic Games

Below Brad Dubberley, of Australia (right), clashes with American Bryan Kirkland during the men's Wheelchair Basketball final.

Below bottom Japan's Toshihiko Oka in action in his Table Tennis Singles match against Yen-Hung Lin of Chinese Taipei.

Right American Shea Cowart sprints to a world record in the women's 100m T44 final at Stadium Australia.

Far right Bin Hou of China celebrates winning gold in the High Jump F42.

Below centre The Netherlands Tandem cyclists Jan Mulder and Jeron Straathof show the meaning of teamwork.

Above Belarus, Spain and Portugal compete in the 4 x 400m Relay T13 final at Stadium Australia.

Below Australia's Louise Sauvage on her way to lighting the Olympic Cauldron during the Opening Ceremony of the Paralympic Games at Sydney's Olympic Park.

Chris Hoy

Hoy got his first bike at the age of six and was competing in – and winning – the national BMX championships at seven. By the time he was 14, he was ranked second in Britain and ninth in the world. He won his first Olympic gold medal at Athens 2004, powering to victory in the 1km Time Trial fractions of a second ahead of world record holder Arnaud Tournant. Four years later at Beijing 2008, Hoy started his Olympic campaign by winning gold in the men's Team Sprint with Jason Kenny and Jamie Staff. Then came the Keirin and a second gold medal. Finally, he overcame teammate and junior world champion Jason Kenny to win the men's Individual Sprint. Already Scotland's most successful Olympian, the first Briton to win three gold medals in a single Olympic Games since Henry Taylor in 1908, and the most successful Olympic male cyclist of all time, Hoy's gaze is now fixed on London 2012 and the Olympic record books.

Hands up for the gold medal winner. Britain's Chris Hoy – now Sir Chris Hoy – celebrates after the presentations for the men's 1km Time Trial at Athens 2004; he would return to the Games at Beijing 2008 to win three events.

'I am in very good shape ... I have very good legs'

Chris Hoy

golds from the 100m, 200m, 400m and 800m – T53 proved an inspiring example for her teammates, with Caroline Innes taking two golds and a silver in the 200m, 400m and 100m – T36 respectively. Deborah Brennan in the 200m – T34 and Hazel Robson in the 100m – T36 also won racing golds, while Lloyd Upsdell shone in an outstanding men's team with gold in the 200m, 100m – T35 and silver in the 4 x 100m Relay – T38. The ever-impressive Robert Matthews took gold in the 10,000m – T11 and silver in the 5000m and Marathon, while gold medals went to Chris Martin (Discus – F33), Ken Churchill (Javelin – F37) and Stephen Miller (Club Throw).

Lee Pearson triumphed in the Equestrian competition, with gold medals in the Mixed Dressage, Freestyle Mixed Dressage and Mixed Dressage Team Open, while swimmer David Roberts continued his dominance of the pool with two golds and two silvers in individual events and a further gold, silver and bronze in relays. This golden Games for the British team was a remarkable achievement for its organisers too. As Tanni Grey-Thompson later observed, this was a defining moment in Paralympic history, 'the time and place when Paralympians genuinely became part of the Olympic Movement'.

The Athens 2004 Games

After the success of Sydney – wildly unexpected by the public and certainly not predicted by the media – there was considerably more pressure on the British team heading to Athens for the 2004 Olympic and Paralympic Games than had been the case for many years. Lottery funding was now flooding into British sport, and a visible improvement across the board had raised the bar. It all took a little getting used to. Britain had made an unambiguous financial commitment to Olympic and Paralympic sports, and now they were expected to deliver.

In Athens that pressure was cranked up further, as the Games were nearly a week old before Great Britain claimed its first gold medal. But it was worth waiting for. Late on 20 August Chris Hoy produced what many still consider to be the ride of his life to win the 1km Time Trial – the Kilo that Jason Queally had won so dramatically in Sydney. The most exceptional aspect of Hoy's ride that evening in Athens was the fact that, seeded to ride last, he had to watch all three riders going immediately before him break the existing sea-level world record before his own chance came. Such formidable competition would have made many people freeze or panic, faced with having to bring that record down yet again to win. Chris Hoy showed that night what an Olympian he was, with the temperament as well as the physical strength to deliver. He was to underline this most impressively in Beijing four years later.

Hoy's win also served to open up the floodgates for Britain, and medals started to flow in as if on tap. Rowing, one of Britain's most consistent success stories in recent years, continued to deliver, with women rowers making a breakthrough in their events. Catherine Bishop and Katherine Grainger took silver in the women's Pairs against stiff competition; only 0.5 seconds separated all boats at 500m, and the British gradually overhauled Belarus to come second to the Romanian pair. In the women's Double Sculls another exhilerating race was won by

Right Tears of joy for Matthew Pinsent after he receives his gold medal – his fourth – at the Athens 2004 Games in the men's Coxless Fours with Ed Coode (right), James Cracknell and Steve Williams.

> 'Four years of emotion went into those six minutes'
>
> James Cracknell, gold medallist in the men's Coxless Fours at the 2004 Games

New Zealand, with Britain's Sarah Winckless and Elise Laverick coming in third behind Germany to take bronze. Meanwhile Britain's Coxed Quadruple Sculls team won silver with Germany taking gold.

The highlight of the Rowing, however, was the men's Four, which, stroked by Matthew Pinsent, took gold in a tightly-fought race. Pinsent, together with James Cracknell, remained from the successful Sydney 2000 Olympic Games and this time they were joined by Ed Coode and Steve Williams as they took an early lead, and at 500m they were 0.44 seconds ahead of the world champion Canadian crew. The Canadians responded to the challenge, and by the third quarter they were in front, putting the British boat under extreme pressure in the final stages of the race. Yet the British fought back to win in a dramatic photo-finish with a time of 6 minutes 6.98 seconds, just 0.08 seconds ahead of the Canadians, with Italy taking bronze.

It was a notable achievement, both for Pinsent,

> 'We knew if we got to halfway and we were with them, they were going to be in more trouble than us. Then we just moved on'
>
> Matthew Pinsent on defeating the world champion Canadian crew to win his fourth Rowing gold medal in Athens

Best of British

Kelly Holmes

'You've won it Kelly, you've won it!' Steve Cram's passionate commentary as Kelly Holmes looked disbelieving after winning the women's 800m at the Athens 2004 Games echoed what millions of Britons were shouting at their television screen. After a career dogged by injury and bad luck, and having run an exemplary tactical race, she had finally done what she had been threatening to do for years: win an Olympic gold medal. Five days later, on 28 August, a newly confident Holmes took to the track again in her signature event, the 1500m. Again running from the back and taking the lead in the final straight, she crossed the line a convincing winner, setting a new British record of 3:57.90. In doing so, she became the first British woman to win a double Olympic gold.

Right Ben Ainslie is the flag-waving hero of the seas after winning the Finn class for Britain in Qingdao at the Beijing 2008 Games. At London 2012, he will be chasing his fourth successive gold.

who had never lost in an Olympic final and now received his fourth gold medal in four Olympic Games, and for the crew as a whole. They had suffered a difficult season affected by injury, with Coode coming into the boat at short notice to replace Alex Partridge who unfortunately suffered a collapsed lung. Jürgen Grobler, the highly experienced German coach who had overseen the resurgence of British Olympic Rowing, was moved to describe the moment of victory as 'the most emotional situation I have ever had. This was maybe the toughest season we have had so far … it is a big relief to me and British rowing.' Pinsent, who retired later in 2004, said merely, 'I thought we rowed a really good race and controlled it nicely in the middle' – a typically understated reaction to becoming an Olympic legend.

Ben Ainslie also won another gold medal after moving up to the heavier Finn class. Despite being the strong favourite for gold, he had to win the hard way following a controversial disqualification on the first day and in only his second race. French opponent Guillaume Florent lodged a belated protest, having declined at the time an offer by Ainslie to put in a penalty turn. 'That evening was

the low point of my sailing career,' confesses Ainslie, who was left trailing in 19th position overall. He now had the bit between his teeth, and what happened next has already become part of Olympic folklore. He hit back with two stunning wins the next day, then added two more for good measure, not to mention two seconds, a third and fourth. Before the last race began it was all over bar the shouting.

'As I walked down to the jetty that second morning in Athens I couldn't wait to race,' Ainslie explained afterwards. 'I'd never felt quite like this before in a boat. For the rest of the week I sailed right on the edge, and loved it …- I wasn't interested in a brave 'battling' finish down the fleet, or even in silver or bronze. I had to show I was the best and take gold despite everything.' And he did.

Great Britain were also successful in the Yngling class with the crew of Shirley Robertson, Sarah Webb and Sarah Ayton taking control early in the regatta and never relinquishing control. In Cycling, Bradley Wiggins won gold in the 4km Individual Pursuit by beating Australian Brad McGee, his nemesis at the Commonwealth Games in Manchester two years earlier. Wiggins also took silver in the men's Team Pursuit and bronze in the Madison, becoming the first British athlete since Mary Rand in 1964 to win three medals in a single Olympic Games. Kelly Sotherton took a bronze in the Heptathlon, coping well with the pressure of being the only British competitor as her teammate Denise Lewis, who had won gold for Britain at the 2000 Games, unfortunately had to withdraw from the competition following injury.

Tales of the unexpected characterised many events. In the Marathon pre-race favourite Paula Radcliffe, suffering from the intense heat, failed to finish, pulling out in distress after 23 miles. Britain's Equestrian team had better fortune. Leslie Law, riding Shear l'Eau, received an Individual gold medal in the Eventing competition after an appeal saw him raised from silver medal position; teammate Pippa Funnell also won an Individual

Britain does indeed rule. (Left to right) Sarah Webb, Shirley Robertson and Sarah Ayton of Britain pose with their T-shirts after winning gold in the women's keelboat Yngling event at the Athens 2004 Games.

' ... it literally felt like I had wings on my shoulders ... I just felt I was in a place where I was so happy – I'd been through so much emotion and pain in my career and fought to get where I got and finally, it all came together'

Kelly Holmes, gold medal winner in the 800m and 1500m in the 2004 Games

bronze. The Court of Arbitration for Sport decided that German rider Bettina Hoy had crossed the starting line twice in the Show Jumping part of the competition and should have been awarded time penalties of 12 points, a verdict which also saw the British team of Law, Funnell, Jeannette Brakewell, Mary King and William Fox-Pitt elevated from bronze to silver medals. Law was delighted by his achievement, Britain's first Equestrian gold for 32 years, commenting that 'I went to Athens looking for a team medal; that was my main job. It was always going to be tough to get an individual medal ... I thought my best chance was a bronze.'

In the swimming pool there was a fine performance from teenager David Davies, who won bronze in the 1500m Freestyle with a new British and European record time of 14 minutes 45.95 seconds. This knocked 12 seconds off Davies's personal best, set only a few days earlier when he became the first man to complete the distance in an Olympic heat in less than 15 minutes. He finished strongly in the final, mounting a late challenge to his hero, Australia's Grant Hackett, who took the gold medal with a new Olympic record of 14:14.04.

Davies, who had won the European Junior Championships and been voted best male newcomer in Europe in 2002, had competed in his first international senior event only two years before Athens, when he reached the 1500m Freestyle final in the 2002 Commonwealth Games. His medal-winning performance, and that of Stephen Parry, who took bronze in the 200m Butterfly, were some consolation for Britain's swimmers, one of the few areas that Britain had met with little success in the 2000 Games. Their celebrated Australian coach, Bill Sweetenham, had in fact predicted just two medals in the 2004 Olympic Games, noting that rebuilding a team to compete at the highest level in the world was not a swift process. And although a haul of two bronze medals did not set the world alight, there were certainly signs of progress. In Sydney British swimmers competed in only five finals, while in 2004

Medal table from the 2004 Olympic Games

Country	Gold	Silver	Bronze	Total
USA	36	39	26	101
China	31	17	14	62
Russian Federation	27	25	38	90
Australia	17	16	16	49
Japan	16	9	12	37
Germany	13	16	20	49
France	11	9	13	33
Great Britain (10th position)	9	9	12	30

they appeared in 14, and in 19 semi-finals, breaking three Commonwealth and nine British records on the way. The prospects for the future were looking good.

In the second week Britain's attention shifted to the athletics stadium and a remarkable 800m and 1500m double by Kelly Holmes, for many *the* British story of the Games. The glorious double was far from expected. Holmes was always a high-quality athlete; she had been an 800m bronze medal winner at Sydney 2000 and was the holder of numerous British middle distance records. However, she had been jinxed by injury and illness throughout her competitive career and at the age of 34 most commentators believed she was past her best. In the build up to Athens, Holmes was barely mentioned as a serious gold medal prospect, but one factor was finally running in her favour.

For once she entered a major Games completely free of injury and experiencing a surge of confidence in that happy state. Having combined athletics and an Army career for many years, working first as a heavy goods vehicle (HGV) driver in the Women's Royal Army Corps (WRAC) and then as a physical training instructor, she had used the Lottery funding available to become a full time athlete in the latter years of her career. In the build-up to Athens she had been on long training camps in Africa with Maria Mutola, the extraordinary talented 800m runner from Mozambique. Holmes considered the 800m very much her second event and almost didn't enter, only confirming her entry five days before the Games began. Despite the late entry she fought a clever and strategic campaign through the rounds, and in the final timed her late surge perfectly to win the gold medal in a very swift 1 minute 56.38 seconds. Her wide eyes of disbelief – 'Am I really winning this race?' – as Holmes crossed the line told the story perfectly, and captured the hearts of British spectators watching at home.

This was followed by the 1500m, her specialist event, but now the dynamic had changed. Holmes

had already achieved the dream of a lifetime and the pressure was off – which as an athlete can either work for you or against you. For Holmes it proved liberating. She won comfortably in a British record and this time was smiling broadly as she crossed the line. She had achieved a double that had eluded Sebastian Coe, Steve Ovett and other legends of the sport. It was a moment of pure delight for Holmes, who knew this would be her last Olympic Games. 'I absolutely felt like I was floating in that race, it was the weirdest thing. I was running and it literally felt like I had wings on my shoulders,' she recalled afterwards. 'I suppose I went into the 2004 Olympics slightly differently because it was the first year in seven that I hadn't had an injury … I had a lot of confidence, my training had gone amazingly well, I had a brilliant team of people working with me … It was the right time and the right place.'

It was probably fitting, given the changing nature of British Olympic sport, that the Athens 2004 Games finished with a gold medal that nobody within athletics had ever dared to dream about. The men's 4 x 100m Relay was traditionally the preserve of the USA and 2004 looked unlikely to be an exception. The USA had three runners in the first four of the 100m final, won by Justin Gatlin in 9.85 seconds, while the British team had failed to qualify a single runner for that final. The team had indeed encountered a lot of criticism over this, and the athletes were probably angry as a result. With even half-decent baton changing the Americans looked certain to win the relay, and they clocked up a comfortable win over second-placed Great Britain in the semi-final.

But no race is over until it's over, and in the final the British quartet of Jason Gardener, Darren Campbell, Marlon Devonish and Mark Lewis-Francis ran a flawless race. The changeovers were slick, and the baton passed smoothly from Gardener to Campbell to Devonish to Lewis-Francis, while the Americans fumbled. They seemed to panic at

Left Every picture tells a story – and what an amazing story this one told. Eye-popping Kelly Holmes cannot believe it as she crosses the line at Athens 2004 after winning the 800m gold medal. Five days later she won her second gold in the 1500m, the first time a British athlete had achieved that double since Albert Hill at the Antwerp 1920 Games.

Below Oh, What A Night! Britain's team are all smiles after winning the 4 x 100m Relay gold. The quartet (left to right) is Marlon Devonish, Mark Lewis-Francis, Darren Campbell and Jason Gardener.

finding a team in such close contention. At the end of the second leg the American Coby Miller went too soon, taking the baton at a virtual standstill. Devonish ran a brilliant final bend to give Lewis-Francis a precious advantage, and somehow he held off the USA's Maurice Greene to win by 0.01 of a second. Teamwork had triumphed, resulting in an incredible victory.

Darren Campbell, the elder statesman of the team, ran the second leg of the relay. He was 30 at the time of the 2004 Games, with a career behind him that lacked only the crown of an Olympic gold medal. Campbell's story powerfully illustrates the impact of Lottery funding on British athletes. In 1994 he was working in Tesco's freezer department; in 2000 he was on the Olympic podium in Sydney receiving a 200m silver medal; and in 2004 he took the 4 x 100m Relay gold on one of the most memorable nights for British athletics in Olympic history. Lottery funding enabled Campbell to train harder and more efficiently, not least by spending more time abroad in climates that made training easier. As he observes, 'it is difficult to criticise athletes when they have to hold down a day job and then train in the evening ... only the chosen few could make it work, and that is why you have to admire those guys so much.' According to Campbell, Lottery funding has transformed individuals' prospects simply by freeing up time for training: 'You don't have to worry about how am I going to pay my bills; instead you can focus on what you are going to do to win.' It continues to make the difference, shown in the fortunes of Olympic and Paralympic competitors in recent years.

Athens also proved another huge success for Britain's Paralympians with the country finishing runners up in the medals table, as they had done at the 2000 Games. This time they won 94 medals including 35 gold medals. China, placed only sixth in Sydney, leaped to the top of the rankings as they began to pour resources into Paralympic sport ahead of staging their own Paralympic Games in 2008.

In contrast to the Olympic Games, British Paralympic swimmers were the dominant force in the pool. They contributed 52 of Britain's medal total of 94, including 16 golds – thus beating the target of 15 set by their performance director Tim Reddish. David Roberts from Swansea was again outstanding, with four gold-winning performances in the 100m and 400m Freestyle S7, the 50m S7 and the 4 x 100m Freestyle Relay 34 pts, as well as silver in the 200m Individual Medley SM7. His feat was equalled by teammate Jim Anderson. The extrovert Scot, a former British wheelchair disco-dancing champion, won his gold medals in the S2 events. First came the 50m Freestyle and Backstroke titles, the same double that he had pulled off in Atlanta eight years before, followed by two more Freestyle events, the 100m and 200m. After his heroics in the pool Anderson received an MBE, and was also voted the BBC Scotland Sports Personality of the Year for 2004. He was awarded an OBE in 2009.

The teenager Oscar Pistorius of South Africa, wearing revolutionary carbon-fibre prosthetic legs, took the 2004 Games by storm, winning gold in the T44 200m in a world record time of 21.97 seconds and bronze in the 100m. It was a statement of intent from the South African, still only 17; his talent was clearly immense, and his carbon-fibre prosthetic legs highlighted the complex issues posed by modern technology. Britain's Paralympic athletes found the going unusually tough in Athens, and had to dig deep. They secured only 17 Athletics medals compared with the bumper haul of 48 in Sydney, and just three of those were gold. Danny Crates, once hoping for a rugby career before losing an arm in a diving accident, beat a highly competitive field to win the T46 800m, adding to his bronze medal for the 400m in the 2000 Games. The relentless Tanni Grey-Thompson took her leave from the Paralympic Games as a competitor with two further gold medals in the T53 100m and 400m,

Best of British

Lee Pearson

Throughout Britain's golden run – between 2000 and 2008 – Lee Pearson was a massive presence in the Paralympic Equestrian team, winning nine gold medals and completing the same hat-trick on all three occasions – Dressage, Freestyle Dressage and Team Dressage. A larger than life character, Pearson was born with arthrogryposis multiplex congenita, which, as he explains, means 'I walk with crutches and my legs are encased in plastic to help me walk, so I'm kind of splintered up... But on a horse, it's more to do with your confidence, your balance and your feel'. A big supporter of gay rights, Pearson says 'I feel lucky that I found my talent, not unlucky that I was born with a disability. When I'm on a horse I'm more worried about what the riding hat is doing to my hair than what my bent legs and arms are doing. What riding has given me is respect. I may daydream occasionally that I've got a gorgeous, muscled body, but I don't have a choice about my disability just as I don't have a choice about being gay.'

bringing her career total to an outstanding eleven gold medals.

Grey-Thompson had become the most decorated British athlete in Paralympic history, but the 2004 Games had not been the easiest for the 35-year-old. Her strategy in the 800m was not successful, and she finished a disappointing seventh of eight, but she went on to win the 100m, probably her least favoured event – it was, by her own reckoning, 'the most emotional race I've ever run.' The 400m, by contrast, was a relatively straightforward affair, broadcast live on breakfast television – a fairytale finale to a career that had spanned four Paralympic Games and made her a household name. Her passion for Paralympic sport is renowned and, already looking to the future, she issued something of a rallying call. 'One of our priorities across all sports must be to get the young talent through. These Games have been a good opportunity for us to increase our awareness of the bigger picture because if we lose that focus, we will be left behind.'

Lee Pearson, as expected, led the way in the Equestrian competition on Blue Circle Boy. He won three gold medals, two individual and one team grade I in Mixed and Freestyle Dressage, a feat repeated by Debbie Criddle riding Figaro IX in the G111 dressage events. Britain led the event medal table, with five gold and three bronze medals, ahead of Norway and Sweden, in joint second, and Germany third. Britain also won its first Wheelchair Tennis medal in the inaugural Quad Singles tournament. Peter Norfolk showed no ill effects of a shoulder injury sustained over the summer in sweeping aside world number two American David Wagner in straight sets to take the gold medal.

Cycling made its presence felt with a double for Darren Kenny in the 1km Time Trial and the Individual Pursuit, while both Powerlifter Emma Brown and Isabel Newstead in Shooting retained their Paralympic titles. The British Wheelchair Basketball team also took a remarkable bronze medal by

defeating the USA, while Britain's archers celebrated a notable double gold. John Cavanagh won the men's Individual W1 title, and Anita Chapman, Margaret Parker and Kathleen Smith triumphed in the women's Open Team competition.

The Paralympic competition had been tougher than anticipated, as competitors and coaches alike acknowledged. Only victory in the final Swimming race, the women's 4 x 50m 20 point Medley Relay, placed Britain ahead of the Sydney total of gold medals. Britain's Paralympians had achieved their target, but all medals had been extremely hard won in a very competitive environment.

'The Great Haul of China'

Just 12 years on from the nadir of the Games in Atlanta, performances at the Beijing 2008 Olympic and Paralympic Games now seem nearly incredible. Britain came fourth in the Olympic medal table with a total of 47, of which an astonishing 19 were gold. It was the nation's best performance for a century; only in 1908 did Britain win more golds, and take more medals overall. As an example of what can be achieved when the right financing and training structures are put in place, such results could hardly

Medal table from the 2004 Paralympic Games				
Country	Gold	Silver	Bronze	Total
China	63	46	32	141
Great Britain	35	30	29	94
Canada	28	19	25	72
USA	27	22	39	88
Australia	26	39	35	100
Ukraine	24	12	19	55
Spain	20	27	24	71

Below Fireworks explode over the Bird's Nest Stadium in Beijing in the Opening Ceremony of the Olympic Games in 2008 – one of the greatest spectacles in the history of the Olympic Movement.

be bettered. Compared with the previous 100 years or so of British Olympic, and later Paralympic, endeavour, this may have lacked a certain romance or spontaneous brilliance. But UK Sport's medal targets and directives were unashamedly couched like business plans, calculated and clinical. In the modern world that's how you have to approach the 'business' of winning if you want to succeed.

Public figures and major new names were to emerge from the 2008 Games. Chris Hoy, soon to become Sir Chris, became the first British competitor to win three gold medals at a single Olympic Games since swimmer Henry Taylor, exactly 100 years earlier. Ben Ainslie, Sailing's powerhouse, won a third consecutive gold medal, and Iain Percy won a second consecutive gold on the Sailing Star class, as did Sarah Ayton and Sarah Webb in the Yngling class. Rebecca Adlington – virtually unknown to general British sports fans before the Games – returned home from Beijing a public figure after her two gold medals. So did cyclist Bradley Wiggins, building upon his success from the Athens 2004 Games. Coaches and administrators also suddenly hit the limelight. Dave Brailsford, for example, was feted as the guru who had 'transformed' Britain into a cycling superpower through shrewd man management of a golden generation of riders, complemented by recruitment of the very best coaches and back up staff in the world. Brailsford continued, and added his own take to, the strategies that Peter Keen had put in place. The result saw Cycling take an extraordinary eight gold medals – seven on the Track and one, splendidly taken by Nicole Cooke, in the women's Road Race.

Brailsford epitomised just about everything that was considered good and progressive about the Great Britain team in Beijing, but he was always his own man. He only ever spoke about the level of performance he demanded, not the outcome, emphasising his belief that if you do 100 simple small things as well as it is possible to do them in

a complicated process, you are likely to be more successful than your opponents. Such an approach extended to fitness and conditioning work and advanced bike technology to squeeze every last fraction of a second of speed out of the bike itself. It even included ways to avoid the stomach bugs and other minor illnesses that seem to plague top athletes. Medical experts lectured the Cycling squad on the absolute necessity of handwashing, almost to an obsessional degree. No stone was left unturned.

In the lead-up to Beijing 2008 Brailsford established the so-called 'secret squirrel' club. It was headed up by Chris Boardman, winner of the Individual Pursuit Olympic gold medal in 1992. This team beavered away, fine tuning and developing the British bikes and aerodynamic race suits and helmets. The regulations of the international governing body Union Cycliste Internationale (UCI) were pushed to the limit, but never beyond. Sporting authorities distrust sudden change so British innovations were brought in unannounced. Backroom technicians quietly videoed unsuspecting UCI scrutinisers as they passed the bikes fit for purpose, to provide documentary evidence of such approval if required. On some occasions bicycles were elaborately hidden under tarpaulins to enhance the air of mystery: had Britain come up with something new or not? The mere suspicion of other competitors that they might have done meant that the psychological battle was half won. Such mental tussles are not new. Exactly 100 years earlier, in the 1908 Games, the American tug-of-war team believed the Liverpool police to have an advantage because they were being allowed to wear their work shoes. As a result the Americans were on the back foot before the contest had even begun.

The British Cycling team became highly skilled at talent spotting across various disciplines. Rebecca Romero, for example, had won a Rowing silver medal at the 2004 Olympic Games, but she wanted to move on from this sport and compete for an individual gold medal. Brailsford approached her for his cycling squad and, four years later, Romero remarkably became the Olympic women's Individual Pursuit champion. Meanwhile former BMX world champion Jamie Staff, who had been trying his hand with mixed fortunes at the Keirin and Kilo, was suddenly switched to be lead man in the Team Sprint. Here all his extraordinary power could be harnessed to maximum effect, enabling him to cover the first lap in just a fraction over 17 seconds from a standing start. Such key decisions were to transform the British squad from medal contenders to Olympic champions and world record holders.

The 2008 Olympic Games was the third held in Asia, following Tokyo 1964 and Seoul 1988. it was to prove an extraordinary sporting occasion which saw 43 new world records and 132 new Olympic records established, many in the brand new stadium in Beijing that became known as the 'Bird's Nest' for its interweaving skeletal framework. The Games featured 28 sports and 302 events, nine of which, including the women's 3000m Steeplechase, the men's and women's 10km Marathon in Swimming and the men's and women's BMX, were new additions. Two athletes dominated the Games overall: swimmer Michael Phelps, who broke the records for the most gold medals in a single Olympic Games by winning eight events in the pool, and Jamaican Usain Bolt, who won both the Athletics 100m and 200m in compelling fashion and set new world records in both.

Athletics was one area where Britain's achievements in 2008 did not quite match expectations. Ultimately there were just four Athletics medals although that did include an exceptional gold for Christine Ohuruogu in the 400m, Britain's 50th Olympic Athletics gold. Elsewhere there were silver medals for Phillips Idowu and Germaine Mason in the Triple Jump and High Jump respectively and a bronze for Tasha Danvers in the 400m Hurdles, in which she set a personal best time of 53.84 seconds.

Archery, Badminton and Shooting also disappointed, but they were in the minority. Britain's success encompassed many sports at the 2008 Games, with Cycling, Sailing, Swimming and Rowing proving particularly strong.

Nicole Cooke won Britain's first medal of the Games, riding a Boardman bike frame in the women's Road Race. Her victory, in difficult conditions caused by torrential driving rain, made her the first woman to win both the World Championships title and an Olympic gold medal in the same year. Also in Cycling, Emma Pooley took silver in the women's Time Trial and Bradley Wiggins again triumphed in the men's Individual Pursuit, the first rider to defend this title successfully in the Olympic Games; his teammate Steven Burke took bronze. In the women's Individual Pursuit Rebecca

Best of British

Bradley Wiggins

Track cyclist Bradley Wiggins has emerged as of one Britain's great Olympians over the last decade having garnered a total of six medals, including three golds. The Belgium-born son of a noted Australian Six Day event rider and an English mother, Wiggins settled in London at the age of two. At Sydney 2000 he won a bronze medal in the Team Pursuit and four years later he recorded a memorable victory over Australia's Brad McGee to take gold in the Individual Pursuit. Wiggins was on a roll and also took a silver medal in the Team Pursuit and a bronze in the Madison with Rob Hayles. At the Beijing 2008 Games he defended his Individual title and was part of the world record-breaking GB squad in the Team Pursuit. His massive achievement was slightly overshadowed by Sir Chris Hoy's remarkable hat-trick, but, with a fourth place in the Tour de France the following year, Wiggins is arguably the best all-round cyclist this country has ever produced.

Medal table from the 2008 Olympic Games

Country	Gold	Silver	Bronze	Total
China	51	21	28	100
USA	36	38	36	110
Russian Federation	23	21	28	72
Great Britain	19	13	15	47
Germany	16	10	15	41
Australia	14	15	17	46
People's Republic of Korea	13	10	8	31

Right Britain's Chris Hoy on his final lap before setting an Olympic record and winning the gold medal in the men's Track Cycling 1km Time Trial final at Athens 2004. It was his first Olympic gold.

'When you cross the line all the pressure that has built up, the expectation and the self doubt, evaporates just like that'

Chris Hoy, cycling phenomenon, describes winning his third gold medal

Romero and Wendy Houvenaghel claimed gold and silver for Britain respectively, and Victoria Pendleton won the women's Individual Sprint.

The incredible run at the Laoshan Velodrome continued with a compelling performance in the men's Team Pursuit. Ed Clancy, Paul Manning, Geraint Thomas and Bradley Wiggins broke the world record in the final qualification ride and pushed the strong Danish team into silver medal position in the final. In the Team Sprint Chris Hoy joined with Jamie Staff and Jason Kenny to take gold. The Britons set the pace from the start, breaking the world record in qualifying with a time of 42.950 seconds; as Hoy observed, 'you have to come in and commit from the word go. You never know how the other teams are going to perform.' He also enjoyed a commanding victory in the Keirin, with teammate Ross Edgar coming second, before fending off another talented colleague, Jason Kenny, to win gold in the Individual Sprint. Kenny took silver. The astonishing team performance placed Britain comfortably top of the event medal table with eight gold medals, four silver and two bronze – 14 in total, leaving France in second with six.

The faces of success in Beijing, Olympic and Paralympic, were many and varied, but foremost among them was Hoy. The incredibly powerful Scot had been consistently successful on the world stage for a decade or more as Kilo rider and a member of the GB Team Sprint. He was forced to reassess his career radically after Track Cycling authorities took the shock decision to drop the Kilo from the Olympic Games. Initially Hoy concentrated on just cementing his place in the Team Sprint squad, but he quickly discovered that he did in fact have the potential of becoming the fastest rider in the world. Just over a year before the 2008 Games Hoy embarked on an ambitious flying visit to La Paz, 12,000 feet up in the Andes. He was attempting to sign off his Kilo career with a world record time at the highest velodrome in the world, Alto Orpavi, a feat on which he missed out. As the crowd went home he staged a record attempt on the world 500m record, almost as an afterthought – but he smashed the record by over a second. Suddenly the way forward had become crystal clear.

Hoy was the lynchpin of Britain's effort on the track. Never has a bike been ridden so fast so often with such certainty, the result of a legendary attention to detail and a scientific approach to his fitness and conditioning work. Hoy was totally dominant, winning all 15 races that he contested at Beijing 2008. Opponents seemed somehow complicit, completely powerless to alter the course of the races. Hoy's victories looked inevitable, achieved with an ease that for many comes close to the definition of sporting perfection. As he came into the pits after his final triumph – in the Keirin – one of the team's mechanics handed him his recovery drink; Hoy automatically gulped thirstily from it, only to nearly choke on the potion. They had filled it with potent Belgian beer, the first alcohol to pass his lips since the last night of the World Championships in Manchester five months previously. Hoy proved himself time and time again Olympian in his attitude as much as his athleticism and competitiveness.

Sailing at the 2008 Games was another event that took place in tricky weather conditions, this time at Qingdao. It also saw Britain top of the regatta medal table, with four golds, a silver and a bronze. Paul Goodison took gold in the Laser class, and Iain Percy and Andrew Simpson did likewise in the Star. Nick Rogers and Joe Glanfield won a silver in the 470 class, and there was gold again for Sarah Ayton and Sarah Webb in the Yngling crew, with Pippa Wilson completing the crew on this occasion. Despite conditions later described by Ayton as 'big wind and big rain', they quickly took the lead in the final race, only to be overtaken by Germany at the third mark. They kept their composure and retook the lead, crossing the line seven seconds ahead of the German boat and one minute before the Dutch.

Ben Ainslie had considered retiring from small boat sailing after the 2004 Games, feeling that he had nothing left to prove in Olympic competition. He relented to compete again in the Finn class, although the route to a seemingly inevitable gold medal was in fact far from straightforward. Three days before competition started he woke up feeling unwell, and was diagnosed with mumps and segregated from the rest of the team. Feeling distinctly groggy and with his reputation at stake, Ainslie responded as a champion does. The final Medal Race race was abandoned due to unsettled wind conditions and postponed for 24 hours, by which time strong winds and heavy rain were lashing Qingdao, causing another two hours' delay. Ainslie battled through the 16-knot winds to go 20 seconds clear by the final mark with his nearest rival, American Zach Railey, well out of the running, and Ainslie finally clinched victory in great style. He finished 13 seconds ahead of the Danish sailor Jonas Hoegh-Christensen to claim his third gold medal and assume Rodney Pattisson's mantle as Britain's most successful Olympic sailor. 'To finally get there, to get some great breeze and win the race after two or three hours of hard work means it's all been worth it – I'm a happy man,' he

commented afterwards in obvious relief.

Rowing was another success story for Britain, as audiences had come to expect in recent years. Zac Purchase and Mark Hunter took gold in the Lightweight Double Sculls, as did Tom James, Steve Williams, Peter Reed and Andrew Triggs-Hodge in the men's Four. The men's Eight crew included Alex Partridge who had been forced to withdraw through injury in 2004; in a nail-biting contest they managed to beat the Americans to the silver medal position, with times of 5:25.11 and 5:25.34 respectively, while the Canadian crew took gold. In the women's events Elise Laverick and Anna Bebington won bronze in the Double Sculls and Annie Vernon, Debbie Flood, Frances Houghton and Katherine Grainger took silver in the Quadruple Sculls – placing Britain at the top of yet another event medal table, with six medals to Australia's three.

And so to Swimming, which had been something of a disappointment to the British team in Athens – but not in Beijing. This time they earned two of each colour to finish third in the overall event table behind the USA for whom Michael Phelps claimed an incredible five individual and three relay golds. The open water events proved profitable for Great Britain with David Davies just missing out on gold in the Men's 10km while in the Women's event it was much the same story with Keri-Anne Payne as she finished second against Russia's Larisa Ilchenko.

Britain's two Swimming golds were won by Rebecca Adlington, first in the 400m Freestyle and then in the 800m Freestyle, where she set a new world record time of 8:14.10. It was 48 years since a British woman had last won an Olympic Swimming gold medal, and Anita Lonsbrough, champion in the 200m breaststroke at the Rome 1960 Olympic Games and now a swimming journalist, was present in Beijing to report on the event. Adlington was also the first British swimmer to win more than one gold at a single Olympic Games since Henry Taylor won three golds in 1908.

Best of British

Rebecca Adlington

Sometimes it just all comes together. Rebecca Adlington was only six months old when American swimmer Janet Evans broke the women's 800m Freestyle record with a time of 8:16.22. Astonishingly, the record would hold until the Beijing 2008 Games, when Adlington, now 19, knocked more than two seconds off it. Adlington took the lead on the second lap of the 16-lap endurance swim and never gave it up. A few days earlier this result would have been unthinkable. But Adlington went into the 800m Freestyle final having already won the 400m, coming from behind to beat pre-race favourite Katie Hoff. It was the first time that a British woman had won a Swimming gold medal in 48 years, and a once-in-a-century result for Britain.

Medal table from the 2008 Paralympic Games

Country	Gold	Silver	Bronze	Total
China	89	70	52	211
Great Britain	42	29	31	102
USA	36	35	28	99
Ukraine	24	18	32	74
Australia	23	29	27	79
South Africa	21	3	6	30
Canada	19	10	21	50

Best of British

David Weir

With his massive shoulders and chest, David Weir could have been a boxer (like two of his brothers) had circumstances been different. But he was born with a spinal cord transection that left him without the use of his legs. A natural athlete, he competed in his first Paralympic Games in Atlanta in 1996 as a raw 17-year-old, but medal success eluded him. Afterwards, Weir was disillusioned with the sport and decided 'to live a little'. But watching Tanni Grey-Thompson on television at the Sydney 2000 Games he realised he needed to get back to the track. Four years later in Athens he won silver in the 100m T54 and bronze in the 200m T54, but a gold medal would have to wait until Beijing 2008. There he finally achieved Paralympic glory, taking gold in the 800m T54 and 1500m T54. In 2011 Weir claimed an unprecedented fifth London Marathon wheelchair title with a perfectly timed sprint finish, powering past Switzerland's Heinz Frei into the history books.

Medals were won across the board as Great Britain comfortably exceeded their minimum target of 35. Canoeist Doctor Tim Brabants won gold in the Kayak Single (K1) 1000m and bronze in the 500m and boxer James DeGale also struck gold in the 64–69kg Middle Weigh Class. Heather Fell battled her way to a silver medal in the Women's Modern Pentathlon and Kristina Cook took a double bronze in Eventing (both individual and as part of a mixed team). It was a breakthrough performance on many fronts, a powerful testimony to the efficacy of Lottery funding which has significantly raised expectations for success in London 2012.

But it was not over yet. The 2008 Paralympic Games were to prove Britain's most successful Games to date, with a remarkable total of 102 medals, 42 of them gold. This tally enabled the British Paralympic team to retain the second place on the final medal table, a spot they had happily occupied after both Sydney in 2000 and Athens in 2004. In the face of increasingly tough competition this was a great achievement, and British Airways honoured it by painting the nose of their plane gold for the team's flight home from China. Many of

Britain's Paralympians – David Roberts, Sarah Storey, Lee Pearson, Mark Bristow, David Weir, Eleanor Simmonds, Darren Kenny and Jody Cundy – were becoming household names, reflecting huge personal achievement across a wide spectrum of events.

Both Cundy and Storey had won Paralympic Swimming medals before switching to Cycling for the 2008 Games, where Cundy was to take gold and break the world record in the men's 1 km Time Trial. – LC2 In March 2011 he would take silver in the 4km Pursuit at the UCI Para-Cycling Track World Championship in Italy, focusing on the Kilo, Team Pursuit and Team Sprint for London 2012. Sarah Storey was the winner of multiple Swimming medals, including two golds and three silvers in Barcelona at the 1992 Games, followed by three more golds in Atlanta four years later. Having turned to Cycling, Storey, who has a congenital abnormality of one hand, won a further two golds in Beijing. Victory in the women's Time Trial LC1-2/CP 4 and the women's Individual Pursuit in the same class brought her remarkable total to 18 Paralympic medals – with the prospect of more to come in 2012.

For many spectators it was sobering to reflect on just how good some of these Paralympic performances were in absolute terms. Cundy's time in the 1 km Time Trial – LC2, for example, would have won the gold medal at the Los Angeles 1984 Olympic Games, while Storey's time in the Individual Pursuit would have brought her seventh place in that Olympic final. The changing nature of Paralympic sport was highlighted in Beijing by South African Oscar Pistorius, the young sensation of the Athens 2004 Paralympic Games. He dominated the Athletics at Beijing 2008 with impressive, gold-medal winning performances in the 100m, 200m and the 400m – T44, setting a new Paralympic world record in the last, his favourite event. Pistorius's success was achieved despite the wet weather affecting the grip on his carbon-fibre blades, particularly at the start.

Beijing also saw the outstanding David Weir finally

Yes! Britain's Sarah Storey celebrates after winning the Women's Individual Pursuit (LC 1-2/CP 4) Cycling at the Laoshan Velodrome during day four of the Paralympic Games in Beijing in 2008. Storey is an amazing athlete who first came to the public's attention 16 years earlier at the Paralympic Games at Barcelona 1992, winning six Swimming medals including two golds.

win the gold medal that had eluded him. In fact he won two of them, in the 800m and 1500m – T54, as well as silver in the 400m (where he lost to a new world record time set by Lixin Zhang of China) and bronze in the 5000m. An exceptional British Paralympian, Weir won his fifth London Marathon in 2011 and currently holds British records in all track distances up to 5000m as well as the 10km road race, the marathon and the half-marathon.

Swimming, traditionally a strong sport for Britain's Paralympians, again delivered results, with 11 gold medals, 12 silver and 18 bronze. A total haul of 41 placed Britain fourth in the event medal table, behind the USA, China and Ukraine. The outstanding David Roberts unsurprisingly took golds in the 50m – S7 Freestyle, 100m Freestyle and 400m Freestyle, as well as in the 4 x 100m Freestyle Relay. Sascha Kindred won gold in the 100m – SB7 Breaststroke and the 200m – SM6 Individual Medley, as well as bronze in the 50m – S6 Butterfly; Sam Hynd did the same in the 400m – S8 Freestyle and also took bronze in the 200m Individual Medley. In the women's events Eleanor Simmonds, aged only 13 and the youngest British athlete in China, won two unforgettable gold medals in the 100m – S6 Freestyle and the 400m Freestyle, as well as taking part in the 200m Individual Medley, in which she came fifth. Her teammate Heather Frederiksen took gold in the 100m – S8 Backstroke to accompany silvers in the 400m Freestyle and 100m Freestyle and a bronze in the Individual Medley, while Elizabeth Johnson, who had travelled to the Games in difficult circumstances after losing her mother to cancer, also won a gold medal in the 100m – SB6 Breaststroke.

Britain also scored highly in the Equestrian events, held in the Hong Kong Equestrian Centre. The team again ended top of the event medal table with five gold and five silver medals, well ahead of second placed Germany with their total of six. Lee Pearson, riding Gentlemen, took golds in the 1b Individual Dressage and Individual Freestyle Dressage, also

joining with Sophie Christiansen, Anne Dunham and Simon Laurens to win the overall Team event. Dunham won the 1a Individual Dressage, with Sophie Christiansen taking silver; their positions were then reversed in the 1a Individual Freestyle Dressage. In the newly introduced Paralympic Rowing competition the nation also headed the results table, with two gold medals (from Tom Aggar in the men's Single Sculls and Helene Raynsford in the women's Single Sculls) and a bronze in the Mixed Coxed Four.

Back in Britain, precisely as the Beijing Handover Ceremony gave the Paralympic Flag to London in anticipation of the 2012 Games, Stoke Mandeville staged a special event of its own. Schoolchildren carried flags of the nations likely to compete around the athletics track, a facility that will provide a training base for many of the competing nations in 2012. So the exciting prospect of the Paralympic Games returning to Britain was celebrated in the movement's birthplace, where it had begun 60 years before.

The 2008 Games, both Olympic and Paralympic, had shown what was possible, but there was still much to be done to prepare for London 2012. Even as the triumphant ParalympicsGB team landed at Heathrow Airport, Chef de Mission Phil Lane was trying to refocus the minds of competitors and spectators alike. 'This is one of the top Paralympic performances we have had and will be a tough act to follow,' he acknowledged, 'but we need to get the recruitment right ... We do need a real effort and a big drive to say, "Come on, this is a great chance for you, look what these guys have delivered in Beijing, you could be part of that team in 2012". The 2008 Games had been a splendid curtain raiser, but the bigger drama of the London 2012 Olympic and Paralympic Games, the focus of so many hopes and dreams, was still to come.

Chapter 9
Great Expectations

Great Expectations

BRITAIN'S PARTICIPATION IN, AND SUPPORT OF, THE OLYMPIC AND PARALYMPIC GAMES HAS BEEN SECOND TO NONE FOR OVER A HUNDRED YEARS. IT HAS TWICE PREVIOUSLY BEEN A SUCCESSFUL HOST NATION, ALBEIT IN FAR FROM IDEAL CIRCUMSTANCES – STEPPING INTO THE BREACH AT SHORT NOTICE IN 1908 AND BEING ONE OF THE FEW EUROPEAN CITIES ABLE TO COUNTENANCE THE TASK IN 1948.

In 1989, Richard Sumray, vice-chairman of the London Council for Sport and Recreation (LCSR), attended a Council meeting at which ways to involve more young people in sport were under discussion. As Sumray puts it, 'Without much thought I said "Bid for the Olympic Games".' The following year, a conference organised by the Association of London Government's Arts and Recreation Committee examined the landscape for arts and recreation in London at the end of the century.

Sumray approached the BOA, who needed to lead a bid. Britain sensibly sat out the bidding process for the 2004 and 2008 Games. In 1997, however, without any fanfare, a small team started to quietly construct the basis of a London bid for 2012. This was simply the bare bones – albeit in a document that eventually ran to 400 pages – but it was important to have a substantial and well founded concept in place whenever the right opportunity arose. Four working groups developed concepts for the sports venues, transport, the Olympic Village

> '**This is just the most fantastic opportunity to do everything we ever dreamed of in British sport**'
>
> Lord Coe relishes the possibilities after winning the London 2012 bid

and the environment. After initially considering options for a west London-based Games, one centred on east London or a combination of the two, it became increasingly clear that east London would offer the greatest potential for regeneration and have a more profound effect given this was where the greatest areas of deprivation were located.

The underlying principles of a 2012 bid were taking shape. East London would host the majority of the venues while the Paralympic Games, which had enjoyed such strong ties with Britain since their inception, would have a major role in an integrated bid. Legacy was also to be an extremely important theme. The massive expenditure required to stage the Games demanded clear lasting benefits, encompassing both sporting facilities and urban regeneration. It was also recognised, that the government and the London city authority of the day had to be fully behind the bid, with key sponsors and commercial partners in place. Any London bid must be able to hit the ground running – the only way to win the ultimate prize of the Games.

The sporting and political tide was beginning to turn by the Millennium, with the success of the Sydney 2000 Games challenging the perception of what could be achieved. Manchester also staged a stunning Commonwealth Games in 2002, banishing at a stroke any fears that modern-day Britain could not stage huge international sports gatherings. The Commonwealth Games, described by Prime Minister Tony Blair as 'probably the best-ever Commonwealth Games', was a triumph from start to finish. Huge crowds attended and the organisation was excellent. The event was delivered on time and on budget, generating a decent working profit. Blair's enthusiasm was evident, and he noted that 'the benefits will be felt for generations to come, including the lasting sporting legacy as well as significant regeneration. The wheels for a 2012 bid were now in motion, with the Commonwealth Games adding real momentum.

Finally, in May 2003, the road was clear and the Government came fully behind the BOA bid, along with London Mayor Ken Livingstone and various big hitting commercial partners. London could now present a strong united front and as such was always going to be a strong challenger. Paris was still the hot favourite, even after two strong losing bids in recent years, while Madrid was also a worthy contender. If the British bid could get everything right, London would have a chance.

Well aware that a great world city such as London automatically has credibility and appeal, the bid initially concentrated instead on the nuts and bolts that needed to be in place. Legacy was a key focus of the bid, and all of the proposed major venues were either earmarked for post- Games use in situ or, in the case of the state-of-the-art Basketball Arena, capable of being taken down and erected elsewhere in the country or even internationally. From the very outset it was envisaged that the Olympic Village would be re-used as relatively low-cost housing in the area, and all forms of transport would

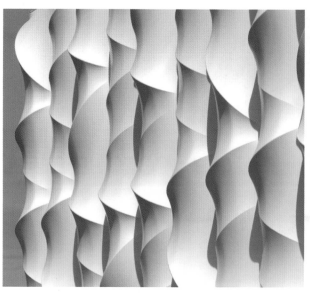

View of the all-white Basketball Arena at the Olympic Park. London 2012 will be the first time Britain has entered a team for the competition at the Games since 1948.

be upgraded.

When Lord Coe, who was one of the three vice-chairmen of the intial team under the leadership of American business woman, Barbara Cassani, assumed control in May 2004, London's campaign really took off and it was Coe's contacts and influence that added significant weight to the bid.

In November 2004 Coe and his team officially handed over the 600 page candidature document to the IOC in Lausanne. It combined emphasis on Britain's historic contribution to the Olympic Games and its deep-rooted Paralympic associations, with a commitment to inspiring young people around the world, underlined with clear and public government support.

The Olympic Park was cleverly designed to include accommodation for athletes in close proximity, allowing many competitors to walk to their events. London itself as a city was woven into the bid as a key player, not a mere backdrop. Iconic sites such as Wimbledon for Tennis and Wembley Stadium for Football balanced bold innovations like Beach Volleyball at Horse Guards Parade in Whitehall, creating an irresistible mix

American duo Jennifer Kessy and April Ross (nearside) against Brazil's Angela Vieira and Liliane Maestrini during the final of the test event of Beach Volleyball at Horse Guards Parade, where Brazil won the tournament.

London 2012 Chairman Sebastian Coe holds the Host City bid book in Singapore on 6 July 2005 after London won the vote to stage the Olympic Games in 2012. The 117th session of the International Olympic Committee voted on whether London, Paris, New York, Madrid or Moscow should host the Games and it became a glorious triumph for London.

overall. Lord Coe, whose passionate 'selling' of the campaign's message was nothing short of inspirational, summed up the bid's determination to create a new and vibrant Games for our times. 'Our vision … is to create the best Games the world has ever seen by unlocking the UK's unrivalled passion for sport, by delivering the best Games for athletes to compete in, by showcasing London's unmatched cultural wealth and diversity and by creating a real and lasting legacy. Our vision is a Games that will inspire, excite, engage and be owned by the next generation. Games that fully reflect the IOC's new thinking – excellence without extravagance.'

The Last Lap

As every athlete knows, and Lord Coe better than most, peaking at the right time is absolutely vital when you are chasing the biggest prize of all; it is a well-timed late run that often results in glory. That's certainly what happened in Singapore

between 4–6 July 2005 when the IOC met to vote on which country should host the 2012 Games. The groundwork had been exceptional, the inspections had gone well and the London bid was looking strong, but the British delegation still arrived at the Raffles Convention Centre in Singapore as second favourites behind Paris, with Madrid not far behind in third place. Three days is a long time in such circumstances, and London travelled, if not in expectation then definitely in hope.

Using his many contacts, in athletics in particular and across sport in general, Lord Coe had already been travelling the world for the previous year drumming up support for the cause. He always knew though that in a close race the final lobbying and presentations in Singapore were going to be vital. He was helped enormously in this late surge by Prime Minister Tony Blair who, despite having to prepare to host the G8 Summit meeting back in Scotland, flew out to Singapore. He went on to work around

'I was in Trafalgar Square when the result was televised live from Singapore. It was hairs on the back of the neck stuff and I realised that with utter certainty that I could never walk away from the Olympics'

Ben Ainslie, contemplating retirement, remembers his reaction in 2005 to the success of the 2012 bid

Above London 2012 Chairman Sebastian Coe (right) hands over the bid book to International Olympic Committee President Jacques Rogge prior to London's triumph in Singapore in winning the 2012 Games.

Above right Born and bred in East London, he might be a global superstar but London 2012 ambassador David Beckham was a key player during the countdown to the Games vote in Singapore. Here with his wife Victoria Beckham, leaving the London 2012 celebration party at the Raffles City Convention Centre in Singapore.

> **'It should be a massive sporting festival and a triumph for the nation, but for all the focus on medals and performance objectives there needs to be a decade of legacy built like concrete behind it'**
>
> Dame Tanni Grey-Thompson describes her hopes for the London 2012 Paralympic Games

the clock for the best part of two days, spreading the message in person to an estimated 40 delegates. The five times gold medallist Sir Steve Redgrave, also in the bid party, reflected later that Blair's involvement was vital. 'To be able to take three days to come out here made the difference The presentations were important, but it's that meeting and greeting and showing that full support right the way through. Hats off to the Prime Minister.'

A strong representation of the great and good of British Olympic and Paralympic history was supporting Blair in the hustings. Sir Steve Redgrave was accompanied by Daley Thompson, Dame Tanni Grey-Thompson, David Hemery, Dame Kelly Holmes and others, as well as global celebrities such as David Beckham. However, Lord Coe and his team had also decided in advance that it was not just going to be a gathering of Britain's sporting glitterati. Of the 100 personnel each bid country was allocated for the lobbying and presentation, London chose to travel with 30 east London school children. Coe

> **'Seb Coe has done an amazing job'**
>
> Sir Steve Redgrave acknowledges his fellow Olympian's vital role in winning London's 2012 bid

was absolutely clear that his personal message in London's presentation would hone in on youth, of both Britain and the world. This had to be an Olympic and Paralympic Games that captured their imagination. His conviction was absolute as he spoke from his heart, not the autocue, and the IOC delegates seemed to like what they heard very much.

The rest, as they say, is history. London came home in the fourth and final round of voting, beating Paris into second place by just 4 votes, 54 votes to 50. Jubilation broke out in Singapore and it was reflected back home in Trafalgar Squarewhere a party had been arranged – with nobody being quite sure whether it would be a celebration or a wake. Blair, now back at Holyrood Palace for the G8 Summit, addressed the throng and the Queen said it was an 'outstanding achievement to beat such a highly competitive field'. Britain's politicians joined in the congratulations. Conservative leader Michael Howard said he was 'delighted' and the Liberal Democrat leader Charles Kennedy said it would unite the nation.

All was well with the world – and then, the very next day, terrorist atrocities in London brought about the deaths of 56 people, including the four perpetrators, and injuring over 700 individuals. At a stroke the winning of the bid in far away Singapore seemed an irrelevance. But as the capital gradually got back to normality Britain's pride in winning the vote returned. It was accompanied by a determination to do the very best job possible. In fact showcasing a bold and undeterred country to the world now seemed more important than ever.

Delivering The Games

London has officially been the Olympic City since 26 September 2008, when the Olympic and Paralympic flags were raised outside City Hall. The huge task of delivering the Games had begun before the Handover Ceremony in Beijing, of course, with all in all a remarkably smooth transition from prospective bid to work in progress. This is no mean feat, given the logistical and day-to-day challenges of fulfilling a building and regeneration programme on this scale – particularly in the teeth of a worldwide economic recession. Construction of the Olympic Park and Olympic Village has constituted the biggest building

project in Europe over the last five years, with more than 10,000 people working on site at the height of the activity and over 26,000 involved in total. Nor is the timeframe negotiable, as the digital countdown clock installed in Trafalgar Square to mark '500 days to go' powerfully underlines. When the Olympic Games opens on 27 July 2012 thousands of competitors from countries across the world will have a right to expect that everything is in perfect working order.

The Olympic Delivery Authority (ODA) started its work with the advantage of an entirely sound and economically costed original bid. The bid had always been a proper working document rather than a theoretical exercise, and from the moment the ODA took over there has been a clear purpose as to exactly what was needed, where and when.

Some outstanding facilities were already in place, of course, and others were relatively easy to organise and fine tune. Nowhere in the world is there a better purpose-built Sailing facility, for both Paralympic Sailing and its Olympic counterpart, than the National Sailing Academy at Weymouth and Portland, where Weymouth Bay provides a perfect location for the sport. Tennis Mecca Wimbledon

Above Left No words are needed, the smiles say it all as the celebrations start in Trafalgar Square after International Olympic Committee President Jacques Rogge announced the word 'London' as the Host City for the 2012 Olympic Games.

Above At that same moment on the stage in Trafalgar Square (from left to right) Paralympian Danny Crates, double Olympic gold medallist Kelly Holmes, 1983 world 1500m champion Steve Cram and Olympic Sailing gold medalist Sarah Webb show what winning London 2012 means to them.

> **... the fact that it's at home is just absolutely massive...'**
> Zoe Smith, teenage weightlifter, sees the potential for achieving a dream in London 2012

Opening Ceremonies

Above Yoshinori Sakai, a student born in Hiroshima on the day the first atomic bomb devastated the city in 1945, carries the Torch up the stairs to light the Olympic Cauldron at the Tokyo 1964 Games.

Above centre An aerial view of the Olympic Stadium during the Opening Ceremony of the Los Angeles 1932 Games.

Above right Torchbearer Cathy Freeman of Australia prepares to light the Olympic Cauldron in Sydney in 2000 at the start of what became an amazing Games for her – and for Australia.

Right Zhang Haidong enters the Olympic Stadium carrying the Torch during the Opening Ceremony of the Beijing 2008 Paralympic Games.

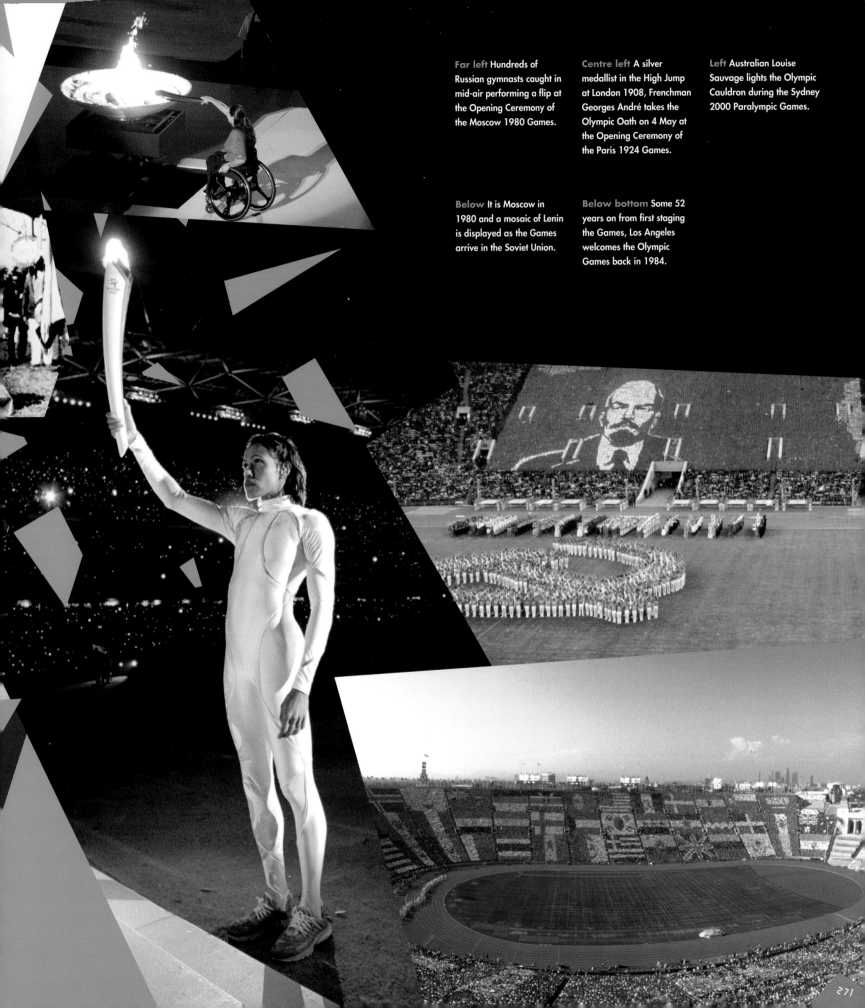

Far left Hundreds of Russian gymnasts caught in mid-air performing a flip at the Opening Ceremony of the Moscow 1980 Games.

Centre left A silver medallist in the High Jump at London 1908, Frenchman Georges André takes the Olympic Oath on 4 May at the Opening Ceremony of the Paris 1924 Games.

Left Australian Louise Sauvage lights the Olympic Cauldron during the Sydney 2000 Paralympic Games.

Below It is Moscow in 1980 and a mosaic of Lenin is displayed as the Games arrive in the Soviet Union.

Below bottom Some 52 years on from first staging the Games, Los Angeles welcomes the Olympic Games back in 1984.

271

speaks for itself, as do the international-standard football facilities around Britain. Horse Guards Parade was an inspired choice for the Beach Volleyball, while the multi-purpose ExCeL fulfils a variety of roles and the Lee Valley White Water Centre, set to host the Canoe Slalom, was completed ahead of schedule and to rave reviews. Equally the Mountain Bike venue at Hadleigh Farm in Essex has impressed many people in an area not exactly known for its mountains! It is a tough, challenging course and very spectator-friendly.

The construction of the Olympic Park and Athletes' Village in Stratford has been the biggest project, and one fundamental to the successful bid. The IOC approved of the basic concept, which placed the accommodation of over 17,000 athletes and officials right on site, enabling many to simply walk to their events every day. The structures subsequently constructed on the Park, and the Village accommodation blocks, constitute a huge part of the legacy in terms of sports facilities and the regeneration of east London.

Without seeking to emulate the grand scale of the Games facilities in Beijing, Britain's Olympic Park has emerged as an attractive, cleverly designed complex. The impression of spontaneous informality is misleading – the positioning of each building has been carefully honed and reviewed, strategic sightlines of the city introduced and a landscaped 'green space' conjured from the derelict wasteland. A half-mile stretch of ground between the Olympic Stadium and the Aquatics Centre celebrates Britain's longstanding love of gardens and semi-mature, mostly native trees and wetland plants are being introduced to create a natural habitat for wildlife.

This green oasis in the city houses the 'big three' buildings of the 2012 Games: the Olympic Stadium, the Velodrome and the Aquatics Centre. The Stadium, an integral part of the bid and a showpiece for both Olympic and Paralympic Games, has been designed to reduce in size after the Games for long-term legacy use. Surrounded by the so-called Bow Back Rivers, small streams in the lower Lea Valley, the Stadium is effectively situated on a small island, with access provided by a series of footbridges around the perimeter. This concept gives the structure an open, accessible feel, allowing it to engage with the rest of the Park rather than being concealed behind fences or walls.

The Velodrome, the first to be situated in an Olympic Park since the 1988 Games in Seoul, has classical simplicity and beauty, both inside and out, establishing it as an iconic venue for the Olympic and Paralympic Track Cycling. London Mayor Boris Johnson sang its praises, and those of the Park around it, at the Velodrome's opening, commenting that 'this place will live and live. The Velodrome will become a place of pilgrimage for cyclists and would-be cyclists to be inspired. It will be the crucible where future champions are forged. My spirits rise every time I visit the Olympic Park which is an unambiguously successful and productive project.'

The designers consulted with riders, including Sir Chris Hoy, at every stage of the Velodrome's design, with some interesting results. The high banking, for example, used to generate speed and a key feature of track cycling, is the standard 42 degrees, but the finishing line is some five metres further down the home straight than is normal, which could make for some exciting late finishes in the sprint events. At Hoy's suggestion they have even installed an 'emergency' lavatory just out of sight down the ramp for nervous competitors who feel the irresistible call of nature before a race.

The structure is exciting, impressive and practical, designed for both competitors and spectators. As British Cycling's Performance Director David Brailsford has observed, 'it has been put together by people who really care about cycling and they have also taken the trouble to consult us along the way.' Natural light floods in from the concourse windows, unusual for an indoor velodrome, in which spectators normally have

Top left Members of Britain's Track Cycling team test out the Velodrome where they will be chasing a clutch of gold medals in 2012.

Top right View of the Velodrome, which will host Track Cycling events during London 2012.

Left British Olympic diver Tom Daley performs at the Aquatics Centre during the One Year to Go festivities on 27 July 2011.

Bottom Left A general view of the London 2012 Basketball Arena court and seating.

Bottom Right The newly finished Velodrome in London's Olympic Park exemplifies simplicity and beauty. Designer Mike Taylor consulted cyclists including Sir Chris Hoy and Paul Manning to make the building as friendly as possible to competitors and spectators alike.

Right The Aquatics Centre at the Olympic Park, London, pictured on 27 July 2011, one year before the Olympic Games are set to open.

Olympic Park Venues

Aquatics Centre: Diving, Modern Pentathlon (swimming), Swimming, Synchronised Swimming, Paralympic Swimming

Water Polo Arena: Water Polo

Basketball Arena: Basketball, Handball, Wheelchair Rugby, Wheelchair Basketball

BMX Track: BMX

Eton Manor: Wheelchair Tennis

Handball Arena: Handball, Modern Pentathlon (fencing), Goalball

Velodrome: Cycling (Track), Paralympic Cycling (Track)

Hockey Centre: Hockey, 7-a-side Football, 5-a-side Football

Olympic Stadium: Athletics, Paralympic Athletics, Opening and Closing Ceremonies

no inkling of whether it is night or day. For once, those in the Velodrome will feel connected, physically and emotionally, with the wider Games – they can view the other splendours of the Olympic Park between races and feel at the heart of London 2012.

The Aquatics Centre, with its distinctively curved wave roof, seemed certain in the early planning stages to become *the* iconic prestige venue of the 2012 Games. For practical purposes the full glory of Zaha Hadid's design has been superimposed with two 'wings' of temporary seating to allow more spectators to watch the popular Aquatics events. After the Olympic and Paralympic Games the wings will be removed and the full impact of the Centre's design revealed. Internally it is a stunning venue which has received wide acclaim, not least from Australia's champion swimmer Ian Thorpe, who has said that a visit to the Aquatics Centre was at the heart of his decision to come out of retirement. From a legacy perspective, the two 50m pools and diving centre will serve the sport and the area far into the 21st century.

Another structure in the Olympic Park with a major 'legacy' role is the Hockey Centre. During the Olympic Games it will host both the men's and women's Hockey competition, switching in the Paralympic Games to host the 5-a-side and 7-a-side

Football competitions, then being relocated to Eton Manor for community use. Another building, the beautiful, copper-clad Handball Arena, re-oriented during construction to allow better views over the site, is facing a busy Games schedule. During the Olympic Games all the Handball preliminary games and quarter-finals will be held there, along with the fencing element of the Modern Pentathlon, while during the Paralympic Games it will host the popular Goalball tournament. After the Games the Handball Arena will remain on the Olympic Park, where it will be adapted for community use.

The Basketball Arena, a remarkable temporary structure on the Park, features a distinctive white 'Christmas cake' exterior which will be illuminated at night. Its arena will stage all the preliminary matches of the Basketball competition, both men's and women's events, and the women's quarter-finals, as well as the semi-finals and finals of the Handball. In the Paralympic Games it will stage Wheelchair Rugby and preliminary games of Wheelchair Basketball. The steep banks of seats should generate a superb atmosphere, with Basketball fans in particular traditionally some of the noisiest in sport. Again, the intention is that it will be reused elsewhere after the Games.

The London bid always promised equal status to the Olympic and Paralympic Games, and the needs of Paralympians have been kept at the forefront as individual venues are constructed. Some necessary adjustments and alterations to stadia and facilities are planned between the end of the Olympic Games and the Opening Ceremony of the Paralympic Games on 29 August 2012, but in other respects the transition will be seamless. The scale of the Paralympic Games, the first since the 2000 Games to authorise participation of athletes with learning disabilities in certain sports, is impressive; competitors from over 150 nations will take part in 20 sports across more than 500 gold medal events. The contrast with the original 16 individuals who gathered for an afternoon of archery on the lawn at Stoke Mandeville on that day in 1948 could hardly be greater or more poignant.

For, despite all that venues and compelling sports can contribute, it is people who bring the Olympic and Paralympic Games to life. From those who have spent years preparing the best possible locations to the volunteers offering invaluable help on the day, those who have contributed over the years through their lottery tickets and the excited spectators who are such a force as the events unfold, the Games is created by them and for them. The sight of hundreds of thousands of fans attending a victory parade in London as the British teams reassembled in October 2008 reflected the nation's commitment to its sportsmen and women – a combination of ambition, pragmatism and desire. There is nothing that succeeds like success, and it is reflected in a new mood of self-confidence among supporters and competitors alike.

There are certainly great expectations for the London 2012 Olympic and Paralympic Games. Established names, already familiar to the general public as well as sports fans, see this as the chance of a lifetime to perform at their very best on their home turf. Tom Daley, Jessica Ennis, Mark Cavendish, Lee Pearson, David Weir, Jody Cundy, Phillips Idowu, Sarah Storey, Eleanor Simmonds, Peter Norfolk, David Roberts, Liz Johnson, Darren Kenny, Dai Greene, Ben Ainslie, Tom Aggar, Mo Farah amongst many others and many more accomplished athletes are waiting in the wings. So too are younger hopefuls such as teenagers Zoe Smith and Hannah Cockcroft, and the up and coming Alistair and Jonny Brownlee, Nathan Stephens, Hannah England, Perri Shakes-Drayton – a native of Bow, about a mile from the Olympic Stadium – and Danielle Brown. All have their own stories of dedication and determination to succeed. For all of them the 2012 Games offers a truly great opportunity to shape an unforgettable part of Britain's Olympic and Paralympic journey.

Sports in the London 2012 Paralympic Games

The numbers in brackets show the total of medals available

Archery (9)
Athletics (170)
Boccia (7)
Cycling: Road (32); Track (18)
Equestrian (11)
Football 5-a-side (1)
Football 7-a-side (1)
Goalball (2)
Judo (13)
Powerlifting (20)
Rowing (4)
Sailing (3)
Shooting (12)
Swimming (148)
Table Tennis (29)
Volleyball (Sitting) (2)
Wheelchair Basketball (2)
Wheelchair Fencing (12)
Wheelchair Rugby (1)
Wheelchair Tennis (6)

'Every athlete's dream is to compete at an Olympic Games, so to get the opportunity to compete in front of a home crowd is so special'

Tom Daley anticipates the Diving competition at the 2012 Olympic Games

---

Following page

In the shape of a wave, the Aquatics Centre for London 2012 will be one of the showpiece venues at the Games – with diver Tom Daley and swimmer Rebecca Adlington set to be among the biggest British stars chasing gold.

Acknowledgements and References

The finest resource of the Olympic and Paralympic Games in the world lies largely hidden in the unheralded LA84 Foundation website (www.LA84foundation.org) where your can, at you leisure, download the complete official reports of every Modern Olympic Games since 1896. As a primary source it is unequalled, giving the official blow-by-blow account of precisely what happened and much more besides as the official correspondents go off on tangents. It is also the repository of endless extraordinary photographs that alas rarely see the light of day. Be warned though, the report for the 1908 Games, for example, runs to 864 pages alone, while London 1948 came in at 766 pages. You could spend a lifetime reading the official reports and never absorb it all.

British hockey legend Sean Kerly celebrates after scoring during the Seoul 1988 Games where his goals led the team to gold.

Also highly recommended:

- www.olympic.org
- www.paralympics.org.uk
- www.london2012.com
- www.sportinglife.com
- www.bbc.co.uk/sport
- www.olympics.org.uk
- www.IAAF.org
- www.FINA.org
- www.ishof.org
- newspapers.bl.uk
- www.telegraph.co.uk/archive
- www.nytimes.com/ref/membercenter/nytarchive.html
- www.uksport.gov.uk

It might be a digital age with a treasure trove of information in cyberspace but no book dealing with the modern Olympic Games in any shape or form can be written without constant reference to the 'Bible', namely *The Complete Book of the Olympics* by David Wallechinsky and Jamie Loucky, updated every four years by Aurum Press. I am not the first journalist – and I won't be the last – to doff a grateful cap in their direction when trying to confirm what actually happened, while their steady flow of priceless, pithy 'did you know?' anecdotes are a constant joy, albeit an occasional distraction from the task in hand.

Thanks also to my favourite second-hand book shop in Penzance which I visited on 11 May 2011 in the company of Getty's chief sports photographer Dave Rogers before a rugby match between the Cornish Pirates and Worcester Warriors. As if by divine intervention, I stumbled across a batch of old newspapers from both 1908 and 1948, almost as if some amateur historian of the Olympic Games was having a clear out. In fact that is clearly what must have happened. Rogers muttered something about 'lucky so and so' while I purchased a job lot.

Mention must finally be made of a number of superb books dealing with the issues and personalities connected with the Olympic Games, which I have either coveted like old friends over the years or rushed to read on publication in recent years.

- Ainslie, Ben, *Close to the Wind*, London: Yellow Jersey Press, 2009

- Bach, Steven, *Leni: The Life and Work of Leni Riefenstahl*, New York: Alfred A. Knopf, 2007

Baker, Keith, *The 1908 Olympics: The First London Games*, Cheltenham: SportsBooks 2008

Beresford, Pat and Long, Tommy, *David Wilkie*, Suffolk: Halesworth Press, 1976

Bland, Ernest A., *Olympic Story*, London: The Burleigh Press, 1948

BOA, *The Official Report of the London Olympic Games 1948*, London: World Sports, 1948

Brittain, Ian, *The Paralympic Games Explained*, Abingdon, Oxon.: Routledge, 2010

Buchanan, Ian, *The Guinness Book of British Olympians*, London: Guinness World Records Ltd, 1991

Burnell, Richard and Page, Geoffrey, *The Brilliants: A History of the Leander Club*, Bath: Bath Press, 1997

Butcher, Pat, *The Perfect Distance: Ovett and Coe*, London: Weidenfeld & Nicolson, 2004

Collins, Mick, *All-Round Genius: The Unknown Story of Britain's Greatest Sportsman*, London: Aurum Press, 2006

Emery, David, *Lillian*, London: Hodder and Stoughton, 1971

Hampton, Jane, *The Austerity Olympics*, London: Aurum Press, 2008

Hemery, David, *Another Hurdle*, London: William Heinemann Ltd, 1976

Ibbotson, Doug, *Sporting Scenes*, London: Weidenfeld & Nicolson, 1980

Jenkins, Rebecca, *The First London Olympics: 1908*, London: Piatkus Books, 2008

Keddie, John W., *Running the Race: Eric Liddell, Olympic Champion and Missionary*, Darlington: Evangelical Press 2007

Kent, Graeme, *Olympic Follies: The Madness and Mayhem of the 1908 London Games*, London: JR Books, 2008

Ljungqvist, Arne, *Doping's Nemesis*, Cheltenham: SportsBooks Ltd, 2011

Llewellyn, Harry, *Passports to Life*, London: Hutchinson and Co./Stanley Paul, 1980

Mandell, Richard D., *The First Modern Olympics*, Berkeley, CA: University of California Press, 1976

McCann, Liam, *The Olympics: Facts Figures and Fun*, Artists' and Photographers' Press, Ltd, 2006

McCarthy, Kevin, *Gold, Silver and Green: The Irish Olympic Journey 1896–1924*, Cork: Cork University Press 2010

McCasland, David, *Eric Liddell: Pure Gold*, Grand Rapids, MI: Discovery House Publishers, 2001

Millar, David, *The Official History of the Olympic Games and the IOC*, Edinburgh: Mainstream Publishing, 2008

Moore, Richard, *Heroes, Villains and Velodromes*, London: HarperCollins Publishers, 2008

Peters, Mary with Ian Wooldridge, *Mary P: Autobiography*, London: Stanley Paul, 1974

Phillips, Bob, *The 1948 Olympics: How London Rescued the Games*, Cheltenham: SportsBooks Ltd, 2007

Quinn, Mark, *The King of Spring: The Life and Times of Peter O'Connor*, Dublin: The Liffey Press, 2004

Reeve, Simon, *One Day in December: The Story of the 1972 Munich Massacre*, London: Faber and Faber, 2007

Rippon, Anton, *Hitler's Olympics: The Story of the 1936 Nazi Games*, Barnsley: Pen and Sword Books, 2006

Scruton, Joan, *Stoke Mandeville: Road to the Paralympics*, Aylesbury: Peterhouse Press, 1998

Smith, Martin, ed., *The Daily Telegraph Book of Sports Obituaries*, London: Pan Macmillan, 2000

Trimborn, Jürgen, Riefenstah,l Leni: *A Life*, London: Faber and Faber, 2002

Watman, Mel, *All-Time Greats of British Athletics*, Cheltenham: SportsBooks Ltd, 2006

Webster, Lt Col F.A.M., *Olympic Cavalcade*, London: Hutchinson and Co., 1948

White, John, *The Olympic Miscellany*, London: Carlton Books Ltd, 2008

Wilson, Peter, *The Man They Couldn't Gag*, London: Hutchinson and Co./Stanley Paul, 1977

Wright, Graeme, *Olympic Greats*, London: Queen Anne's Press, 1980

Index